A MODERN HISTORY OF THE SUDAN

A MODERN HISTORY

OF THE

SUDAN

From the Funj Sultanate to the Present Day

by P. M. Holt

GROVE PRESS, INC.   NEW YORK

CONTENTS

CONTENTS

Part IV: The Republic of the Sudan

Conclusion

ILLUSTRATIONS

The Land and the People

Under Turco-Egyptian Rule

The Republic

Foundations of the Future

A*

PREFACE

THE FIRST steps towards the making of the modern Sudan were taken, nearly a century and a half ago, when the soldiers of Muhammad 'Ali Pasha, the Ottoman sultan's viceroy in Egypt, brought under their master's rule the Muslim cultivators, merchants and tribesmen of Nubia, Sennar and Kordofan. A common administration, the shared glories and disasters of the Mahdist Revolution, and renewed experience of alien rule under the Anglo-Egyptian Condominium, welded the Sudanese peoples together, and stimulated the development of Sudanese nationalism. On New Year's Day, 1956, the Sudan emerged into independent statehood.

This is in brief the story which the following pages attempt to tell in more detail. Three factors predominate in modern Sudanese history. The first is the indigenous tradition, itself the product of the intermingling of Arab Muslims with Africans. The fusion began over a thousand years ago, and, as allusions to the problem of the southern Sudan will show, is still a continuing process. This lies at the base of Sudanese nationality, religion and culture. I have therefore dealt at some length with the earlier stages of the fusion in the Introduction, and have returned to the theme of the indigenous tradition in the Conclusion.

The two other factors are the influence of Egypt, which in its earlier phases was late Ottoman rather than purely Egyptian in quality, and the influence of Britain. The effect of these two influences upon the Sudan is seen in its history from the time of Muhammad 'Ali's conquests until the present day. Egyptian rule ended with the Mahdist Revolution, British administration with the coming of independence, but the modern Sudan is politically and materially very largely the heir of these earlier regimes. The cultural influence of both Egypt and Britain is unaffected by the transformation of their former dependency into a sovereign state. The play upon each other of these three factors is the theme of this book.

In the difficult problem of the transliteration of Arabic words, I have adopted a compromise. For the place-names of provinces and larger towns, I have used conventional forms, e.g. Khartoum, Kordofan, El Obeid. The conventional Kassala and Bahr El Ghazal have, however, been slightly modified to the more accurate forms Kasala and Bahr al-Ghazal. Personal names (except for Neguib and Nasser, which have a firmly established conventional spelling) and technical terms are rigorously transliterated, but diacritical marks have been omitted for the sake of simplicity. Ottoman titles which are not purely Arabic in origin, e.g. *defterdar*, *hükümdar*, are spelt according to modern Turkish conventions.

In conclusion, I wish to express my gratitude to all those who have helped me in the preparation of this book; in particular the General Editor of this series, Professor Bernard Lewis; my former colleague, Mr A. B. Theobald, and Sayyid Osman Sid Ahmed Ismail of the University of Khartoum. All these read the book in draft, and assisted me with their comments and criticisms. Dr G. N. Sanderson, also of the University of Khartoum, kindly provided information on the diplomatic background to the Reconquest. While acknowledging their very real help, I accept, of course, all responsibility for the statements and opinions expressed in my book. Material for the illustrations was generously provided by Dr J. F. E. Bloss and Mr F. C. A. McBain from their private collections of photographs, and by Mr R. L. Hill from the Sudanese archive of the University of Durham. Sayyid Mohamed Kamal El Bakri, First Secretary of the Sudan Embassy in London, was most helpful in making available, or obtaining, further photographic material. I am grateful to the following publishers for permission to reprint short passages from copyright works: Oxford University Press for *Egypt in the Sudan* R. Hill, Messrs D. van Nostrand Inc., New York for *Diplomacy in the Near and Middle East* J. C. Hurewitz, and Cambridge University Press for *Sudan: Arabic Texts* translated by S. Hillelson. Lastly, I am forever indebted to the Sudanese people for the many happy and formative years which I spent in their land.

P. M. HOLT

Great Missenden, 1961

INTRODUCTION

THE BACKGROUND TO MODERN SUDANESE HISTORY

'*The Sultan of the Muslims, the Caliph of the Lord of the Worlds; who undertakes the affairs of the world and the Faith; who is raised up for the interests of the Muslims; who supports the Holy Law of the Lord of the Prophets; who spreads the banner of justice and grace over all the worlds; he by whom God corrects His servants and gives light to the land; the repressor of the race of unbelief and deception and rebellion, and the race of oppression and corruption; the mercy of God (praised and exalted be He!) to the townsman and the nomad; he who trusts in the King, the Guide: the sultan, son of the sultan, the victorious, the divinely aided Sultan Badi, son of the deceased Dakin, son of the Sultan Badi.*

    May God, the Compassionate, the Merciful, grant him victory by the influence of the great Koran and the noble Prophet.   Amen. Amen. O Lord of the Worlds.'

From a charter of
Sultan Badi VI (1791)

CHAPTER I

THE LAND AND THE PEOPLE

The territories comprising the modern Sudan

THE MEDIEVAL Muslim geographers gave the name of *Bilad al-Sudan*, 'the land of the Blacks', to the belt of African territory lying south of the Sahara Desert. In the more restricted sense of the territories lying southwards of Egypt, which formed the Anglo-Egyptian Condominium from 1899 until 1955, and which now constitute the Republic of the Sudan, the term is of nineteenth-century origin, a convenient administrative designation for the African empire acquired by Muhammad 'Ali Pasha, the viceroy of Egypt, and his successors.[1] The Sudan in this sense excluded the vast regions west of Darfur which in the late nineteenth and early twentieth centuries were to pass under French and British colonial rule; on the other hand it included territories which did not form part of the Sudan as traditionally understood—Nubia, the land of the Beja, and the Ottoman ports of the Red Sea coast.

Traditionally the name of Nubia was applied to the whole riverain region from the First Cataract to the Sabaluqa Gorge, not far north of the confluence of the Blue and White Niles. It fell into two portions, which had separate histories from the early sixteenth to the early nineteenth century. Lower Nubia, called by the Ottomans *Berberistan*, 'the land of the Barabra',[2] extended from the First to the Third Cataract, and thus included territory both north and south of the modern Egyptian-Sudanese frontier. It was, nominally at least, dependent upon the Ottoman viceroys of Egypt. Upper Nubia, above the Third Cataract, was under the suzerainty of the Funj rulers of Sennar.

East of Nubia, in the Red Sea Hills, were the Beja, recognized by medieval Muslim writers as a distinct ethnic group, not Nubians, nor Arabs, nor *Sudan* ('Blacks'). Suakin and its sister-port of Massawa (which was annexed by Italy in 1884) were the attenuated remains of the Ottoman province of *Habesh*[3] (Abyssinia) and looked to the Red Sea and Arabia, rather than to the Nile valley, from which they were separated by the barrier of the Red Sea Hills and the intractable Beja.

The area of the present-day Republic of the Sudan is very nearly one million square miles—about one-quarter the size of Europe. Geographically, the greater part of the country is an immense plain. This may be divided into three zones: in the north is rocky desert and semi-desert; south of this is a belt of undulating sand, passing from semi-desert to savanna; south of this again a clay belt, which widens as it stretches eastwards from the south of Darfur to the rainlands and semi-desert lying east of the Blue and main Niles. The Red Sea Hills, a northerly prolongation of the Abyssinian highlands, separate the great plain from the narrow coastal strip.

The Sudanese plain is drained by the Nile and its tributaries. Both the White and Blue Niles rise outside the country. The White Nile enters the Sudan (where its upper reaches are known as *Bahr al-Jabal*, 'the Mountain River') at Nimule, and after a course of a hundred miles, passes into the clay plain. Here it is obstructed, and enlarges into an enormous swampy area, known as the Sudd (Arabic: *sadd*, 'barrier'). After a winding course of four hundred miles, it is joined by its western tributary, the Bahr al-Ghazal, which collects the waters of a multitude of smaller rivers, draining the south-western plain and originating in the ironstone plateau which forms the Nile-Congo divide. About eighty miles further on, it is joined by the Sobat from the east.

A broad, slow river, the White Nile emerges from the swamps into a region of acacia forests which at one time fringed its banks as far as Khartoum, but now the last part of its journey lies through open, almost treeless plains. From the confluence of the White Nile and Bahr al-Ghazal to Khartoum is a distance of about six hundred miles. The Blue Nile is a shorter, swifter and more beautiful river. Its course within the Sudan covers nearly five hundred miles. The peninsula which lies between the Blue and White rivers, as they converge at Khartoum, is known as the Gezira (Arabic: *jazira*, 'island' or 'peninsula'). Once the

4

granary of Khartoum, the Gezira is now the site of the principal cotton-growing area of the Sudan.

The main Nile flows in a generally northward direction from Khartoum through increasingly arid country. Two hundred miles below Khartoum, it receives the seasonal waters of the Atbara, its last tributary. About a hundred and fifty miles further on, at Abu Hamad, it makes a great bend to the southwest before resuming its northerly course by Dongola to the Egyptian frontier.

The tribes of the Sudan

There exists a broad distinction, which is nevertheless slowly being modified by the processes of history, between the northern and southern parts of the modern Sudan. The north is, with certain important exceptions, Arabic in speech, and its peoples are largely arabized in culture and outlook. Its indigenous inhabitants are universally Muslim; a minority of Arabic-speaking Christians is composed of the descendants of immigrants from Egypt and Lebanon since the Turco-Egyptian conquest. The southern Sudan contains a bewildering variety of ethnic groups and languages. Unlike the northerners, its peoples are not generally Muslims, nor do they claim Arab descent; although there has been some degree of islamization and arabization. These tendencies were restrained during the Condominium period, when European and American missionaries effected a limited christianization of the region.

Three southern tribes will appear fairly frequently in the following pages. The Shilluk now occupy a comparatively small area on the western bank of the White Nile, but formerly their range was much more extensive. As late as the mid-nineteenth century their northern limit was the island of Aba, thirty years later to be the cradle of the Mahdia. Until the early years of the Turco-Egyptian regime, they raided the Arab settlements down the White Nile, and one such raid is said to have led to the foundation of the Funj kingdom by a band of Shilluk warriors. Until the coming of firearms and steamers, they were able to meet their northern neighbours on equal terms.

The Dinka occupy a much more extensive territory than the

present-day Shilluk, but lack their unity: they are a group of tribes, some of which dwell on the eastern bank of the White Nile, others, the majority, in the grassy flood-plains of the Bahr al-Ghazal, where they herd their cattle. Further south, on the higher land of the Nile-Congo divide, live the Azande, now divided by the international boundary between the Republic of the Sudan and the former Belgian Congo.

The arabization of the northern Sudan resulted from the penetration of the region by tribes who had already migrated from Arabia to Upper Egypt. The process will be described in the following chapter. With certain comparatively minor exceptions, those northern Sudanese who claim Arab descent belong to one or other of two extensive, if somewhat artificial, divisions: the arabized Nubians, mainly sedentaries of the main Nile, composed of the Barabra and the Ja'ali Group; and the mainly nomadic or semi-nomadic Juhayna Group.

The Barabra, as we have seen, inhabit Lower Nubia. Their representatives in the modern Sudan are the Sukkut and Mahas, who still speak related Nubian dialects. South of them are a series of tribes, inhabiting the old Upper Nubia, who belong to the Ja'ali Group. These tribes claim as a common ancestor an Arab named Ibrahim Ja'al. Whether this eponym is historical or not, the traditional pedigree indicates an element common to all these tribes. Since the Arab irruption into this region, Arab descent has been a source of pride and distinction: hence it is not surprising that stress is laid on a common Arab ancestor. A further genealogical sophistication makes Ibrahim Ja'al a descendant of al-'Abbas, the Prophet's uncle. Thus the epithets Ja'ali and 'Abbasi have become virtually synonyms in the genealogies of the eastern *Bilad al-Sudan*. In spite, however, of the anxiety of the genealogists to provide the Ja'ali Group with a common Arab ancestor, it would be more realistic to regard the submerged Nubian substratum as the common ethnic element among these tribes. This hypothesis does not, of course, reject the undoubted historical fact of Arab ancestry as such: the result of intermarriage between Arab immigrants and the older Nubian population. From this intermingling the present Ja'ali Group derive their markedly Arab characteristics and their Muslim cultural inheritance.

6

The name of Ja'aliyin (plural of Ja'ali) is specifically applied to one tribe of this Group, dwelling between the Atbara confluence and the Sabaluqa Gorge. The Ja'aliyin in this restricted sense formed from the sixteenth century until the Turco-Egyptian conquest a tribal kingdom, dominated by a royal clan known as the Sa'dab. North of them, the region of Berber is the homeland of the Mirafab, another tribe of the Ja'ali Group, who also used to form a tribal kingdom. Further north still are other tribal members of the same Group, the Rubatab and Manasir, inhabiting the banks of the Nile down to and beyond the great bend at Abu Hamad.

The reach of the Nile between the Fourth Cataract and al-Dabba is the homeland of a tribal confederacy, the Shayqiyya, which does not claim Ja'ali origin. Many observers have noted what their history confirms, the difference between their character and that of their neighbours. In the eighteenth century the predatory, equestrian aristocracy of the Shayqiyya dominated Nubia. In 1821, they alone of the riverain tribes resisted the Turco-Egyptian invasion. Their subsequent service to the new regime as a quasi-feudal irregular cavalry led to the establishment of Shayqiyya colonies around the junction of the Niles and elsewhere.

The most northerly tribes of the Ja'ali Group lie downstream of the Shayqiyya, between al-Dabba and the country of the Barabra. Their homeland is the historical region of Dongola (Arabic: *Dunqula*), whence these tribesmen are known collectively as *Danaqla* (singular: *Dunqulawi*), i.e. 'men of Dongola'. Among them there is far more consciousness of Nubian origin than among the tribes of the southern Ja'ali Group, and a Nubian dialect continues to be spoken.

The arabized Nubians are primarily sedentary cultivators, inhabiting the narrow strip of riverain land and the islands (some of which are very extensive) which can be watered by the Nile flood or irrigation. Their territories lie outside the normal rain-belt. Hence the pressure of population on the land has always been heavy, especially among the Danaqla and Barabra. This economic limitation, in association sometimes with political instability, has made temporary or permanent emigration a recurrent feature of the history of these peoples.

7

The Barabra have provided Egypt with its 'Berberine' servants. In the sixteenth century, Mahas migrated to the confluence of the Niles and established themselves as religious teachers.

Various ruling groups, basically neither Nubian nor Arab, have claimed a Ja'ali (or, synonymously, an 'Abbasi) ancestry. The royal family of Taqali, a small Muslim state in the pagan Nuba Mountains, derives its origin from the marriage of a Ja'ali holy man with an indigenous princess. A similar story is told of the origin of the Nabtab, the dominant clan of the Beja Banu 'Amir. The royal Kayra clan amongst the Fur claimed 'Abbasi ancestry, as did the neighbouring rulers of Wadai. The rise of the Shayqiyya in the eighteenth century produced an emigration of Danaqla to Darfur, which seems to have led to a development of trade between that state and Egypt. In the nineteenth century Ja'ali *jallaba* (petty traders) were ubiquitous in southern Kordofan and Darfur, on the southern fringe of Arab territory, while Danaqla and other members of the great Ja'ali Group played a prominent part in the opening-up of the White Nile and Bahr al-Ghazal. Al-Zubayr Rahma, the merchant-prince of the western Bahr al-Ghazal in the reign of Khedive Isma'il, prided himself on his 'Abbasi descent.

Mention should also be made of several tribes, outside the confines of ancient Nubia, which claim membership of the Ja'ali Group. These are probably synthetic tribes, formed by the accretion of heterogeneous fragments around Ja'ali leaders. It is significant that five of them have names derived from the Arabic root *jama'a*, 'to collect'.

In Sudanese genealogical usage, the term *Juhayna* is practically a comprehensive term for all tribes claiming Arab descent but not asserting a Ja'ali-'Abbasi origin. Arabs of the Juhayna of Arabia, who had migrated to Upper Egypt, played a leading part in the break-through into Nubia in the fourteenth century, and there has been a tendency for elements of varied (and even non-Arab) origins to link themselves with this successful tribe.

Even the confused and sometimes tendentious genealogical materials available today make it clear, however, that at least two important sub-groups can hardly be linked ancestrally with the Juhayna. The Rufa'a, found on the Blue Nile, preserve some memory of a distinct origin. Their ancestors lived in geographical proximity to the ancestral Juhayna, both in the Hijaz and in Upper Egypt; and this has probably led to their inclusion in the Juhayna Group. In the late fifteenth century an Arab population, probably of varied origins, became sedentarized at the junction of the Blue and White Niles under a chief from the Rufaʻa named ʻAbdallah Jammaʻ. He and his successors, the ʻAbdallab, became prosperous from the tolls levied on the desert Arabs during their annual nomadic cycle, and were recognized by the Funj rulers of Sennar (1504–1821) as paramount chiefs of the Arabs. The bulk of the Rufaʻa were almost entirely nomadic until the nineteenth century, when the northern section became partly sedentarized. The town of Rufaʻa on the Blue Nile was originally a tribal settlement. The southern section, on each side of the upper Blue Nile, is still largely nomadic.

A second sub-group which can hardly belong to the Juhayna by descent is the Fazara. This term, now obsolete in Sudanese usage, included until the last century most of the camel-nomads of northern Kordofan and Darfur. The historical Fazara tribe was of north-Arabian origin, whereas the Juhayna were south-Arabian.

Among the numerous tribes of the Juhayna Group, two have played a sufficiently important part in Sudanese history to be given specific mention. The leading tribe of the southern Butana (i.e. the quadrilateral bounded by the main Nile, the Atbara, the Blue Nile and the Abyssinian foothills) is the Shukriyya, camel-owning nomads. They rose to importance during the eighteenth century as Funj power declined, under the leadership of the Abu Sinn family. Ahmad Abu Sinn (*circa* 1790–1870) lived on good terms with the Turco-Egyptian regime, was given the rank of bey, and for ten years was governor of Khartoum. Their territory included the grain-producing rainlands of the Qadarif, where a tribal market developed. This place, originally called Suq Abu Sinn ('Abu Sinn's Market') has now taken over the name of the region, anglicized as Gedaref.

Another important nomadic tribe is the Kababish. These inhabit a region suitable for sheep and camel rearing in the semi-desert north of Kordofan. They are a synthetic tribe, formed from diverse elements by a common way of life, which is reflected in their name (from Arabic: *kabsh*, 'a ram'). Their wide range, across the north-western trade-routes, made the tribe a factor of some importance in the commercial and political history of the Sudan, especially during the nineteenth century.

An important sub-group of tribes claiming origin from the Juhayna is the Baqqara of southern Kordofan and Darfur. As their name (from Arabic: *baqar*, 'a cow') implies, these are cattle-nomads: the frontier-tribes of Arabdom, inhabiting regions where camel nomadism is climatically impossible. The route by which they arrived in their present habitat is a subject of controversy, but broadly speaking they seem to be a southern offshoot of the great Arab irruption into the lands west of the Nile. The furthest wave of these immigrants was carried as far west as Lake Chad, whence a return-movement towards the east deposited the ancestors of the modern Baqqara tribes.

Between the Baqqara in the south and the camel-Arabs of the north were enclaves of non-Arab sedentaries. From one of these, the Fur, protected by the mountainous bastion of Jabal Marra, developed the important Muslim sultanate of Darfur ('the land of the Fur'). The non-Arab tribes to the south of the Baqqara country were frequently raided for slaves, and inter-marriage has considerably modified the physical type of the Baqqara, although they have preserved their Arabic speech and tradition. Two tribes played a particularly important role in the history of the last century: the powerful Rizayqat of southern Darfur, athwart a principal route from the Bahr al-Ghazal region to the north; and the Ta'aisha, an unimportant tribe until the Mahdia, when they were used by their kinsman, the Khalifa 'Abdallahi, as an instrument of his domination in the Sudan.

The Beja are Hamitic-speaking tribes, now inhabiting the Red Sea Hills and parts of the plains sloping down to the main Nile. Their ancestors confronted and, to some extent, inter-married with the Arab immigrants into Upper Egypt in the early Middle Ages. They are camel-nomads, although there has been some degree of sedentarization, especially in connection with the modern agricultural development of the Gash and

Tokar deltas. Like the riverain Nubians, the Beja became Muslims, and have undergone varying degrees of arabization. In its lightest form, this amounts to little more than claiming an Arab pedigree; the early Muslim heroes, Khalid ibn al-Walid and al-Zubayr ibn al-'Awwam being preferred as adoptive ancestors.

The most northerly of the modern Beja, the 'Ababda, now divided between Upper Egypt and the Sudan, are, however, Arabic-speaking. As protectors of the route across the Nubian Desert, from Sudanese territory to the Nile at Kurusku, a clan of the 'Ababda played a part of some importance before the construction of the railway, and their chiefs were in close relations with the Turco-Egyptian administration. The more southerly and less arabized Beja underwent a period of expansion in the eighteenth century, moving south-westwards from their mountainous habitats towards the plains of the Atbara and the Gash. The most aggressive of these tribes, the Hadendowa, had established itself in the Taka, the region of the Gash, by the early nineteenth century.

Of the other non-Arab peoples of the northern Sudan, the Fur have already been mentioned. Although surrounded by a flood of immigrant Arab tribes, they succeeded in establishing a dynastic Muslim state which was not finally extinguished until 1916. Between Darfur and the White Nile, the hilly region of the Nuba Mountains provided a refuge for another indigenous people as Arab tribes gradually occupied the plain of Kordofan. The name of Nuba is applied in Arabic both to these people and to the historical Nubians of the main Nile. The nature of the relationship between these two homonymous groups has long been a matter of controversy. Here it is enough to note that the hill-Nuba never succeeded in asserting themselves against the Arabs, as did the Fur. Their hill-top communities were divided and isolated. They remained for the most part pagan, although the greater security of the present century has opened the way both to organized Christian missionary activity and the more amorphous but effective influence of contact with Muslims. In the north-eastern foothills lay the kingdom of Taqali, whose rulers encouraged the immigration of settlers and established their suzerainty over a considerable area. The kingdom continued to exist in semi-autonomy after the Turco-Egyptian conquest; and was integrated into the local government system of the Condominium.

The ancient trade-routes

The territories which now form the northern Sudan were traversed by a number of trade-routes. These found their outlet through Upper Egypt and the Red Sea. The commerce of the eastern *Bilad al-Sudan*, extending to Darfur or a little further west, was thus quite distinct from that of the central *Bilad al-Sudan*, which found an outlet by way of the Fezzan to North Africa.

The routes of the eastern *Bilad al-Sudan* lay along two main axes. One, running roughly from south to north, linked Sennar with Egypt. The other, roughly from west to east, linked Darfur with Suakin. Commercial relations existed between Sennar and western Abyssinia, centring on Gondar. From Sennar a route ran along the western bank of the Blue Nile through the Gezira to the ancient market-town of Arbaji.[4] Further to the north, the river was crossed, and the way continued along the eastern bank of the Blue and main Niles by al-'Aylafun and Halfayat al-Muluk ('Halfaya of the Kings'), the later capital of the 'Abdallab chiefs.

Beyond Qarri, the old 'Abdallabi capital, there were alternative routes to the north. The western route was apparently the more used in the earlier Funj period. The Nile was crossed near Qarri or al-Dirayra (i.e. either above or below the Sabaluqa Gorge), and travellers then struck across the Bayuda Desert in a north-westerly direction, cutting off the great bend of the Nile and avoiding the country of the predatory Shayqiyya. Before the rise of the Shayqiyya, in the late seventeenth century, caravans may well have followed the river all the way. The desert route met the Nile again at Kurti, and continued along its western bank, through the vassal-kingdom of Dongola, to the frontier-post of Mushu, some way south of the Third Cataract. Here the caravans turned into the desert.

At the Salima Oasis, the Nile route was joined by the great artery of trade between Darfur and Egypt, the *Darb al-arba'in* ('the Forty Days' Road'). This began at Kubayh, the principal commercial centre of Darfur, ran to the frontier-post of Suwayna, and thence went north-eastwards across the desert to Salima. From Salima the route went by way of the alum-producing watering-point of Shabb to the Kharja Oasis, which was an outpost of Ottoman Egypt. Thence it ran to the Nile at Asyut.

The eastern route seems to have developed during the eighteenth century, in consequence of increasing political instability in the riverain territories downstream of Berber. From Qarri it went along the eastern bank to Shendi and El Damer, and over the Atbara into the territory of Berber. It then left the river, and crossed the Nubian Desert until Ottoman territory was reached in the neighbourhood of Aswan. After Muhammad 'Ali's conquests, a shorter desert-crossing was usual, from Abu Hamad, at the great bend of the Nile, by the wells of al-Murrat to Kurusku in Lower Nubia. The line of the modern railway, between Abu Hamad and Wadi Halfa, is the latest variant of this historic route.

The routes of the west-east trade axis were also liable to vary in accordance with political conditions. Kordofan was a debatable land between the rulers of Sennar and Darfur, and the situation of the untamed Shilluk on the White Nile combined to render unsafe the direct route from Kubayh to Sennar via El Obeid. Caravans therefore took a more northerly route from El Obeid to Shendi. From Shendi caravans went to Egypt by the desert-crossing described above. Merchants travelling from Shendi to Suakin went up the river Atbara to Quz Rajab, a market-town ruled by an 'Abdallabi chief. A direct route from Sennar also ran to Quz Rajab, but this was rendered dangerous by the Shukriyya nomads. From Quz Rajab, one route went direct to Suakin, while another made a diversion into the Taka.

By the early nineteenth century, Shendi, the point of intersection of the two route-axes, had become the principal commercial centre of the eastern *Bilad al-Sudan*. In the years immediately preceding the Turco-Egyptian invasion it was under the strong autonomous rule of *Makk* Nimr,[5] the Sa'dabi chief. Its populace was composed of indigenous Ja'aliyin and merchant settlers from Sennar, Kordofan, Darfur and Dongola, the last being the most numerous. In spite of the commercial activity over which they presided, neither the Sa'dab nor any other Sudanese dynasty coined their own money. Millet and *dammur*, the local cotton cloth, the staples of local commerce, formed the media of exchange, while foreign silver coins (in Burckhardt's time[6] the Spanish dollars of Charles IV) were used for larger transactions.

Shendi was a centre both for the internal trade of the various regions of the eastern *Bilad al-Sudan*, and for external trade. Among the principal commodities produced and consumed within the region were millet and *dammur*, while slaves were of pre-eminent importance, both in internal and external trade. The slaves were not, of course, taken from among the Muslim peoples, but were obtained chiefly by raiding the pagan fringe of Abyssinia and the tribes to the south-west of Darfur. A certain number of them came from servile families settled in the neighbourhood of Sennar. Although many slaves were retained permanently in the Sudanese territories, as domestic servants, field workers and armed bodyguards, there was a considerable export trade to Egypt and Arabia. A smaller, more specialized trade, was in horses from Dongola, which were exported to the Yemen.

Although there was little commercial intercourse between the eastern *Bilad al-Sudan* and the countries west of Darfur, a steady stream of Muslim pilgrims, known generically as Takarir, or Takarna (singular, Takruri), passed from the central and western *Bilad al-Sudan* into Darfur, where their numbers were still further augmented from the local peoples. From Darfur they went eastwards by a variety of routes. Some went north, to Asyut and Cairo, where they joined the Egyptian Pilgrimage Caravan. Others made their way to Sennar and Gondar, and thence to the seaport of Massawa. The most favoured route in the early nineteenth century was however the great commercial artery, by way of Shendi to Suakin. This pilgrimage-route, linking the central and eastern portions of *Bilad al-Sudan*, can hardly have been older than the sixteenth century, when Muslim dynasties were established in Sennar, Darfur and Wadai.

Many of the pilgrims were excessively poor, and depended on charity or earnings from manual labour to complete their journey, which in some cases lasted for years. Their successors in the present century, now generally called Fallata, have provided much of the labour force for the cotton-fields of the Gezira, and are a semi-permanent element in the population of the modern Sudan. At some time, probably in the early nineteenth century, a colony of Takarna established a vigorous frontier-state in a district of the Abyssinian marches known as the Qallabat. The name of their territory is perpetuated in the modern frontier-town of al-Qallabat, anglicized as Gallabat.

CHAPTER II

BEFORE THE TURCO-EGYPTIAN CONQUEST

The coming of the Arabs

WHEN THE Muslim Arabs under 'Amr ibn al-'As invaded and conquered the Byzantine province of Egypt, between 639 and 641, the Nubian territories south of the First Cataract formed two Christian kingdoms. The more northerly, itself the combination of the two older kingdoms of Nobadia and Makuria, is generally known as al-Maqurra. Its capital was Old Dongola, and it extended to a point on the main Nile south of the Atbara confluence. Beyond it lay the kingdom of 'Alwa, which extended southwards up the Blue and White Niles for an indeterminate distance. The capital of 'Alwa was the town of Suba, on the right bank of the Blue Nile, some miles upstream from its confluence with the main Nile.

Frontier raiding south of Aswan began at once, and in 651-2 the Arab governor of Egypt, 'Abdallah ibn Sa'd ibn Abi Sarh, led a Muslim army to besiege Dongola. He did not succeed in effecting a conquest, if this had been his intention, but withdrew after concluding a treaty which established for some six hundred years trading relations and a *modus vivendi* between Muslim Egypt and Christian Nubia.[1] This forbade the permanent settlement of Nubians in Muslim territory, or of Muslims in Nubia. It provided for the maintenance of a mosque in Dongola, and required the payment of an annual tribute of 360 slaves to the Muslim governor of Aswan. By a convention, not expressed in the treaty, the Nubians received gifts of cereals and other goods from the Egyptian authorities, and these at times exceeded the value of the slave-tribute.

The transient military success of 'Abdallah ibn Sa'd's expedition set a pattern which was to recur in the following centuries. Until the time of Muhammad 'Ali Pasha, no expedition from Egypt succeeded in making any extensive permanent conquest in the Sudan. The threat to Christian Nubia came less from the remote Muslim rulers in Cairo than from the nomad Arab tribes, imperfectly controlled by the administration, which gradually penetrated into Upper Egypt, formed with indigenous groups an arabized frontier society, and ultimately, as Nubian defences weakened, infiltrated into the region of the Cataracts and beyond.

Many of the details of this historical process are forever lost, but medieval Arabic sources preserve a few records of the main stages. Arab immigration into the region of the First Cataract seems to have become politically significant about the time of the autonomous governor of Egypt, Ahmad ibn Tulun, in the last third of the ninth century. An Arab adventurer, named al-'Umari, with followers from the tribes of Rabi'a and Juhayna, made an expedition into Nubia but then turned his attention to the eastern desert. Here, where opposition came only from the less sophisticated Beja, existed mines of gold and emeralds, beyond the reach of settled administration. Subsequently Rabi'a intermarried with the Beja of the desert, and with the Nubians of the region of the First Cataract. Between the eleventh and fourteenth centuries, the Banu Kanz,[2] as the ruling clan of this mixed Arab-Nubian society were called, were powerful marcher lords, virtually autonomous of the rulers of Egypt.

Apart from the expedition of al-'Umari in 969, and another commanded by Turan Shah, brother of Saladin, in 1172, direct hostilities between the rulers of Egypt and of Nubia seem to have been unknown between the time of 'Abdallah ibn Sa'd and that of the Mamluk sultan of Egypt, al-Zahir Baybars (1260–77). Baybars's intervention in Nubian affairs may have been partly due to mistrust of an autonomous power on the upper Nile, a recurrent fear of Egyptian rulers, but partly also to a desire to turn the activities of the insubordinate Arab tribes of Egypt into channels less dangerous to his administration. The expeditions sent by Baybars and his successors in the late thirteenth and the fourteenth centuries into al-Maqurra, usually with the object of installing a puppet ruler, sapped the political and military strength of the Nubian kingdom. The northern part, at least, fell under the control of the Banu Kanz. The Juhayna immigrated southwards, intermarried with the local dynasts and, owing to the Nubian custom of matrilineal succession, took over their territories in the next generation. Settled government disintegrated and, when Ibn Khaldun wrote in the late fourteenth century, Juhayna were masters 'from Aswan and beyond it as far as the land of the Nubians and that of Abyssinia'.

Ibn Khaldun's phraseology implies that in his time there were still Nubian territories outside Arab control. The name of Berber[3] suggests an ancient linguistic frontier, or an enclave of non-Arabic speech, of which now no memory remains. Sudanese tradition has however preserved the recollection of the fall of the southern kingdom of 'Alwa. Unlike al-Maqurra, 'Alwa, or at least its metropolitan region, did not disintegrate as a result of gradual infiltration but was conquered by an Arab confederation under a leader named 'Abdallah Jamma' (i.e., 'Abdallah 'Gatherer').[4] It is noteworthy that, whereas Old Dongola continued to be a leading town and was the residence of a vassal-king in the Funj period, Suba completely lost its importance, and the descendants of 'Abdallah Jamma' made their capital on the main Nile at Qarri. Sudanese tradition also asserts that the Nubians largely abandoned this conquered region: this is borne out by the persistent report, in later times, that Hajar al-'Asal, north of Qarri, was the southern frontier of Nubia.

From the later fourteenth to the early sixteenth century is a dark age in Sudanese history. At the end of this period, however, new political groupings appear. The Funj rulers of Sennar established their hegemony over the Gezira and the main Nile. The Ottoman conquest of Egypt was followed in due course by the establishment of a frontier-province against the Funj in Lower Nubia. Ottoman rule was also established on the Red Sea littoral, in the province of *Habesh*. At a rather later date the indigenous Muslim sultanate of Darfur came into being.

The Funj Sultanate

The Funj were a mysterious people, who appeared suddenly in

history in the Muslim year 910 (i.e., A.D. 1504–5) when their first ruler, 'Amara Dunqas, founded his capital at Sennar on the Blue Nile. Of their origin, perhaps the only thing that can be said with certainty is that they were neither Arabs nor, at first, Muslims, and even this has been obscured by later genealogical legend, which, following a common pattern amongst the Muslim fringe-peoples, sought to ennoble the newly islamized rulers by deriving their pedigree from an Arab, in this case an Umayyad refugee. To the Sudanese, their dynasty is traditionally known as the Black Sultanate. The Scottish traveller, James Bruce, who visited Sennar in 1772, records a tradition that the Funj were by origin Shilluk raiders from the White Nile. This is not inherently improbable. Bruce's tradition has been criticized by recent writers, and various alternative hypotheses have been proposed. A rigorous investigation of the problem of Funj origins has yet to be made.

At the time of the coming of the Funj, the hegemony over the Arab tribes in the northern Gezira and around the confluence of the Blue and White Niles was held by a sedentary clan, the 'Abdallab, whose chief resided at Qarri on the main Nile. There are many obscurities around the person and date of the eponymous ancestor of the clan, 'Abdallah Jamma', but the early relations of Funj and 'Abdallab appear to have been hostile.

The 'Abdallabi chief, 'Ajib I, who ruled from about the middle of the sixteenth century, was appointed by the Funj ruler and bore the non-Arab title of *manjil* or *manjilak*, conferred by the Funj on their principal vassals. According to 'Abdallabi tradition, however, he revolted against his overlord and temporarily drove the Funj into the Abyssinian marches. The Funj regained their lost dominions under King Dakin who 'came from the east' and is remembered even in the meagre chronicle of the period as an administrator and lawgiver. Many years later, 'Ajib revolted again and was killed in the battle of Karkuj (1607–8) on the east bank of the Blue Nile, near its confluence with the White. This time the 'Abdallab ruling family were expelled from their territory and sought refuge in Dongola. Ultimately a settlement was effected through the mediation of a celebrated religious teacher, Shaykh Idris ibn

19

Arbab, whose disciple the reigning Funj monarch was. The *status quo* was restored, and the descendants of 'Ajib ruled as hereditary, and virtually autonomous, princes of the Arabs. The patronymic *Wad 'Ajib* ('Son of 'Ajib') was used almost as a title for these chiefs.[5]

When Bruce passed through the kingdom in 1772, the 'Abdallabi chief ruled as far north as Hajar al-'Asal on the main Nile. Below this point, to the frontier of Ottoman Nubia, above the Third Cataract, was a succession of tribal chieftaincies, strung out along the banks of the river. Of these riverain tribal states, the most important were those of the Sa'dab Ja'aliyin, with their capital at Shendi, the Majadhib theocracy of El Damer, the Mirafab of Berber, and the kingdom of Dongola in the far north. During the sixteenth century, the Shayqiyya confederacy had asserted their independence of the Funj suzerain, and, as the Funj state passed into decline, they preyed increasingly on the territory of their riverain neighbours.

After the rather misleading wealth of tradition on the foundation of the Funj kingdom, the records of early rulers become very sparse. The dynasty and its warriors were soon converted to Islam; the second (or third) king, 'Abd al-Qadir, bore a Muslim name, although non-Arabic names preponderate in the king-lists until the end of the dynasty. Bruce states that the conversion was 'for the sake of trading with Cairo': it would probably be more true to see in it a consequence of trading, political and cultural relations with Upper Egypt. The early Funj period was one of considerable Muslim missionary work in the riverain Sudan, as we shall see.

From about the middle of the seventeenth century we are more fully informed of the activities of the Funj kings. The dynasty was at its highest point under Badi II Abu Daqn who reigned from 1644–45 until his death in 1680. He made a great campaign across the White Nile, raiding the Shilluk as he passed, and penetrated the Nuba Mountains. Here the Muslim kingdom of Taqali was besieged and its ruler became tributary to the Funj. Although the nature of the tribute is not specified, it is reasonable to assume that it was paid in slaves, since the Nuba Mountains were one of the principal slave-raiding areas.

In any case, Badi brought back numerous prisoners whom he settled in villages around Sennar. The prisoners and their descendants, later augmented by raiding and purchase, formed a slave-army for the protection of the capital and its ruler. This shift in the military basis of the dynasty's rule, from the band of free warriors, the Funj aristocracy, to slave-troops directly dependent on the monarch,[6] is paralleled in other Islamic states, notably in the Ottoman Empire itself. The tensions produced by this innovation appeared in the reign of Badi II's second successor. A section of the Funj revolted against him and tried to depose him, but were defeated in battle. Further troubles occurred under his son, who was faced by a military revolt of the southern Funj, and compelled to put to death his vizier (possibly a slave); and then was himself deposed. This was the end of the direct line of 'Amara Dunqas. The new ruler and his successors were connected with the dynasty on the mother's side.

The second monarch of this branch, Badi IV Abu Shulukh (1724–62), was the last effective Funj king. The earlier part of his long reign was successful and prosperous, although in these years, significantly, the management of affairs was in the hands of viziers. Thereafter the king assumed personal power. He began with a proscription of the old ruling clan, from which the kings preceding his father had come, and set up an arbitrary rule with the support of his Nuba slave-troops, 'whom he made chiefs in place of the men of old lineage and rank'. By such actions he antagonized the Funj notables.

In 1747 Badi sent a great army across the White Nile on campaign against the Musabba'at, the ruling tribe of Kordofan. Since the king did not himself accompany this expedition, he may have meant to rid himself of potential opponents, much as the Khalifa, in the following century, despatched 'Abd al-Rahman al-Nujumi on the *jihad* against Egypt. The Funj army was worsted in its first encounter with the Musabba'at, but the troops were rallied by the notable, Shaykh Muhammad Abu Likaylik, who inflicted a crushing defeat on the enemy. Thereafter Abu Likaylik seems to have ruled Kordofan as viceroy for fourteen years.

The existence of this remote and successful military force,

B

however, constituted a threat to Badi. The crisis came to a head in 1760–61, when the Funj notables in Kordofan, perturbed by reports of the king's actions towards their clients in their absence, persuaded Abu Likaylik to head a revolt. Accompanied by his troops, the Funj notables and even some of the royal slaves, Abu Likaylik recrossed the White Nile. He negotiated with a son of the king, whom the rebels set up as their figurehead. Sennar was besieged, but Badi was finally allowed to leave under an amnesty for exile in Suba. With him the power of the Funj dynasty passed away. The remaining kings down to the Turco-Egyptian conquest were puppets of their hereditary viziers, who were in effect regents of the kingdom.

The first of these was Shaykh Muhammad Abu Likaylik himself. Although he had been brought to power by a revolt of the Funj aristocracy, he belonged to the Hamaj. This seems to be one of a number of terms applied by the immigrant Arabs to the indigenous peoples: it should not be assumed that all the Hamaj formed a single, homogeneous, ethnic group.[7] The Hamaj hegemony, inaugurated by Abu Likaylik, is therefore an interesting revival of an element in the population which had for two and a half centuries been politically submerged by immigrant ruling groups, the Arabs and the Funj.

The Regent Muhammad Abu Likaylik ruled until his death in 1776–77. He had deposed the puppet-king at the end of 1769 and appointed his brother Isma'il as king in his place. Isma'il was king in Sennar at the time of Bruce's visit. Bruce describes him as light in colour, about thirty-four years of age. 'He had a very plebeian countenance, on which was stamped no decided character; I should rather have guessed him to be a soft, timid, irresolute man.'[8] On Abu Likaylik's death, he was succeeded as regent by his nephew. Once again the Funj revolted, but the regent was too strong to be shaken, and the result of the rebellion was the deposition and exile of another king.

The Funj kingdom was however visibly decaying. The last forty years of its history are filled with the quarrels of rivals for the regency, kaleidoscopic combinations of Funj aristocrats and 'Abdallab chiefs, petty wars and all the symptoms of political instability. The Hamaj regents soon went the way of their Funj sovereigns. The fourth regent, Nasir, a son of the great Abu Likaylik, handed over the management of affairs to the *Arbab*⁹ Dafa'allah and gave himself up to luxury. A revolt against him was joined by his own brothers: he was captured and put to death in 1798 as an act of vengeance by his cousin, the son of the second regent, Badi. Although his brother and successor restored order, he held power for only five years, and after his death the disruptive tendencies in the Hamaj dynasty reasserted themselves.

The ninth and last of the Hamaj regents, Muhammad wad 'Adlan, a grandson of Muhammad Abu Likaylik, was a strong ruler who used violence and treachery to consolidate his position. He seized power in August 1808 and held it until the troops of Muhammad 'Ali Pasha advanced on Sennar. At the news of their approach, his followers scattered and Wad 'Adlan was treacherously attacked and killed by his cousin, Hasan wad Rajab. The collapse of the regency left no effective authority in the kingdom of Sennar, and the titular ruler, Badi VI, surrendered without resistance to Isma'il Pasha.

The Ottoman Fringe

Although Sultan Salim I overthrew the Circassian Mamluk sultanate, occupied Cairo and annexed Egypt to the Ottoman Empire in 1517, he did not attempt a territorial conquest of his new province in detail. The remoter parts of Upper Egypt were beyond effective administration from the centre, even though the great tribal chiefs accepted the sultan's suzerainty. Lower Nubia at this period was similarly loosely dependent upon the Funj king (or perhaps more accurately upon the 'Abdallabi chief), so that there was at the outset no reason for a clash between the Ottomans and the Funj.

The extension of Ottoman power into Nubia occurred late in the reign of Sultan Sulayman the Magnificent (1520–66) through the agency of Özdemir Pasha. Özdemir was a relative of the Circassian Mamluk sultan, Qansuh al-Ghawri, who had been defeated in 1516 by Selim. He served the new Ottoman rulers and ultimately became governor-general of the Yemen. He resigned this office about the year 1550 and returned to Egypt by way of Suakin. He went on to Istanbul, where, in an

interview with the sultan, he proposed an expedition to conquer Abyssinia. The sultan approved the proposal and authorized Özdemir to enrol troops in Egypt.

He did so, and the expedition set out by way of Upper Egypt
overland to Suakin. This was a curious and arduous route to
choose. It was probably dictated by an opportunity of intervening in the affairs of Lower Nubia, where a struggle for the
hegemony was proceeding between two local tribes, the
Jawabira and the Gharbiyya. The Jawabira, in alliance with
the Funj (or, more probably, the vassal-king of Dongola) had
won the upper hand, when the Gharbiyya sought Ottoman
support. Özdemir captured the key-fortress of Ibrim from the
allies, and garrisons of Bosniak troops were installed there, and
also at Aswan and Say, which lies between the Second and
Third Cataracts.

The administration of the district, primarily the collection
of revenue, was committed to an official, who, like his counterparts in Egypt, bore the old Mamluk title of *kashif*. His residence was at Dirr. The office became hereditary in the family
of its first holder. The clan formed by his descendants were
known as *Ghuzz*, a term originally applied to the free Turks
but in Egypt at this time, by a curious shift of meaning, used
for the Mamluks. The Bosniak troops likewise intermarried
locally, and their descendants formed a privileged class, known
as *Kal'ejis* (Turkish; 'men of the fortress') or *Osmanlis* (Ottomans), ruled by their own *aghas* and independent of the *kashifs*.

There appears to have been further fighting before the Ottoman frontier was finally established at the Third Cataract. There
is an 'Abdallabi tradition of a victory on 'the Egyptian border'
over Ottoman troops armed with firearms, but the chronological indications are hopelessly muddled. This may be a
suitably modified version of another tradition which describes
the overwhelming defeat of a 'Funj' force by a Ghuzz governor
at Hannak, just above the Third Cataract. The Ghuzz leader is
called Ibn Janbalan, and may be identified with Sulayman
Janbulad, a Mamluk bey who, about the year 1620, became the
first governor of Upper Egypt, and thereby the immediate
overlord of the *kashif* of Dirr. Henceforward Hannak was the
border between Ottoman and Funj territory.

From Nubia, Özdemir proceeded to the Red Sea coast, to establish a base for Ottoman power against the Portuguese on the one hand and the Abyssinians on the other. Suakin, which already recognized some degree of control from Egypt, passed into his hands. Massawa was taken in 1557, and became his administrative centre. Zayla was taken from the Portuguese. In collusion with a revolted vassal of the Abyssinian king, Özdemir conquered some inland territory and seized Debaroa. There he died and was buried in 1559–60, but his body was later removed to Massawa.

After the heroic age of Özdemir Pasha, Ottoman power in the so-called province of Abyssinia (*Habesh*) rapidly declined. The Portuguese threat passed away, and the Red Sea became, in the seventeenth century, a quiet backwater of Muslim commerce. When Bruce visited Massawa in 1769, it no longer had an Ottoman governor but was ruled by a tribal chief, with the title of *na'ib* (Arabic; 'deputy'). As in Nubia, the Ottoman garrison had intermarried with the local people and their descendants formed an hereditary military caste. Although the *na'ibs* were nominally subordinate to the Ottoman governor of Jedda, they were in practice much more dependent on the rulers of Abyssinia, with whom they shared the customs revenue, while they had ceased to pay tribute to the sultans.

Burckhardt, in 1814, found a similar condition of affairs in Suakin. Suakin was governed by an *amir* chosen from the local patrician families of the Hadariba, a tribe of mixed Arab-Beja origin. The descendants of the Ottoman garrison-troops, who here claimed mostly a Kurdish ancestry, formed another element in the population. Ottoman authority in the port was limited to the granting of recognition to the *amir* by the governor of Jedda, and the appointment of a customs-officer, who had the title of *agha*.

Darfur

The creation of a Muslim kingdom in Darfur was the work of a line of rulers belonging to the Kayra clan of the Fur. The early traditions are conflicting and obscure. There seems to have been intermarriage between ancestors of the dynasty and Arabs; a folk-hero named Ahmad al-Ma'qur plays a prominent, if ambiguous role, while the first clearly historical ruler, Sulayman, is called *Solong*, 'the Arab', and is said to have been the son of an Arab mother. Although tradition glorifies the Arab ancestors of the Kayra by linking them with the 'Abbasid caliphs or the Banu Hilal, whose exploits in North Africa are commemorated in a legendary cycle, it is more probable that they belonged to the Fazara camel-nomads of the vicinity. Another tradition links the Kayra with the Musabba'at who ruled in Kordofan, and with the royal house of Wadai.

Sulayman Solong is the Furawi counterpart of 'Amara Dunqas, the founder of the dynasty and first Muslim ruler, a conqueror who fought in alliance with the nomad Arabs. His dates are uncertain, but it seems likely that he flourished around the year 1640. His immediate successors are shadowy figures, who seem to have been largely occupied in hostilities against the sister-kingdom of Wadai. One interesting tradition concerns Abu'l-Qasim, the sixth sultan, who lived about the middle of the eighteenth century. He, it is said, 'showed a great inclination to the Blacks, and incurred, in consequence, the hostility of his relations, who urged him to take the field against Wadai, and having advanced, suddenly deserted him with the army, leaving him with the Blacks only.'[10] Here is probably a reminiscence of the development of a royal bodyguard of slave-troops which, as in the Funj sultanate, produced tension between the ruler and the old free military aristocracy.

Fuller traditions begin with the seventhsultan, Muhammad Tayrab, who, towards the end of his reign (i.e. rather before 1787) went to war against the Musabba'a sultan of Kordofan. The Musabba'at must have returned to power there after the withdrawal of Muhammad Abu Likaylik in 1760–61, although Bruce still speaks of it as a dependency of Sennar in 1772. There is some resemblance between Tayrab's expedition and that which Badi IV sent into Kordofan, since Tayrab's motive seems to have been to remove from Darfur his brothers and members of the old ruling aristocracy. He hoped thereby to clear the way to the succession for his son, Ishaq. While the king took the field, his son with a shadow administration was left as viceroy in the royal residence. Hashim, the sultan of Kordofan, was expelled and sought refuge in Funj territory.

The Fur troops occupied Kordofan, which remained a dependency of Darfur until the Egyptian conquest. Tayrab himself died at Bara; it is said that he was poisoned by his grandees.

A dispute over the succession now developed between the partisans of Ishaq and those of the brothers of Tayrab. The political director of the latter group was a young eunuch named Muhammad Kurra. He induced the princes to recognize as their candidate their youngest brother, the pious and scholarly 'Abd al-Rahman al-Rashid, whose youth and temperament no doubt made him seem an ideal figurehead. In the subsequent fighting, Ishaq and his faction were defeated, and 'Abd al-Rahman was recognized as sultan. Muhammad Kurra became his chief minister.

The reign of 'Abd al-Rahman marks the highest point of the old Kayra sultanate. It was a time of progress in both commercial and religious development, both of which were stimulated by the immigration of riverain Sudanese into Darfur in consequence of growing political instability along the main Nile. Increased contact with the outside world, through trade with Egypt along the *Darb al-arba'in*, is indicated by an exchange of presents between 'Abd al-Rahman and the Ottoman sultan, by the visit of an English traveller, W. G. Browne, in 1793–96, and by correspondence with Bonaparte in 1799, during the French occupation of Egypt. Browne, who had an audience of the sultan, describes him as

'. . . a man rather under the middle size, of a complexion adust or dry, with eyes full of fire, and features abounding in expression. His beard is short but full, and his countenance, though perfectly black, materially differing from the negro; though fifty or fifty-five years of age he possesses much alertness and activity.'[11]

On 'Abd al-Rahman's death in 1800–1, the old kingmaker, Muhammad Kurra, installed his master's young son as sultan. The new ruler, Muhammad Fadl, ruled for nearly forty years, but his was a period of decline. Early in his reign, he developed suspicions of Muhammad Kurra, who was killed in 1804. In 1821 Muhammad 'Ali's troops, commanded by the *Defterdar*[12]

Muhammad Bey Khusraw, invaded Kordofan, defeated the Furawi governor, the *Maqdum* Musallim,[13] and annexed the province. Henceforward the rulers of Darfur were to dwell in the shadow of their powerful neighbour until the Kayra sultanate was overthrown and Darfur annexed to the Egyptian Sudan in 1874.

The establishment of Islam in the Sudan

Although the Arab tribes, whose infiltration caused the collapse of Christian Nubia, were nominally Muslims, there is no reason to suppose that their Islam was any less superficial than that of other nomads. The passing of power into the hands of their chiefs turned Nubia from a 'land of war' (*dar al-harb*)[14] to a 'land of Islam' and, as Ibn Khaldun notes, the payment of tribute to the Muslim rulers of Egypt ceased, but it is unnecessary to assume that the new masters were fanatical proselytizers for their faith.

The true islamization of the region was the work of quite other persons; individual teachers, who came from, or had studied in, the older lands of Islam, and brought to the Sudanese some knowledge of the precepts and Holy Law, and instilled the practices of piety common to the Muslim world. The earliest of these men of whom there is record was a Yemeni Arab, Ghulamallah ibn 'A'id, who came from al-Luhayya by way of the Red Sea and ultimately settled in Dongola, because, in the words of a Sudanese genealogical work, 'it was in extreme perplexity and error for lack of learned men. When he settled there, he built the mosques, and taught the Koran and the religious sciences.' It has been computed that the date of Ghulamallah's settlement was in the second half of the fourteenth century. His descendants and kinsmen by marriage developed into a tribe, the Rikabiyya, called after one of his sons.

About a century later, a teacher of a different kind settled in the district of Berber. This was Hamad Abu Dunana, who, like Ghulamallah, claimed to be descended from the Prophet. Abu Dunana was primarily a missionary of the Shadhiliyya order of Sufis,[15] and is said to have been the son-in-law of al-Jazuli, who propagated the order in Morocco. The settle-

28

ment of Abu Dunana in the Sudan is dated 1445, and one of his daughters is said to have married 'Abdallah Jamma'. Another was the mother of Idris ibn Arbab.

With the establishment, in the sixteenth century, of greater political stability in the riverain Sudan, by the Funj and 'Abdallab, conditions favoured the work of Muslim teachers and holy men. The first of these, Mahmud al-'Araki, was born on the White Nile, studied in Egypt, and then returned to instruct the people of his native district. He sought to inculcate the Holy Law, of which the people were totally ignorant. He may, however, also have been a Sufi missionary, since a building which he erected is called in one account a *ribat*, i.e., a convent for Sufis. The White Nile flourished as a centre of Muslim learning and devotion: there were seventeen schools between the confluence with the Blue Nile and al-Ays, near the modern al-Kawwa, but these were all destroyed by Shilluk raiders and *Umm Lahm*, the memorable year of famine and disease, 1684.

About the middle of the sixteenth century, Ibrahim al-Bulad began his teaching. He was one of four brothers, 'the Sons of Jabir', who were all distinguished for their learning and piety, and were descendants in the fifth generation of Ghulamallah. Like Mahmad al-'Araki, Ibrahim al-Bulad studied in Egypt and returned to teach in his homeland, the territory of the Shay-qiyya, and also in the Gezira. He was a teacher of law, not a Sufi missionary, and introduced the two standard text books which became the staple of Muslim legal learning in the Sudan; *al-Risala* of Ibn Abi Zayd al-Qayrawani, a jurist who died in 996, and 'Khalil', i.e. *al-Mukhtasar* of Khalil ibn Ishaq (d. 1365), a compendium of Muslim law according to the Maliki school.[16]

There was something approaching a formal reception of Muslim law into the Funj and 'Abdallab territories in the second half of the sixteenth century. King Dakin (?1568–86) instructed the 'Abdallabi chief, Shaykh 'Ajib al-Manjilak, to appoint four judges. The most celebrated of these was Dushayn of Arbaji, known as *Qadi al-'adala*.[17] The jurisdiction of these four was on a territorial basis, the Sudanese in general follow-ing the Maliki school of legal doctrine. Dushayn, however, was a Shafiʻi, and served as judge for this school in general, as well as judging the district of Arbaji.

The next of the early teachers, Taj al-Din al-Bahari, was a Sufi, not a jurist. A member of the Qadiriyya order, he came from Baghdad, its centre, and, while on Pilgrimage, met a Sudanese from the Gezira and accepted his invitation to visit the Funj territories. He spent seven years in the Gezira, shortly after Ibrahim al-Bulad, and introduced the teachings of the Qadiriyya. Another immigrant teacher of the same period is remembered only as al-Tilimsani al-Maghribi, 'the man of Tlemcen in north-west Africa'. The route by which he reached the Sudan is unknown. His speciality was scholastic philosophy, the Koranic sciences and the recitation of the Koran. He was also a Sufi, and initiated his principal disciple, Muhammad ibn 'Isa, called *Suwar al-dhahab* ('Gold bracelet'), into the Qadiriyya. Suwar al-dhahab belonged to the Bidayriyya tribe of Dongola, and was himself a celebrated teacher. He lived well into the seventeenth century.

By this time Sudanese holy men were becoming numerous. They were at the same time Sufi leaders and teachers of law and theology. The distinction which existed in the Ottoman Empire between the hierarchy of *'ulama'*—judges, jurists and teachers—which formed part of the governmental system, and the unofficial but influential hierarchies of the Sufi orders, had no counterpart in the Funj dominions or in Darfur. The title of *faki*, a dialect form of *faqih* (which in general usage means a student of *fiqh*, a jurist), was applied indiscriminately to these holy men.

Some of them, especially the local heads of Sufi orders, possessed considerable political influence. Idris ibn Arbab, a Qadiri teacher, of Mahasi descent, who is said to have lived from 1507 to 1651, acted as a kind of oracle to both Funj and 'Abdallab rulers. Badi II Abu Daqn granted the *faki* Bishara al-Gharbawi, a holy man in the Shayqiyya territory, exemption from all taxes and dues throughout the Funj dominions; these privileges were confirmed in the following century by Badi IV Abu Shulukh to his successors.

Other *fakis* were endowed with grants of land and, perhaps in connection with these, were invested with Funj symbols of authority, the stool and turban, and even in one case with the *taqiyya umm qarnayn*, the horned cap which was the distinctive sign of secular authority. The holder of this exceptional privilege, Shaykh Hasan ibn Hassuna, who died in 1664–65, was the grandson of a Tunisian immigrant. He was possessed of great herds and traded in horses. He dominated the country around the village which still bears his name, north-west of Khartoum, like a feudal lord, having a private army of slaves, 'each one of whom bore a sword with scabbard-tip and plate and pin of silver'.[18]

In the eighteenth century, when Funj-'Abdallab control over the main Nile was weakening, the Majadhib, a family of hereditary *fakis*, established a tribal theocracy among the Ja'aliyin, south of the Atbara confluence. The founder of the state was Hamad ibn Muhammad al-Majdhub (1693–1776), who, after studying under Sudanese teachers, made the Pilgrimage and was initiated into the Shadiliyya order. He acquired enormous prestige among the Ja'aliyin as a teacher and ascetic, and became the effective ruler of a district centring upon his residence at El Damer.

Burckhardt, who visited El Damer in 1814, has left a description of the Majdhubi theocracy in its last phase. Its ruler, *al-faki al-kabir* 'the great teacher', was Muhammad al-Majdhub (1796–1831), a grandson of the founder. Burckhardt comments on the neatness, regularity and good condition of El Damer. It contained several schools, drawing pupils from a wide area in the Sudan; the teachers had many books on theology and law, brought from Cairo. Many of the *fakis* had themselves studied at Cairo, in al-Azhar, or at Mecca. The great religious prestige of the Majadhib was widely acknowledged and served as a passport to travellers on the route to Suakin.

The early nineteenth century, before the Egyptian conquest, saw the appearance of new influences in the religious life of the Sudan. These were the repercussions of that great wave of revival and reform, which arose in the heart of Islam during the late eighteenth century, and which produced, among other less-known phenomena, the fanatical Wahhabi movement in Arabia. One aspect of the revival was the appearance of a new, activist spirit in the Sufi orders. The Khalwatiyya order, founded in the fourteenth century, took on fresh life in the eighteenth, when missionaries were sent to propagate its teachings in Africa. One of these, al-Sammani (1718–75) established a new sub-order, which was brought to the Sudan about 1800, by a Sudanese, Ahmad al-Tayyib al-Bashir, who had been initiated in Medina. He won many adherents in the Gezira, particularly along the White Nile.

Another religious teacher whose followers were to have great influence in the Sudan was Ahmad ibn Idris al-Fasi, who originated from Fez in Morocco but spent much of his career in Arabia, where he died in 1837. Like the Wahhabis, he was a reformer, who sought to restore the primitive model of Islam, purged of superstitious innovations. He influenced Muhammad al-Majdhub, when the latter was an exile in Mecca, after the Turco-Egyptian conquest. Another of his disciples was Muhammad 'Uthman al-Mirghani (1793–1853), who was sent by Ahmad ibn Idris as a missionary to the Sudan. He won an enormous following among the Nubian tribes between Aswan and Dongola, and in 1816–17 reached Sennar. Here he seems to have gained little success, and he left the Sudan, never to return. While on his missionary journey, however, he had married a woman of Dongola, by whom he had a son, al-Hasan.

After Ahmad ibn Idris's death, al-Mirghani organized his own adherents, in Arabia and the Sudan, as a new order, the Mirghaniyya or Khatmiyya. Further proselytization was carried out in the Sudan by his son, al-Hasan, and the order was favourably viewed by the Turco-Egyptian rulers. But the coming of the Egyptians had brought an important change into the structure of Sudanese Islam, as will appear.

PART 1

THE TURCO-EGYPTIAN PERIOD
1820–81

'You are aware that the end of all our effort and this expense is to procure negroes. Please show zeal in carrying out our wishes in this capital matter.'

Muhammad 'Ali to the *defterdar*
(23 September 1825).

'I have granted you . . . the government of the provinces of Nubia, Darfour, Kordofan, and Sennaar, with all their dependencies—that is to say, with all their adjoining regions outside of the limits of Egypt. Guided by the experience and wisdom that distinguish you, you will apply yourself to administer and organize these provinces according to my equitable views, and to provide for the welfare of the inhabitants.'

Ferman of Sultan 'Abd al-Majid
to Muhammad 'Ali Pasha
(13 February 1841).

CHAPTER III

THE INAUGURATION OF THE
TURCO–EGYPTIAN REGIME: 1820–25

MUHAMMAD 'ALI'S conquest of the Sudanese provinces has some similarity to Özdemir Pasha's conquest of Lower Nubia and the Red Sea littoral, nearly three centuries previously. Both expeditions were primarily private ventures of ambitious servants of the Ottoman sultan. Their armies fought in the sultan's name, the territories acquired were formally annexed to his dominions, but lay in practice outside the bounds of his effective control. But there were certain differences between Özdemir's status and that of Muhammad 'Ali which were to affect the future history of their conquests. In 1820 Muhammad 'Ali Pasha was the autonomous viceroy of Egypt, and could draw on considerable military and economic resources in order to secure his rule over the Sudanese provinces. Unlike Özdemir, he was the founder of a dynasty, which, until the double calamity of the Mahdist revolution and the British occupation of Egypt, held tenaciously to the territories he had acquired. He was, in the third place, influenced by current European ideas, and sought not merely to acquire territory in the traditional Ottoman fashion, but to exploit its resources of men and its natural products.

Muhammad 'Ali's primary motive in undertaking the invasion of the Sudan was probably political. In the early days of his rule over Egypt, his most dangerous opponents had been the Mamluks, the survivors of the military and governing *élite* whose chiefs had been, in the previous century, the real masters of Egypt. By massacre and proscription, he had succeeded in 1811 in breaking their power in Egypt, but a remnant of the Mamluks had escaped beyond his control and established themselves in the petty state of Dongola, at that

35

time a dependency of the Shayqiyya confederation. Their headquarters, which they called *Ordu* (Turkish; 'the Camp', a name corrupted by the Sudanese to *al-'Urdi*), and which is more generally known as New Dongola, stood on the west bank of the Nile, not far south of the old frontier between *Berberistan* and the Funj dominions. Here they built a walled town, recruited black slaves to replenish their own dwindling numbers, and clashed with the Shayqiyya for the control of the region.

The history of the previous century had many times demonstrated the extraordinary vitality and tenacity of the Mamluks; it was commonplace for a defeated faction to withdraw upstream until a convenient opportunity occurred for a descent on Cairo and a political revolution. Although the Mamluks of Dongola were perhaps too insignificant in numbers and too remote to follow the traditional pattern, their inviolability was certain to cause anxiety to the viceroy of Egypt.

In 1812, therefore, Muhammad 'Ali Pasha sent an embassy to urge the Funj sultan to expel the Mamluks from the dominions he nominally ruled. Neither the sultan nor the Hamaj regent any longer possessed effective authority in Dongola, as Muhammad 'Ali was doubtless well aware. The embassy served a more practical purpose in spying out the military weakness and political fragmentation of the Nilotic Sudan. The situation was also made known to the viceroy by *Makk* Nasr al-Din, a member of the ruling family of the Mirafab of Berber, who sought the support of Muhammad 'Ali against his dynastic rivals. The political disorder on the middle Nile had almost stopped trade with Egypt, and the desire to revive commerce was one of Muhammad 'Ali's motives in making the conquest.

The viceroy had, however, greater ambitions than simply to restore the old trading relations. A conquest of the Nilotic Sudan would bring under his control a principal channel of the slave-trade. At this time Muhammad 'Ali's military situation was precarious, and the idea of a slave-army, docile, trained in the European manner and personally loyal to him, was most attractive. The Albanian troops, who had raised him to power in Egypt, were dangerously insubordinate, and could well be put to the arduous task of conquering and pacifying the remote Sudan. A further attraction of the region was its fabled gold-mines, which, could they be located and exploited, would provide the viceroy with the means to assure his position in Egypt and his independence of the sultan.

It is difficult to find a convenient designation for the conquest of 1820–21. It was prepared in Egypt by the ruler of Egypt. Yet to speak of 'the Egyptian conquest' is liable to call up anachronistic associations. The Arabic-speaking Egyptian nation-state with its national army did not then exist: the government of the Ottoman province of Egypt was in the hands of Turkish-speaking Ottoman subjects, a ruling *élite* linked by a complicated web of ties to the Arabic-speaking population.

On the other hand, to speak of 'the Ottoman conquest' is equally unsatisfactory. It was, as has been said above, a private venture by Muhammad 'Ali. Although after the conquest the new provinces were governed by the same Turkish-speaking *élite* that ruled Egypt, and although Ottoman suzerainty was recognized, the sultan's power was even more tenuous in the Sudan than in Egypt itself. Perhaps the clumsy adjective 'Turco-Egyptian' best describes both the conquest and the administration which followed.

To the Sudanese, at any rate, the invaders and the new rulers were *al-Turk*, 'the Turks', and their regime was *al-Turkiyya*. These terms, which at first were linguistically justifiable, subsequently came to include all members of the ruling and military *élites* who were not of Sudanese origin. It lost its linguistic connotation and never acquired a purely ethnic significance: the Condominium administration set up in 1899 was 'the second *Turkiyya*' and, to the unsophisticated Sudanese at any rate, the British officials were 'Turks'.

The force, which left Cairo early in July 1820, was composed of about four thousand actual combatants. Different sources give varying accounts of the strength of the contingents, but all bring out their extraordinarily varied composition. Albanians and 'Turks' of unspecified origin were prominent. Another element was the Maghribis—Arabs of north-west Africa, who had long provided soldiers of fortune for the Ottoman Empire.

The most genuinely Egyptian element in an ethnic sense was the Bedouin tribal forces, but the Egyptian *fallahin*, as yet unconscripted, had no part in this military venture. Of particular importance, because of their knowledge of the Nubian marches, were the 'Ababda tribesmen, who provided the camel-transport. The commander of the expeditionary force was the viceroy's third son, Isma'il Kamil Pasha, who was then about twenty-five years of age. He was accompanied by the usual household staff of a governing pasha, including a secretary, Muhammad Sa'id Efendi, who was to play a part of some importance. Three *'ulama'* travelled with the expedition, to summon the Sudanese Muslims to obey the agent of the Ottoman sultan. The officers included George Bethune English, a renegade American, who served as an officer of artillery and wrote an account of the expedition. A much more detailed and scientific description was written by a French observer, Frédéric Cailliaud, a distinguished traveller and archaeologist. Two English amateurs of antiquities, George Waddington and the Rev. Barnard Hanbury, also attached themselves to the advancing army and penetrated as far as Marawi, whence they were peremptorily ordered to return by Isma'il Pasha.

On 20 July 1820, Isma'il and his staff joined the army at Aswan. The timing of the start of the campaign was governed by the flood of the Nile, during which season alone it would be possible to haul the boats over the Cataracts. The *kashiflik* of Lower Nubia had long been autonomous of Cairo, and Husayn *Kashif*, one of the brothers who ruled the region, would have disputed the advance of the expedition but, finding himself unsupported, he fled to Kordofan. His brother, Hasan *Kashif*, submitted to Isma'il, and was confirmed in office.

The Second Cataract was passed, and the ruler of Say made his submission, only to revolt later and to be killed in the fighting. English was not a little surprised to find the people of Say, the descendants of the Bosniak *kal'ejis*, 'as white as the Arabs of Lower Egypt, whereas the inhabitants of Nubia are quite black, though their features are not those of the Negro.'[1] The Mamluks of New Dongola made no resistance. A few came in to surrender, but the majority of them fled further south and sought refuge with the Ja'ali ruler, *Makk* Nimr of

Shendi. The petty rulers of the Danaqla submitted to Isma'il, and were confirmed in their positions.

The destruction of the military power of the Shayqiyya had been a principal object of the expedition. A summons was sent to their chiefs to surrender their horses and arms, but this was rejected. The Shayqiyya confederacy was at this time headed by two chiefs, *Makk* Subayr, the principal ruler of the Hannakab, in the western part of the territory, and *Makk* Jawish, whose capital was Marawi. On 4 November a battle took place near Kurti, in which the Shayqiyya were defeated. The remnant of their forces, which escaped from the battlefield, crossed the Nile and took refuge in a stone fortress at the foot of Jabal Dayqa (now called Jabal Ibn 'Awf), where they were bombarded by Isma'il, and routed once again.

This was the end of serious military resistance. *Makk* Subayr submitted to the pasha, while Jawish fled southwards, to seek asylum among the Ja'aliyin. Isma'il's victory over the Shayqiyya was largely a consequence of his superior armament. The Shayqiyya were armed principally with long swords and lances. They carried shields of hippopotamus or crocodile hide, while some of their leaders wore coats of mail.

'A very few had pistols; but the possession of guns was confined to the Chiefs, and it is a singular proof of their attachment to the weapons of their fathers, that having it always in their power to be tolerably supplied with fire-arms ... they would never consent to adopt them.'[2]

One is reminded of the similar conservatism of the Mamluks of Egypt, whose cavalry were routed by the fire-power of the Ottomans in 1516. Faced with this resistance, Isma'il showed for the first time a degree of ruthlessness, but an amnesty was offered to all who would surrender themselves, and in the vicinity of his camp order and security prevailed.

Having concentrated his forces, Isma'il prepared for a further advance. A river column of boats, with a protective escort moving along the bank, was sent upstream, while the pasha marched with the bulk of his troops across the peninsula of the Bayuda Desert on the left bank of the Nile. He set out on

21 February 1821, and reached the river seven days later at al-Buqayr. On 5 March the desert column reached al-Ghubush, opposite the residence of *Makk* Nasr al-Din, the ruler of Berber,[3] who made his submission and was confirmed in office.

Isma'il was in the meantime negotiating with *Makk* Jawish and the fugitive Mamluks at Shendi. All made their submission, with the exception of a small remnant of the Mamluks, who continued their flight and vanished from history. The amnestied Mamluks returned honourably to Egypt. On 19 May *Makk* Jawish made a capitulation no less final than honourable. 'I have fought against you,' he said to Isma'il, 'to the utmost of my means and power, and am now ready, if you will, to fight under the orders of my conqueror.'[4] He was given an army rank and accompanied Isma'il on the rest of the expedition, while Shayqiyya cavalry were enlisted under the command of their chiefs as irregulars (*bashi bozuq*).

The two rulers of the Sa'dab Ja'aliyin, *Makk* Nimr of Shendi and *Makk* al-Musa'id of Metemma, also submitted and were confirmed in their positions. A similar submission was made by the sick and aged chief of the 'Abdallab, Shaykh Nasir wad al-Amin. His son and *Makk* Nimr accompanied Isma'il as hostages. Hitherto the advance had been up the western bank of the Nile, but it was now necessary to cross into the Gezira. The passage of the White Nile took from the early morning of 20 May to the afternoon of 1 June, and was a difficult operation since only nine small boats had been able to pass the Third Cataract. The horses and camels were swum across, or floated with inflated water-skins. Had the kingdom of Sennar possessed an effective army, Isma'il's troops could have been caught at a serious disadvantage, but there was no enemy in the vicinity, the passage was unopposed, and the remainder of the advance was a military parade.

The Regent Muhammad wad 'Adlan, who had sent a defiant message to Isma'il, had been killed by conspirators supporting his cousin, Hasan wad Rajab, about the beginning of April. The following weeks were wasted by an internecine struggle between the two factions. From this, Hasan emerged victorious only to flee to the Abyssinian frontier on hearing of the approach of Isma'il. Such authority as remained in Sennar was held by the old minister, the *Arbab* Dafa'allah, and the brother of the murdered regent. As the expeditionary force approached Sennar, they began to negotiate a capitulation. English describes the arrival of Dafa'allah and his colleague as ambassadors:

'I saw these personages when they arrived. They were two, one a tall thin elderly man of a mulatto complexion, dressed in green and yellow silks of costly fabric, with a cap of a singular form,[5] something resembling a crown, made of the same materials, upon his head. The other was the same young man who had come a few days past to the Pasha. He was dressed today in silks like the other, except that his head was bare of ornament. They were accompanied by a fine lad about sixteen, who was, it is said, the son of the predecessor of the present Sultan. All three were mounted on tall and beautiful horses, and accompanied by about two hundred soldiers of the Sultan, mounted on dromedaries, and armed with broadswords, lances and shields.[6]

On the next day, the last Funj sultan, Badi VI, came in person to Isma'il's camp to make his submission. He was well received and honourably entertained. He apparently obtained recognition of his position from the pasha, like the other Sudanese rulers, but politically this meant nothing. A pension, granted to him and the royal family, continued to be paid until the Mahdist revolution. On the following day, probably 13 June, the expeditionary force entered Sennar. The town was far gone in ruin and decay. Even the mosque had been profaned by the scrawled drawings of pagan raiders. The old royal palace was derelict, and Badi's own residence was a large courtyard containing low brick buildings. The condition of Sennar was visible evidence of the debility of the Funj state at the time of the conquest.

After the reduction of Dongola and the Shayqiyya country, Muhammad 'Ali Pasha sent out a new expeditionary force of three or four thousand troops and a battery of artillery to conquer the sultanate of Darfur. The commander of this second army, Muhammad Bey Khusraw, the *defterdar*, left Cairo to join his troops on 20 April 1821.[7] The force assembled at al-Dabba, on the left bank of the Nile, below Kurti, and, with the assistance of Shaykh Salim, the chief of the Kababish, struck south-westwards across the Bayuda Desert towards Kordofan. The Furawi governor, the *Maqdum* Musallim, was invited to surrender and replied with a letter protesting against this unprecedented invasion of a Muslim country which was not subject to the Ottoman sultan. The two armies clashed at Bara, where the horsemen of Darfur and tribal warriors of Kordofan were routed by the firearms and artillery of the invaders. The *maqdum* was killed in the fighting, and the *defterdar* entered El Obeid, the provincial capital.

On hearing of the loss of Kordofan, Sultan Muhammad Fadl sent an army to recover the province. This too was defeated. The inhabitants of the plain of Kordofan were soon reduced to submission and the harsh brutality of the *defterdar* and his troops was long remembered,[8] but the Nuba hillmen of Jabal al-Dayir, as well as those of the remoter mountains to the south, remained unsubdued. The ultimate objective of the expedition, the subjection of Darfur itself, was also beyond the powers of the invaders. Muhammad 'Ali Pasha later tried to gain his end by supporting the claims of a brother of Muhammad Fadl, named Abu Madyan, but this attempt to install a puppet sultan in El Fasher[9] also ended in failure.

The first impressions which the people of Sennar had of their new ruler were by no means wholly unfavourable. The conquest had been achieved practically without bloodshed, and Isma'il Pasha deliberately presented himself as a mild and accessible administrator. His coming was to mark a new era: he would listen to no petitions concerning events before his arrival. To this rule, however, one important exception was made: Hasan wad Rajab and the killers of the Regent Muhammad wad 'Adlan were pursued and captured. Hasan himself was imprisoned and treated with leniency, but some of his underlings were put to death by impalement—a punishment that was a disagreeable innovation to the Sudanese.

The conquerors had already attained their military objec-

42

tives; the destruction of the independent power of the refugee Mamluks and the Shayqiyya. Muhammad 'Ali Pasha could now seek to realize his further aims: the exploitation of the wealth of the Sudan, especially its gold and slaves. Towards the end of 1821, Isma'il was joined at Sennar by his elder brother, the famous Ibrahim Pasha, as commander-in-chief of the troops of Sennar and Kordofan. They were repeatedly urged by Muhammad 'Ali to send slaves to Egypt. The two brothers decided to make expeditions into the pagan territories to the south of Sennar, but Ibrahim soon fell ill and returned to Cairo. Isma'il went on and established his authority over the auriferous region of Fazughli, where a levy of gold was laid on the traders.

Meanwhile preparations were going forward for the taxation of the riverain districts. A census of the slaves and flocks held by the Sudanese had already been made, but apart from a levy of fodder no taxes had yet been demanded. During Isma'il's absence, however, the arrangements were completed. The fiscal system was organized by a committee of three, the pasha's secretary, Muhammad Sa'id Efendi, the *Mu'allim*[10] Hanna al-Tawil (a Coptic financial official) and the *Arbab* Dafa'allah. Taxes were to be paid by owners of slaves and animals at the rate of fifteen dollars per slave, ten dollars per cow, and five dollars per sheep or donkey.[11] The burden would fall on the settled people of the riverain villages, not on the nomads (there was no mention of a camel-tax), who were still virtually outside the control of the regime.

It has rightly been said that this taxation appears 'almost unbelievably onerous, and to amount to something approaching confiscation'.[12] Confiscation rather than revenue was indeed probably the real intent. Specie was rare in the Sudan, and the taxes could be paid in strong male slaves instead of cash. Thus Muhammad 'Ali's incessant demand for slaves to train as soldiers could be met by draining the reservoir of slave-labour available in the newly conquered provinces, until such time as sufficient recruits could be obtained by raiding the pagan tribes of the upper Blue and White Niles and the Nuba Mountains.

This device, if carried out, would however have grave social and political consequences. It would destroy the slave-retinues of the petty rulers who had accepted Muhammad 'Ali's suzerainty, and it would jeopardize the livelihood of all but the very poorest families, since slaves were universally employed in the households and the fields. The results were curiously similar to those which ensued from Khedive Isma'il's attempts to abolish slavery, nearly sixty years later. The Sudanese rose in rebellion.

The first symptoms of revolt appeared at once. A rumour spread that Isma'il Pasha was dead in the southern mountains, and there were sporadic attacks on Egyptian troops. The situation was saved for the time being by the return of Isma'il to Sennar. He acted with wisdom and discretion. The rebellious Sudanese were treated with clemency, and he tried to modify the assessment. He was too late; the books had already been sent to Cairo. Among his troops disease was widespread, and he removed his headquarters downstream from Sennar to Wad Medani, supposedly a healthier site. But the mortality continued, among those who died being the *Qadi* Muhammad al-Asyuti, who had been sent as judge with the invading army. While Isma'il was at Wad Medani, Hasan wad Rajab escaped from confinement to play a part in the crisis which was developing.

In October or November 1822 the incident occurred which sparked off the rising. Isma'il left for the north and arrived by river at Shendi. Here he demanded a heavy contribution of money and slaves from the Ja'aliyin, and insulted their chief, his former hostage, *Makk* Nimr. The following night his quarters were set on fire and he perished among his retinue.

At once revolt flared out among the riverain Sudanese from Shendi southwards to Wad Medani. The small local garrisons on the main and Blue Niles, at Karari, Halfaya, Khartoum, al-'Aylafun and al-Kamlin, evacuated their posts and made their way, not without difficulty, to general headquarters at Wad Medani. Here the secretary, Muhammad Sa'id Efendi, who had been appointed deputy governor (*Kâhya*) by Isma'il Pasha before his departure, assumed command. He fortified his position and sent a reconnaissance party to the confluence of the Niles.

Alarming though the situation was, two factors favoured the

Turco-Egyptian regime. Its troops, although inferior in numbers, were superior in their possession of firearms and their military experience to their opponents—a mixture of settled peasantry, tribal warriors and the private slave-armies of the Sudanese magnates. Secondly, the revolt was never either a general or a unified movement. Mahu Bey held the province of Berber against the rebels upstream. Dongola and the far north were totally unaffected. The Shayqiyya remained loyal to their new masters, and their irregulars served in the operations against the rebels. Even within the area of the revolt, the garrison of Khartoum was assisted by the people of the nearby village of al-Jirayf, whose chief guided the troops to Wad Medani.

The rebels never had unity of leadership. There were three principal centres of revolt, each dominated by local magnates. The Ja'aliyin had as leaders their chiefs *Makk* Nimr and *Makk* al-Musa'id. The 'Abdallab revolted under the *Wad 'Ajib*, Nasir wad al-Amin. In the Gezira the resistance was headed by those two survivors of the Funj-Hamaj regime, Hasan wad Rajab and the *Arbab* Dafa'allah. The latter, on the outbreak of the revolt, had fled from Wad Medani to 'Ibud, whither the rebels began to muster.

In these circumstances, it was possible for Mahu to hold out in Berber, and for Muhammad Sa'id to undertake local operations in the vicinity of Wad Medani. A cavalry squadron was sent from Wad Medani to 'Ibud, and the rebels there dispersed without a fight. The *arbab* fled up the Blue Nile, and joined forces with his old enemy, Hasan wad Rajab. The deputy governor sent out another force, which included Shayqiyya levies, which defeated them at Abu Shawka, south of Sennar. Hasan wad Rajab was killed. The *Arbab* Dafa'allah escaped and made his way to the Abyssinian marches.

Neither Mahu nor Muhammad Sa'id was, however, strong enough to undertake the general suppression of the rebellion. This was the work of the *defterdar* who, on hearing of the death of Isma'il hastened from Kordofan with a body of his troops and a contingent of Fur warriors. Entering the Ja'ali country, he found that Nimr and al-Musa'id were blockading Mahu in Berber, but their sons and a large number of followers were at

Metemma. They negotiated an amnesty, but an unsuccessful attempt by a tribesman to assassinate the *defterdar* provoked him to fury and a massacre ensued. He then marched north to relieve Berber. The Ja'ali chiefs advanced to meet him, crossed the Nile, and were defeated in a battle on the west bank. Freed from the blockade, Mahu left Berber and met the *defterdar* at El Damer.

After their conference, the *defterdar* advanced along the east bank into the 'Abdallabi country. He found Halfaya deserted, and burnt it. Another massacre took place on Tuti island, at the confluence of the Niles, while al-'Aylafun, which offered resistance, was burnt and looted. The *Wad 'Ajib* had fled before him, but as the *defterdar* continued to pursue him up the Blue Nile, he doubled back to Qubbat Khujali, near the modern Khartoum North, and crossed to Omdurman, where he was joined by the survivors of the battle of Abu Shawka. Having reached Wad Medani, the *defterdar* sent out an expeditionary force which completed the task of reducing the Gezira to submission. Meanwhile the *defterdar* returned to Kordofan.

During his absence another force had dispersed the concentration of 'Abdallab and Hamaj at Omdurman, but the rebels fled to Shendi, to which *Makk* Nimr had returned. It was clear that further measures would be needed to suppress the revolt among the Ja'aliyin, and the *defterdar* again set out for the river. On hearing of his approach the rebels dispersed, but the main body of them under Nimr and al-Musa'id fled to al-Nasub in the Butana, near Abu Dilayq. Here they were defeated. Nimr and al-Musa'id fled, and a vast number of prisoners, including many members of Nimr's family, were taken.

Returning to the river, the *defterdar* made his camp at Umm 'Uruq, a site now uncertain.[13] A last rebel force under al-Musa'id and the *Wad 'Ajib* was still at large east of the Blue Nile. In September 1823 the *defterdar* advanced against it. The rebels were defeated at Makdur, between the rivers Rahad and Dinder. The *defterdar* now struck north-eastwards as far as Sabderat, just across the present Eritrean border, whence he returned to the Nile.

His term of command was drawing to a close. In January

1824 Muhammad 'Ali Pasha informed him of his impending recall. In his last few months the *defterdar* ordered all the prisoners of war, whether slaves or freemen, to be sent to Cairo. A new deputy-governor was appointed to Wad Medani, while Muhammad Sa'id Efendi returned to Cairo with the remainder of the household and possessions of Isma'il Pasha. At Umm 'Uruq the *defterdar* awaited the arrival of his successor; then, at the beginning of the new Muslim year (August–September 1824) himself departed for Egypt.

He was succeeded as commander-in-chief (in effect, as military governor) by 'Uthman Bey the Circassian, who was accompanied by five regiments of infantry. These were soldiers of a new type, the *Jihadiyya*, regular troops recruited from the slaves obtained in the Sudan, and drilled on European lines in the training camp established at Aswan in 1821. Muhammad 'Ali's great project of a new model army in place of the motley troops of Egypt was only partially achieved: the slave recruits perished by hundreds in the Egyptian climate, and by 1824 conscription of the Egyptian peasantry had begun. Nevertheless, the Negro *Jihadiyya* could fulfil a useful function as garrison troops in the Sudanese provinces. Henceforward the military strength of the Turco-Egyptian regime was mainly derived from two sources, the regular *Jihadiyya*, of slave origin, originating from what would now be called the southern Sudan; and the Shayqiyya irregulars, serving mainly as cavalrymen under their own chiefs.

'Uthman Bey realized at once the strategic importance of Khartoum, the trunk of land[14] at the confluence of the Blue and White Niles. He decided to build a fort and garrison a regiment there. This was the beginning, from which in a few years Khartoum was to develop as the military and administrative capital of the Egyptian Sudan. As yet, however, army headquarters remained at Wad Medani, whither 'Uthman proceeded. The new commander-in-chief, an elderly Mamluk, regarded his task with the eyes of a soldier rather than of an administrator. To repress revolt and get in the taxes were his sole aims, and he emulated the *defterdar* in harshness and brutality. The consequence was a flight of cultivators from the Nile valley to the remote district of the Qadarif in Shukriyya territory. Here they were pursued by government troops and shot down.

'Uthman's few months in office were made more difficult by natural calamities. An epidemic of smallpox coincided with drought, famine, and the migration of refugees to produce severe depopulation. The commander-in-chief was ailing and left the responsibility of government to a deputy. But this man was a mere subaltern and the high-ranking officers refused to obey his orders. The army was drifting into anarchy, with consequent suffering for the people of the Sudan, when 'Uthman Bey died on 11 May 1825. The deputy-governor prudently concealed the fact of his death until he had summoned the experienced governor of Berber, Mahu Bey, to take over the command.

CHAPTER IV

SETTLEMENT AND STAGNATION

1825–62

MAHU BEY, who had been governor of Berber since 1822, was a cavalry officer of Kurdish origin. His fortitude during the great revolt had prevented his province from falling to the rebel Ja'aliyin. He took over the command of troops in the province of Sennar: the command in Kordofan, which had been held by the *defterdar* and 'Uthman Bey jointly with Sennar, was now detached.

Mahu's brief period of authority marks a turning-point in the history of the Turco-Egyptian regime. He adopted a policy of conciliation towards the frightened and resentful Sudanese. Taxes were reduced, and the licence of the *Jihadiyya* was repressed. The novelty of his approach appeared when he summoned an assembly of the remaining Sudanese notables in the Gezira, and consulted with them on the means of restoring order and bringing back the emigrants. He particularly approved of the advice of a minor shaykh, 'Abd al-Qadir wad al-Zayn, whom he raised in rank and employed as his adviser on native affairs. Shaykh 'Abd al-Qadir accompanied Mahu on a tour to the Qadarif, the asylum of many of the refugees. Mahu sent grain from the Qadarif to the stricken Gezira, thereby winning the gratitude of its people.

The rule of Mahu Bey marks another stage in the advance of Khartoum to the status of a capital. It was his habitual residence, and he stationed his troops at Qubbat Khujali, across the Blue Nile. His period of office ended in June 1826, when 'Ali Khurshid Agha arrived at Omdurman after serving under Ibrahim Pasha against the Greeks.

Khurshid's exceptional ability as an administrator is indicated

49

by his long term of office in the Sudan, as well as by the successive extensions of power and elevations of rank conferred on him by the grateful Muhammad 'Ali. His appointment seems to have been designed to inaugurate a new period of civil administration, rather than military rule: he bore at first the title of 'governor of Sennar', whereas his predecessor had been commander-in-chief. His authority did not at this time extend to the northern provinces of Dongola and Berber, nor to Kordofan, but his own province of Sennar, including the Gezira and surrounding territories, the heart of the old Funj-'Abdallab dominions, presented administrative and political problems of far greater gravity than those which confronted his colleagues.

His policy was essentially the continuation and fulfilment of that practised by Mahu, a continuity symbolized by the circumstances of the meeting of the two men in Omdurman:

'The Amir Mahu Bey met him in Omdurman, and they conferred together in private there for a while. Then Mahu Bey ordered Shaykh 'Abd al-Qadir to be brought forward, and he presented him with his own hand to Khurshid Agha, saying, "If you desire the prosperity of the country, then act according to the opinion of this man." '[1]

The restoration of prosperity was indeed the first object of the new governor. To achieve it, the lands abandoned during the revolt and subsequent repression had to be brought back into cultivation, and the thousands of emigrants, many of whom had made their way to the hill-country of the Abyssinian marches, persuaded to return to their villages. In the Ja'ali districts, much riverain land was given to the loyal Shayqiyya, who paid no taxes but received a forage ration in consideration of their service as cavalry.

Khurshid's new deal was devised with the assistance of Shaykh 'Abd al-Qadir, who was instructed to convoke an assembly of notables, and draw up a list of the villages, showing whether they were inhabited or lying waste. Letters of amnesty were sent out inviting the fugitives to return, and promising them freedom from disturbance. One of the most inveterate opponents of the Turco-Egyptian regime was Shaykh Idris wad 'Adlan, the brother of the murdered Regent Muhammad wad 'Adlan, who had fled at the conquest to the mountains up-stream of Sennar, and had unflinchingly refused to recognize the new masters of his country. To him as an envoy came Shaykh 'Abd al-Qadir in the summer of 1826, with the offer of an amnesty from the governor. Idris accepted the invitation, and accompanied 'Abd al-Qadir to Berber, where he was wel-comed by Khurshid and formally recognized as shaykh of the Funj mountains.

In the following twelve months, another assembly of Sudanese notables was held in Khartoum. Its purpose was to advise the governor on taxation, but before proceeding to this, the members were instructed to elect one of their own number as paramount shaykh, to be their official intermediary with the governor. Not surprisingly, their choice fell on 'Abd al-Qadir, who was invested with the paramountcy from Hajar al-'Asal to the further limits of the Funj mountains. The election really did no more than regularize 'Abd al-Qadir's position as native adviser to the governor. Khurshid had also a corps of experi-enced officers, the *mu'awins* (assistants), who formed a kind of intelligence branch. He regularly consulted them and also his Coptic financial intendant.

In 1828 Khurshid began a serious attempt to bring back the refugees from the Abyssinian marches. Some of them came in to him while he was on tour in that region. He was advised by Shaykh 'Abd al-Qadir to exempt the chief notables and *fakis* from taxation, in order to gain their support for his policy. He did so, and the stratagem proved highly successful. Under the influence of the Sudanese notables, many of the emigrants returned, to the great benefit of cultivation and the profit of the revenue.

A refugee leader of particular importance was Shaykh Ahmad al-Rayyah al-'Araki, a member of a family which had great religious prestige. During the troubles, he had led thousands of his tribesmen, the 'Arakiyin, from their homes on the Blue Nile, into exile in the Abyssinian marches. He now came in to submit to Khurshid. After an honourable reception, he was sent back to proclaim an amnesty to the emigrants, and

51

took letters from Shaykh 'Abd al-Qadir promising freedom from disturbance. But the governor also threatened that he would shortly make an expedition to the region, and kill those who had not submitted. He quickly fulfilled his promise and, freely or under compulsion, thousands of emigrants returned to the Blue Nile. Another consequence of this expedition was the extension of Egyptian rule over the Qallabat and its colony of Takarir settlers from the western *Bilad al-Sudan*.

Another crisis threatened in 1835. Khurshid returned from a visit to Cairo during which he had been instructed by Muhammad 'Ali Pasha to conscript Sudanese freemen for military service. This project, no doubt devised because of the pressure laid on Muhammad 'Ali's man-power by his occupation of Syria, appeared administratively simple, since it merely extended to the Sudanese provinces a system which had been applied in Egypt proper since 1824. The appearance was deceptive, and the rumour of Khurshid's intention filled with dismay an assembly of administrative officials and Sudanese notables which he summoned to meet in Khartoum. After two days of private consultation with Shaykh 'Abd al-Qadir, who insisted that conscription would start a fresh wave of emigration and damage the new prosperity of the country, Khurshid abandoned the project. Instead an alternative proposal was accepted, that the people of every locality should contribute a quota of their slaves as recruits for the *Jihadiyya*.

Khurshid devoted much energy to the development of Khartoum. Settlers in the town were rewarded with grants of privileges, and the population rose so rapidly that the mosque which he had built in 1829–30 was demolished seven years later to give place to a larger one. A barracks and military storehouse were constructed for the *Jihadiyya* garrison, and a dockyard was set up on the Nile. The townspeople were encouraged to build permanent houses in place of their tents of matting and hides, and were provided with building materials. Commerce was encouraged: trade routes were protected and Khurshid resisted Muhammad 'Ali Pasha himself to prevent the revenue and products of the Sudan being exploited for the benefit of Cairo. His period of office witnessed a local boom in trade, some petty merchants making great fortunes. But the

The Land and the People

1. Ferryboat at Dongola. Sailors and traders from Dongola played a leading part in the opening-up of the southern Sudan in the nineteenth century.

2. Beside the Nile in Nubia. Driven by oxen, the creaking *saqia* raises water for irrigation.

3. A street in Suakin. This ancient Red Sea port, so different from any other Sudanese town, is now used only by pilgrims on their way to Mecca. Its great houses are slowly falling into ruin.

4. A market scene in Kasala. Behind the town, which developed in the nineteenth century from a Turco-Egyptian garrison-station, rises Jabal Kasala, a notable landmark.

5. Beja tribesmen, of the Red Sea Hills. Men like these, the 'Fuzzy-Wuzzies' of Kipling's poem, were 'Uthman Diqna's warriors in the Mahdia.

6. A family of Baqqara. These Arabic-speaking cattle-nomads provided the mass of the tribal warriors in the Mahdia. Under the Khalifa 'Abdallahi they dominated the Sudan.

7. Ploughing in the Gezira. The plain between the White and Blue Niles is one of the Sudan's chief agricultural areas. Formerly the granary of the central Sudan, it now produces most of the Sudan's cotton. (See also No. 36.)

8. A Fur family. The Fur, a non-Arab people, have their home around Jabal Marra. From the sixteenth to the twentieth century, they maintained an independent Muslim sultanate in Darfur. (See also No. 26.)

9. Shilluk in an *ambatch* (reed-pith) canoe. Warriors under a dynasty of divine kings, the Shilluk dominated the White Nile until the nineteenth century. A Shilluk war-band may have founded the Funj kingdom of Sennar.

Under Turco–Egyptian Rule

10. The castle of the kings of Shendi. At the time of the Turco-Egyptian invasion, Shendi was the commercial centre of the eastern *Bilad al-Sudan*, but this picture indicates the precarious state of security in the region.

11. Makk Nasr al-Din (1761–*c*. 1837). The king of Berber, he was deprived of his throne by a usurper, but was reinstated as a result of the Turco-Egyptian invasion.

12. Sennar in 1821. This drawing shows the old capital of the Funj kingdom as it was at the time of the Turco-Egyptian invasion. On the left is the mosque; on the right, the dilapidated tower of the royal palace.

13. Khedive Isma'il (1830–95). As Ottoman viceroy of Egypt (1863–79) he saw the second phase of Egyptian expansion in the Sudan. The upper White Nile, the Bahr al-Ghazal and Darfur were all added to his empire.

14. General Charles George Gordon (1833–1885). A British soldier who became the most famous of Khedive Isma'il's foreign servants. He strove to establish administration and suppress slave-trading in the newly acquired territories. The last khedivial governor - general, he died when the Mahdi took Khartoum.

15. Aba Island in 1852. In 1852 Aba was a Shilluk island at the extreme limit of Turco-Egyptian control: in 1881 it was to be the cradle of the Mahdia. This is how it was seen by Bayard Taylor, the first American tourist in the Sudan.

16. Muhammad 'Ali Pasha (1769–1849). As Ottoman viceroy of Egypt from 1805, he founded the dynasty which ruled until 1952. His conquests of Nubia, Sennar, Kordofan and the Taka were the nucleus of Egyptian rule.

17. A slave-raid in southern Kordofan. In the early Turco-Egyptian period, the acquisition of slaves was a function of the administration. The scene shows an encampment of slave-raiders, headed by the governor of Kordofan, who is seated and smoking a pipe in the left-hand corner.

18. The Palace of the *Hüküm-dars*, Khartoum. This residence of the Turco-Egyptian governors-general fell into ruin after the Mahdi's capture of Khartoum. Rebuilt after the Reconquest to house the governors-general of the Condominium, it is now the Republican Palace.

The Mahdia

19. Autograph of the Mahdi. This is the sole document known to be an authentic autograph of the Mahdi. It is a formal legal document, written four years before his announcement of the Mahdia. It bears his signature as a witness above his seal in the bottom left-hand corner.

20. The Battle of 'Abu Klea' (Abu Tulayh, 17 January 1885). An incident in the advance of the Desert Column, which was sent to relieve Gordon in Khartoum. The sketch was made by a British officer present at the engagement.

21. The Khalifa's House, Omdurman. Erected near the Mahdi's Tomb, the Khalifa's House is a complex of buildings. It is now a museum of the Mahdia. On the left is the original cupola of the Mahdi's Tomb.

22. The Mahdi's Tomb, Omdurman. The erection of a domed tomb over the Mahdi's grave was carried out, as a work of piety, by the Khalifa 'Abdallahi. Ruined and desecrated at the Reconquest, the Tomb was rebuilt in the last years of the Condominium by the Mahdi's son, Sayyid 'Abd al-Rahman.

23. Mahmud Ahmad (*c.* 1865–1906). A nephew of the Khalifa 'Abdallahi, Mahmud commanded the army sent against the Anglo-Egyptian forces at the Reconquest. Although lacking in generalship, he fought with desperate courage against Kitchener in the Battle of the Atbara (8 April 1898). He died a prisoner in Rosetta.

24. Umm Diwaykarat, 24 November 1899. In the foreground lies the body of the Khalifa 'Abdallahi; on his right hand, his general, Ahmad Fadil.

The Condominium

25. Sir Reginald Wingate, Bt. (1861–1953). Succeeding Kitchener as governor-general of the Anglo-Egyptian Sudan (1899–1916), he was chiefly responsible for laying the administrative foundations of British rule.

26. Palace of Sultan 'Ali Dinar, El Fasher. A view of the gateway to the palace of 'Ali Dinar, last sultan of Darfur (ruled 1898–1916).

27. Sir Douglas Newbold (1894–1945). As civil secretary from 1939 until his death, Newbold initiated the movement of the British administration from paternalism towards self-government and ultimate independence.

28. The Legislative Assembly. The member speaking is 'Abdallah Bey Khalil, at that time minister of Agriculture and leader of the Assembly; he was later (1956–8) prime minister of the Republic. The European on the front bench is Sir James Robertson, then civil secretary, and subsequently governor-general of Nigeria.

29. The Anglo-Egyptian Agreement, 12 February 1953. Sir Robert
Howe, the governor-general, announcing the signature of the
Agreement to the Sudanese people in Khartoum.

The Republic

30. Independence, New Year's Day, 1956. The flag of the new Republic is hoisted at the Palace in Khartoum, watched by Sayyid Isma'il al-Azhari, the prime minister, and Sayyid Muhammad Ahmad Mahjub, leader of the opposition.

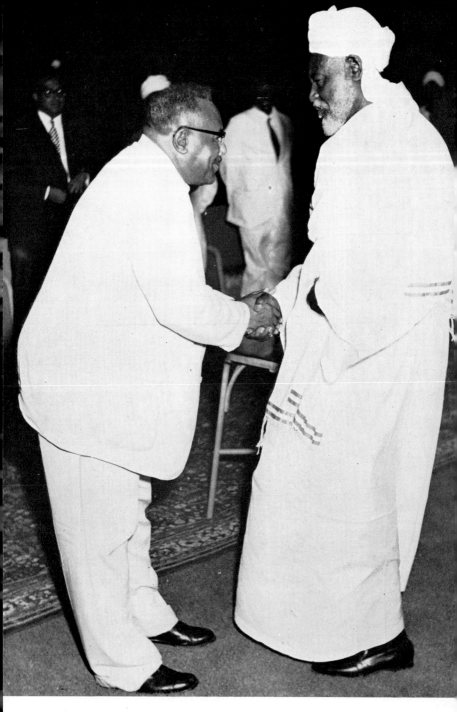

31. Sayyid 'Abd al-Rahman al-Mahdi (1885–1959). The post-humous son of the Mahdi, Sayyid 'Abd al-Rahman was the head of the religious sect of the Ansar, and the patron of the Umma Party. He is shown being greeted by Sayyid Isma'il al-Azhari.

32. Sayyid 'Ali al-Mirghani (b. 1879). The descendant of a family of religious leaders, Sayyid 'Ali is the head of the Khatmiyya sect, the rivals of Sayyid 'Abd al-Rahman al-Mahdi's Ansar.

33. President Ibrahim 'Abbud (b. 1900). As the general commanding
the Sudanese army, Ibrahim 'Abbud assumed the headship of the
state after the military *coup d'état* of 17 November 1958.

Foundations Of The Future

34. and 35. (Above) A nursery school and (below) Intermediate
schoolboys and their teacher in Omdurman.

36. The main canal of the Gezira Scheme, which irrigates a large cotton producing area.

37. President Ibrahim 'Abbud opened the new railway-line to Darfur in April 1959.

prosperity of the Sudan was always precarious, being linked closely with the state of the harvest in the areas of rain cultivation. The inception of Khurshid's new deal had been favoured by the good rains of the summer of 1826: the difficulties of his last years were increased by drought and famine, beginning in 1836 and accompanied by a cholera epidemic.

Khurshid was less distinguished as a soldier than as an administrator. In the late summer of 1827, he led an expedition from al-Rusayris, on the upper Blue Nile, into the Dinka country. As a slave-raid this was no great success, only five hundred captives being brought in, while the Dinka put up a very stiff resistance, using arrows and spears, and routed Khurshid's cavalry. Nevertheless, Khurshid pushed on by force of arms as far as the Sobat, whence he returned to al-Rusayris. Three years later, in the autumn of 1830, he organized a river expedition against the Shilluk, whose raids in canoes were still troubling the Arabs of the White Nile as they had done in the sixteenth century. As Khurshid's ships moved upstream, the Shilluk deserted their islands and fled to the interior, and the expedition penetrated as far as the mouth of the Sobat. On the return journey, the Shilluk attacked the expedition with arrows. Artillery fire dispersed them and the troops were able to take booty and slaves, but the Shilluk returned to the attack, recovered their booty and compelled the expedition to withdraw with a mere two hundred slaves.

Khurshid's third great expedition, in 1831–32, was against the Hadendowa of the Taka. Sabderat was his objective, but he seems never to have got so far. After crossing the Atbara at Quz Rajab, the expedition became entangled in the bush, and was heavily defeated by the Hadendowa under their chief, Muhammad Din. Unable to advance, Khurshid established a fortified camp and beat off another attack, but he was glad to be able to extricate himself and return to Khartoum.

The last years of his rule were marked by a series of frontier wars with Kanfu,[2] the Abyssinian ruler of the district of Kwara. The Abyssinian marches were always a critical area, remote from the centres of Turco-Egyptian power and a convenient refuge for malcontents. One of these was Shaykh

Rajab wad Bashir al-Ghul, a chief of the Hammada Arabs, whose brother, Abu Rish, had been preferred by the authorities as head of the tribe. Rajab conspired with Kanfu to invade the Egyptian Sudan, and warning of the plot was sent to Khurshid by Ahmad *Kashif* Ghashim, the district officer of the Qadarif. Khurshid at the time was slave-raiding in Fazughli, and could not personally lead an expedition to the threatened area, but he sent off reinforcements. In the battle which took place, the Abyssinians were completely defeated and Rajab fled. He was, however, betrayed by Kanfu to Khurshid, who had him put to death in Khartoum in the spring of 1836.

Ahmad *Kashif* now took the initiative and raided Abyssinian territory. His first expedition was successful in capturing a number of prisoners, but on his second raid he was unexpectedly confronted by a large army under Kanfu. Ahmad's own troops had been augmented by reinforcements sent by Khurshid, but their commander resented his subordinate position and would not co-operate with Ahmad. The Turco-Egyptian troops were heavily defeated, but Ahmad escaped with his life, and the Abyssinians withdrew. This engagement, the battle of Wad Kaltabu, took place in April 1837.

Khurshid was now thoroughly alarmed. He believed that Kanfu was seeking to annex the frontier districts around the Qallabat, which would then once more become an asylum for emigrants. He asked Muhammad 'Ali to send him reinforcements, so that he could mount a counter-attack on Kanfu. The viceroy agreed to do so. In the meantime, Khurshid gathered his own forces, and marched from Wad Medani to the Qallabat. Here he paused, and his campaign came to an inglorious conclusion. The British government intervened to warn Muhammad 'Ali against attempting conquests in Abyssinia. The reinforcements had, however, been despatched under the command of Ahmad Pasha Abu Widan,[3] who met Khurshid on his return from the Qallabat.

Khurshid's rule was now near its end, although he continued to enjoy the favour of Muhammad 'Ali Pasha. In February 1834 he had been raised to the rank of bey and appointed governor (*mudir*) of the four Sudanese provinces, Sennar, Berber, Kordofan and Dongola. In the following year he paid a visit to Cairo and was created a pasha. The unique nature of his appointment was indicated by the grant of a special title (*hükümdar*,[4] usually translated governor-general), which differentiated the head of the administration in the Sudan from the governors (*mudirs*) of the provinces of Egypt proper. In May or June 1838 he was recalled to Cairo and Ahmad Pasha Abu Widan took over as acting governor-general. Khurshid was expected to return after medical treatment. He never did so,[5] and some six months later Abu Widan was confirmed in office as *hükümdar*.[6]

Under Abu Widan, the administration continued on the lines laid down by Mahu and Khurshid. Shaykh ʿAbd al-Qadir was again commended by the outgoing ruler to his successor, and continued as the governor-general's chief native adviser. Abu Widan soon distinguished himself by a rigorous investigation of the fiscal system, which had been relaxed under Khurshid to the great profit of the financial officials. Several of these suffered distraint and punishment. An edict, issued soon after Abu Widan's accession to power, ordered all tenants of riverain land to bring their holdings fully under cultivation. Derelict land was to become the property of the first claimant who cleared and irrigated it, while land thus brought into cultivation was given a three years' exemption from tax.

Abu Widan's stringency in fiscal matters produced two serious incidents. The first was with the Shayqiyya settlers, who had been allowed to colonize the derelict lands of the Jaʿaliyin rebels and emigrants. Abu Widan cancelled the forage allowance which these cavalrymen had received, and demanded the payment of land-tax with arrears from the time they had taken possession. The chiefs of the Shayqiyya produced their charter, but Abu Widan refused to relent. They then proposed to abandon their lands, but undertook to pay the arrears of tax if they might still receive their fodder rations. This compromise was also rejected by the governor-general, who insisted that they should continue to occupy their holdings. Very reluctantly, the Shayqiyya accepted the order, with the exception of one chief, *Makk* Hamad, who with his family and two hundred followers set off from Shendi for the Abyssinian marches.

On the way, the emigrants fell in with Shaykh Ahmad Abu Sinn, the chief of the Shukriyya, who informed the governor-general. Abu Widan set out in pursuit, attacked Hamad, and captured his baggage together with most of the women and children. Hamad himself escaped, with a few followers, and raided the camp of Abu Widan. The governor-general was himself accompanied by a contingent of Shayqiyya, whose chief, *Makk* Kanbal[7], he suspected of having a secret understanding with Hamad. Kanbal was shot, probably at Abu Widan's instigation, and the Shayqiyya troops were sent home. Failing to catch up with the refugees, Abu Widan consulted his Sudanese advisers, Shaykh 'Abd al-Qadir, Shaykh Ahmad Abu Sinn and Shaykh Abu Rish of the Hammada. On their advice, he offered an amnesty to the refugee chief, who finally submitted on condition that the Shayqiyya should be allowed to vacate their lands, while those who wished to remain should pay a fixed annual tax, but without arrears. The fodder allowance remained cancelled.

The second crisis over taxes concerned Shaykh Abu Rish himself. When, probably early in 1842, Abu Widan demanded a double payment from the Hammada, the chief fled to the Abyssinian marches, and joined forces with a band of freebooters. He and his allies re-entered Sudanese territory, and inflicted a defeat on the local district officer. Although it was now the rainy season and movement in the region was extremely difficult, Abu Widan set out from Wad Medani to punish the raiders. At this juncture Abu Rish was abandoned by his allies and decided to submit to the governor-general. He came to Abu Widan's camp, and was pardoned after the intervention of Shaykh 'Abd al-Qadir and other notables.

The last important territorial expansion of the Egyptian Sudan in the reign of Muhammad 'Ali Pasha was achieved by Abu Widan's occupation of the Taka. Although the area had been invaded by the *defterdar* and also by Khurshid, neither of them had succeeded in establishing their authority permanently, and Khurshid's campaign against the Hadendowa had been, as we have seen, an ignominious military failure. In 1840 Abu Widan determined to make a fresh expedition and to obtain the payment of tribute by the Beja. The two tribes which formed his principal objective were the Hadendowa under Shaykh Muhammad Din, in the wooded country of the northern Gash, and the Halanqa further south around Jabal Kasala.

Troops were assembled at El Damer, and on 20 March 1840 Abu Widan began his advance up the Atbara. On the way he was joined by Muhammad, the son of the *Arbab* Dafaʿallah. In spite of his father's turbulent career, Muhammad wad Dafaʿallah had been received into favour and was an important notable of the Gezira.[8] He brought with him his private retinue of troops. The expeditionary force halted at Quz Rajab, and then continued its advance in the direction of Jabal Kasala.

Although Muhammad Din had sent his son as an envoy, the first tribal chief to come in was Shaykh Muhammad Ila of the Halanqa. He was a parvenu to power, a *faki*, not related to the old chief, who had fled on the news of Abu Widan's approach. On 12 April the Turco-Egyptian force encamped on the Gash, near the village of Aroma, and two days later Muhammad Din arrived to make his submission in person. But to extract tribute from the unwilling and elusive Hadendowa was no easy matter, although Abu Widan seized Muhammad Din and other chiefs as hostages.

Finally the expeditionary force moved on to Jabal Kasala and encamped near the holy village of al-Khatmiyya, the headquarters of the Mirghani family. On the camp-site the town of Kasala subsequently developed, and became the chief administrative centre of the eastern Egyptian Sudan. Abu Widan now tried to defeat the Hadendowa by stratagem. Muhammad Ila suggested the damming of the river Gash, in order to prevent its floods from reaching the Hadendowa. Deprived of water for their lands and their crops, they would, the governor-general hoped, be compelled to submit and pay tribute. The device however failed: the floodwaters breaking the crudely constructed dam. An advance made against the Hadendowa was rendered ineffective by the scrub of the lower Gash. Abu Widan patched up an agreement with his opponents, and returned to Khartoum.

Although Abu Widan had failed to reduce the Hadendowa to submission, his campaign had been much more successful than that of Khurshid. Muhammad Din, the leader of the Hadendowa, was taken as a prisoner to Khartoum, where he died of smallpox in the following year. More important still, the Turco-Egyptian administration had obtained at Kasala a permanent foothold. The extension of the Egyptian Sudan towards the Red Sea inevitably gave a new importance to the old Ottoman ports of Suakin and Massawa, at that time nominal dependencies of the vilayet of the Hijaz. Abu Widan himself raised the question of their status, demanding that the governor of Suakin should pay taxes to the Sudanese treasury. In the face of opposition, both from the governor of the Hijaz and the Ottoman government, Muhammad 'Ali Pasha withdrew this claim. This was in 1843, but in 1846 the Ottoman Sultan 'Abd al-Majid granted the ports to Muhammad 'Ali on an annual lease. Three years later the lease was terminated and not until 1865, in the reign of Khedive Isma'il, were the two ports permanently annexed to the Egyptian Sudan.

Ahmad Pasha Abu Widan was a strong and effective governor: the Sudanese chronicler declares that his period of office was better than that of Khurshid, good though this was. He was perhaps too successful: it was rumoured that he was seeking to make himself independent, or alternatively that he was plotting with Sultan 'Abd al-Majid to separate the Sudanese provinces from Muhammad 'Ali's dominions. When he died suddenly in Khartoum, on 6 October 1843, the story quickly spread that he had been poisoned by his wife, the daughter of Muhammad 'Ali.

Whether or not Muhammad 'Ali instigated the death of Abu Widan, he took advantage of the situation to prevent his successor from attaining so powerful a position. A special commissioner, Ahmad Pasha Manikli, was sent to decentralize the administration. The appointment of *hükümdar* was abolished. Each province would be autonomous, under a governor of the rank of pasha, who would correspond directly with Cairo. A few months later, Muhammad 'Ali changed his mind. Manikli, who had remained in the Sudan to report on the gold of Fazughli, was ordered to reintegrate the administration. He himself was appointed *hükümdar*, a post which he held until 1845. His period of office was chiefly notable for a punitive

58

expedition against the Hadendowa, carried out with a brutal vigour that won him the nickname of *Jazzar*, 'butcher'.

Muhammad 'Ali's uncharacteristic vacillation over these administrative changes marks the beginning of nearly two decades of feeble administration in the Egyptian Sudan. These are the years of the great viceroy's senility, of the retrogressive reign of 'Abbas I (1849–54), and of the capricious rule of Muhammad Sa'id (1854–63). Eleven representatives of the viceroy sat at Khartoum during the twenty years following the death of Abu Widan. Their abilities varied, but few of them held office long enough to rule effectively. The Sudanese chronicler has little to say of them. One of the greatest pioneers of Western culture in Egypt, Rifa'a Bey Rafi' al-Tahtawi, spent a few unhappy years in Khartoum, nominally organizing a school, in fact a victim of 'Abbas Pasha's jealous obscurantism. Bayard Taylor, the first American tourist in the Sudan, met him there in 1852 and heard the long tales of his woes. In the early months of 1857 an epidemic of cholera broke out, which claimed, among many less distinguished victims, the great counsellor, Shaykh 'Abd al-Qadir wad al-Zayn.

At this juncture the Viceroy Muhammad Sa'id Pasha himself visited the Sudan. He went no further than Khartoum, but what he saw horrified him and he resolved at first to abandon the Sudanese provinces. By the time he had reached the capital, however, he had modified his views. The administration was again decentralized. Four provinces were established, one combining Khartoum and the Gezira, another uniting Dongola and Berber, the others being Kordofan and the Taka. These were to be linked more closely with Egypt by a camel-post, while a railway from Wadi Halfa to Khartoum was projected. This second decentralization lasted until 1862, when Musa Pasha Hamdi was appointed *hükümdar*.

Two major issues of later years were foreshadowed in Muhammad Sa'id's reign. In December 1854, he ordered the governor-general to stop the slave-trade, and in the following year he sought to check the transport of slaves down the White Nile by establishing a control-post at Fashoda, far to the south of the previous limit of Egyptian administration.[9] This policy was not very successful, but it was to be taken up with greater effect (and disastrous consequences for Egyptian rule in the Sudan) by Khedive Isma'il. Muhammad Sa'id Pasha also appointed the first Christian governor in the Sudan, Arakil Bey the Armenian, a relative of Nubar Pasha who played so prominent a part in the history of Egypt under Khedive Isma'il and his successors. Arakil was the first governor of Khartoum and the Gezira under the system of decentralization. The appointment of a Christian almost provoked a revolt of the powerful Shukriyya tribe, a threat which Arakil overcame by his personal courage. His rule was short, since he died in Khartoum in 1858.

The picture of political stagnation in these years is repeated in the field of economic history. Muhammad 'Ali began with an optimistic view of the resources awaiting development and exploitation in the Sudan. A period of disillusionment followed. The limited success of his attempts to recruit a slave army has already been described. Even more disappointing than the slave-soldiers was the gold of the Sudan. This was sought principally in two regions, around Fazughli and at Jabal Shaybun in the Nuba Mountains. European experts, pushed on by Muhammad 'Ali himself, prospected these areas, but to little purpose. The search was to be resumed in the Condominium period, but the profits were small. The iron deposits of Kordofan were slightly more productive, and provided nails for the government shipyard. An attempt to improve their exploitation, with the aid of English iron founders, was, however, a failure. The copper deposits of Hufrat al-Nahas, on the border between Darfur and the non-Arab peoples, were outside the range of Egyptian control until long after Muhammad 'Ali's time.

Attempts to improve Sudanese agriculture were rather more successful. In the early years after the conquest, Egyptian peasants were sent into the new territories to teach their methods to the Sudanese cultivators. Something was done to increase the irrigable areas by the main Nile. New fruit-trees were introduced, while plantations of sugar-cane and indigo were developed. The spread of cotton-production lay in the future, but Mahu Bey is said to have obtained from the Abyssinian frontier the seed which bears his name, and which was the parent of Egyptian cotton. One of the most valuable exports of the Sudan was, as it is today, the gum-arabic of Sennar and Kordofan, while ivory, traded from the still-unconquered south, was acquired by government agents. Cattle and camels, brought from the Sudan, augmented Egyptian livestock, depleted by epizootics and warfare.

From 1824 onwards, Muhammad 'Ali attempted to place all Sudanese exports under a government monopoly. In this he was for many years successful, although his measures ran counter to the official trading-policy of the Ottoman Empire. In his years of weakness, towards the end of his reign, however, he was no longer able to resist the pressure of the European powers for free trade, and by the end of Abu Widan's period of office, in 1843, the various monopolies had been abolished. The end of the monopoly led to the development of a European trading community, at first mostly Greek and Italian, in Khartoum. Under 'Abbas I, they became an influential pressure-group, which succeeded in opening the White Nile to private navigation and commerce. The momentous consequences of this will be considered in the next chapter. Otherwise the reigns of 'Abbas I and Muhammad Sa'id were a period of stagnation in the economic as well as the political history of the Sudan.

CHAPTER V

THE ERA OF KHEDIVE ISMA'IL
1862–81

THE REIGN of Khedive Isma'il (1863–79) marked the culmination of Turco-Egyptian power in the Sudan. Under him the administration regained the vigour which it had lost since the later years of Muhammad 'Ali. In his time the territories of Egypt's African empire were enormously increased. But with all his ability, Isma'il lacked the caution of his grandfather. Moreover he ruled at a time when international interest in Egypt, and in Africa generally, was far more marked, and the issues at stake far greater, than they had been while Muhammad 'Ali lived. Hence the last years of Isma'il's reign are a period of increasing difficulty ending in disaster. Three years after his deposition, the fortunes of the khedivate reached their nadir, when his successor Muhammad Tawfiq was a pawn in the hands, first of 'Urabi Pasha[1] and his militant nationalists, and then in those of the victorious British invaders.

Three characteristic themes emerge from the story of the Egyptian Sudan during the two decades which may broadly be called the era of Isma'il. The first is a great expansion of the territories ruled by the khedive. The second, closely connected with this, is a prolonged struggle against the slave-trade. The third, which again is linked with the two preceding themes, is the increasing employment in high military and civil offices of men who were neither Muslims nor Ottoman subjects, but for the most part Europeans and, at least nominally, Christians.

Although Muhammad 'Ali, as we have seen, valued his Sudanese possessions largely because they tapped a reservoir of slaves whom he could use in his army, the lucrative and flourishing slave-trade became increasingly an embarrassment to his successors. Muhammad Sa'id and Isma'il were westernized rulers, with some genuine sympathy for that nineteenth-century humanitarianism to which Muhammad 'Ali had paid no more than occasional lip-service. The combination of anti-slavery idealism with schemes for colonial expansion, a frequent phenomenon of European imperialism in the last decades of the century, was, at a rather earlier period, characteristic of Khedive Isma'il. It is easy to dismiss his measures against the slave-trade as hypocrisy, a mere pretext for the acquisition of territories that he could not effectively govern, but this is an over-simplification. The campaign against the trade was begun years before the khedivial government had made any attempt to extend its power over the great slave-acquiring areas of the Upper Nile and the Bahr al-Ghazal, while the first suggestions of such an extension seem to have come from the British consul in Cairo.

The campaign against the slave-trade resulted not only from the change of heart of the Egyptian government, and its greater susceptibility to European pressure, but from the new magnitude of the problem in the middle years of the century. The traditional slave-raiding areas, the products of which Muhammad 'Ali had sought to monopolize, lay on the fringe of the old Muslim territories of the northern Sudan. The situation of the fierce Shilluk warriors on the White Nile, and the hazards of navigating the river itself, had long prevented the penetration of Negro Africa from the north. After the Turco-Egyptian conquest, these obstacles were gradually overcome. Khurshid and Muhammad 'Ali had discussed an expedition up the White Nile in 1836, but the scheme was cancelled, and it was not until 1839 that a flotilla of sailing-boats under the command of Salim Qabudan reached a point on the river about 6° N. Two further expeditions, made in the following years, attained a site at about latitude 5° N., where the post of Gondokoro was later to develop. Meanwhile the possession of firearms was to give the men from the north the means of ultimate victory over the Shilluk and other tribes.

Although Salim Qabudan's expeditions failed to realize Muhammad 'Ali's hopes of discovering the source of the Nile and the metals which he was convinced must be there, they opened the way to the traders of Khartoum. At first government restrictions prevented their access to the Upper Nile, but their abolition in 1853 let in a swarm of merchants from Europe, Egypt and the Egyptian Sudan itself. They penetrated, not only the main stream of the Nile itself, where Gondokoro marked their farthest south, but also the western region of the Bahr al-Ghazal. It was not a case of trade following the flag: Aba Island, whence the Mahdi was to launch his revolt in 1881, lay at this time beyond the sphere of Turco-Egyptian rule. The merchants were beyond the control, as they were beyond the assistance, of settled government. Each principal had his agents and servants, his private army of armed retainers, recruited largely from the Danaqla and Shayqiyya of the north. Each had his fortified stations (*zaribas*), encampments surrounded by thorn-fences, which served them as headquarters, entrepôts for their goods, and garrison-posts in time of need. Originally they came to seek ivory, but they turned imperceptibly into slavers. Slaves were needed as concubines and porters, while slave-troops (*bazingers*) usefully augmented their private armies. With the local chiefs and tribes they established curious predatory alliances, and inter-tribal warfare passed into slave-raiding. At the outset the position of the 'Khartoumers' was precarious, but in the end their firearms and organization gave them the mastery over the tribal chiefs. The most powerful of them were merchant-princes, effectively ruling great areas. Meanwhile the ready market for slaves in the north turned them from a profitable sideline to the staple of the Khartoumers' trade.

Although Muhammad 'Ali Pasha had issued edicts against the slave-trade, the first practical measures against it were taken by Isma'il as regent of Egypt for Muhammad Sa'id in October 1862. The *hükümdar* Musa Hamdi Pasha, who had been appointed earlier that year, notified the merchants that boats would only be allowed to leave for the south for trade in ivory. At the same time a capitation tax equivalent to one month's pay was placed on all personnel taking part in trading voyages, while an officer with a small company of troops was appointed to control the traffic on the river.

These measures were a pitiful failure. The slave-trade proceeded as vigorously as ever, since the source of the trade lay beyond the control of the administration. Further steps were taken late in 1863. A new province was constituted on the White Nile with its headquarters at Fashoda, in Shilluk territory. This to some extent strengthened the hand of the authorities. Of the two merchant-princes who dominated the area, one fled while the other made terms with the administration. At the same time Musa Hamdi tripled the capitation tax on personnel. This action, coming just when the traders' boats were about to leave Khartoum, provoked a great outcry from the European trading community, who suspected that the governor-general was trying to drive them off the river. Within the next few years, in fact, the Europeans withdrew from their establishments in the south, which fell into the hands of Egyptians, Sudanese and other Ottoman subjects.

A further measure against the slave-trade, inaugurated in June 1864, was the establishment of a force of river-police. This was equipped with four steamers and half a dozen armed sailing-ships, which intercepted the traders' boats on their return downstream. After the first shock, the river-police seem rapidly to have lost their efficaciousness. An official inquiry in 1866 revealed that in spite of the seizure of 3,538 slaves, the traders had quickly learnt to elude or bribe the patrols, and that their operations were continuing on a large scale. The good intentions of the khedive were, in fact, being defeated by three factors: the existence of powerful and wealthy vested interests in the mercantile community; the lack of honest and well-paid officials; and the absence of any provision for the future of the confiscated slaves. Although in theory these should have been repatriated at the expense of the traders, they were in fact brought to Khartoum where many of them were enrolled in the army. Thus the administration itself was led to connive at a veiled form of slave-recruitment.

The withdrawal of the European traders from the White Nile and the Bahr al-Ghazal was followed by the emergence of a new generation of merchant-princes in the extensive regions still outside khedivial control. On the White Nile, the most successful of these was Shaykh Ahmad al-'Aqqad, who, probably with the financial backing of Isma'il himself, bought up most of his competitors' establishments. The enormous expenses of the trade in ivory led al-'Aqqad, as it had led his predecessors, to have recourse to slave-trading to recoup his losses. He sheltered under a khedivial decree which authorized the personnel of expeditions to bring their Negro concubines and children to Khartoum: a loophole which made possible the transport and sale of thousands of slaves annually.

The only answer to this recurrent problem seemed to be a further extension of khedivial rule, and the appointment as officials of men who stood outside the circle of vested and corrupt interests. The khedive sought to attain both these objectives when, in April 1869, he took into his service the distinguished British explorer, Sir Samuel Baker. Baker drew up his own contract of employment, which was however modified in some details by Isma'il. His tour of duty was to last for two years, during which he was to lead an expedition with the objects of annexing to Egypt all the territories in the Nile basin, suppressing the slave-trade and establishing a chain of military posts in the newly-acquired regions. Baker was given a princely salary and equipment, and provided with a flotilla of six steamers and several sailing-ships.

If strength of body and force of character had sufficed for the task, Baker would have been an admirable choice. But he was deficient in administrative qualities and, a more serious defect in the circumstances, totally blind to his delicate and invidious situation. He was an Englishman and a Christian in the employ of a Muslim ruler. His mission was odious to the powerful and entrenched slave-trading interest with its numerous ramifications in the administration, the army and Sudanese society generally. As it was, he quarrelled with the governor-general, Ja'far Mazhar Pasha, with the slave-traders and with the tribes whose interests he was supposed to protect. Nevertheless, he carried the flag to the borders of Uganda, and left garrisons to mark the authority of the khedive along the Upper Nile.

While Baker was thrusting his way irascibly up the Nile, another expedition was marching to establish the khedive's authority in a different region. The Bahr al-Ghazal was dominated by the merchant-princes, whose *zaribas*, strung out along the routes to the north, were stages for the slave-caravans going to Kordofan and Darfur. Dar Fartit, to the south of Darfur, was an ancient slave-raiding area. About the middle of the century a Muslim named Muhammad al-Hilali, who claimed to come from Morocco, had acquired power in this region and established an autonomous kingdom, under the overlordship of Darfur. Trouble had subsequently developed between the vassal and his suzerain, and Hilali sought asylum with Jaʿfar Mazhar, who proposed to the khedive to support his rights in Dar Fartit. Ismaʿil agreed, seeing in Hilali an instrument by which he might extend his power over the whole Bahr al-Ghazal. Hilali was formally appointed chief of the district of the Bahr al-Ghazal and, in spite of the protests of the sultan of Darfur, was sent off to bring the territory into submission.

The principal opposition which he had to fear was not from the enfeebled sultanate of Darfur, but from the powerful and independent merchant-princes of the Bahr al-Ghazal itself. Amongst these, the most important was a Jaʿali, al-Zubayr Rahma Mansur, who had made himself, the principal trader in the western part of the Bahr al-Ghazal and sent his caravans into Darfur. Zubayr's relations with Hilali were at first friendly, but they soon deteriorated. The difficulties which the slave-trade was experiencing on the Nile worked to the profit of the traders in the remote Bahr al-Ghazal, who were unwilling to accept Hilali's credentials as the agent of the administration. In 1871 Hilali asked Khartoum for reinforcements, and when they arrived he began to attack and reduce the *zaribas* of the traders. Zubayr marched to the aid of his friends and kinsmen. The unfortunate Hilali was killed in battle. The khedive saved appearances, realizing that Zubayr was beyond his power, by constituting the Bahr al-Ghazal a province and appointing Zubayr as its governor (December 1873).

The Upper Nile and the Bahr al-Ghazal had thus been added, at least in name, to Ismaʿil's African empire. The administrative organization of the newly acquired territories on the Nile was the work of another Englishman, Charles George Gordon, who had already made a name for himself as an unorthodox but successful soldier in China. Appointed to succeed Baker, with the title of governor of the Equatorial province, in 1874, he established a provincial capital at Lado, organized the series of riverain garrisons which tenuously held the region, and strove to reconcile the tribes, rendered angry and resentful by the depredations of the slave-traders and the heavy-handed methods of Baker. When he resigned in 1876, Egyptian authority was still feeble. Once again, a basic problem was that of personnel. Although there were advantages in employing foreign admini-strators, their salaries were high, and they succumbed to the climate. The Danaqla, who filled many of the civil and military posts, had long been inured to the region; they were hardy and intelligent, but they felt little loyalty towards the administra-tion, or sympathy for the campaign against the slave-trade.

Meanwhile Zubayr ruled in the Bahr al-Ghazal. As the principal operator in this region, he made an agreement with the Rizayqat tribe of Baqqara in southern Darfur to ensure a safe passage for his caravans. In 1873 the Rizayqat broke their agreement. Zubayr complained to their overlord, Sultan Ibrahim Muhammad of Darfur, and at the same time invaded the territory of the Rizayqat and defeated them. The strained relations that followed, between the sultan and Zubayr, led to further hostilities. Zubayr covered his aggression by informing the governor-general, Isma'il Ayyub Pasha, and through him the khedive, of a project to invade and conquer Darfur in the name of the Egyptian government.

While Isma'il Ayyub concentrated his forces in Kordofan, Zubayr struck into Darfur from the south. A Fur army was defeated in January 1874, and in October Sultan Ibrahim was killed at the battle of Manawashi. On 2 November, Zubayr entered El Fasher, where he was joined a few days later by Isma'il Ayyub. Thus Darfur became a province of the Egyptian Sudan, over half a century after Muhammad 'Ali had originally planned its conquest. Zubayr was granted the title of pasha, but his great triumph was rapidly to be followed by eclipse. A clash with Isma'il Ayyub was inevitable. When it occurred, Zubayr went to Cairo, to plead his cause in person, and there he was detained. He did not return to the Sudan until after the Anglo-Egyptian Reconquest. With his removal, the Bahr al-Ghazal lost its master, at a time when the khedive's authority in the province was little more than nominal.

The reign of Khedive Isma'il witnessed also an expansion of the Egyptian empire in the east, when in 1865 the ports of Suakin and Massawa were finally ceded by the Ottoman government to the viceroyalty of Egypt.[2] The acquisition of the Red Sea ports opened a new phase in the relations of Egypt and Abyssinia. In 1871 Isma'il appointed as governor of Massawa a Swiss, Munzinger, whose authority was subsequently extended over the whole Sudanese coast. Munzinger began to prepare for war against King John IV of Abyssinia. He died in an ambush, but Isma'il's aggressive policy continued. The outcome was unfortunate for Egypt. Two Egyptian expeditionary forces in succession were overwhelmed and defeated in the Eritrean highlands in 1875 and 1876 respectively.

Isma'il's failure in Abyssinia was the first of a series of calamities. The following year, 1877, saw a crisis in the three characteristic developments of his reign. In February Gordon was appointed governor-general of the Sudan, the first Christian and European to hold this post. At the outset he was faced with the legacy of Isma'il's expansionist policy—an unsettled frontier with Abyssinia, revolt in Darfur, and anarchy in the Bahr al-Ghazal. Finally, in August 1877, the khedive concluded the Anglo-Egyptian Slave Trade Convention, which provided, amongst other things, for the termination of the sale and purchase of slaves in the Sudan by 1880. Meanwhile the khedive's growing financial involvement was leading to increasing difficulties with his European creditors and the great powers that stood behind them. It was in the years following 1877 that the revolutionary situation was created which ultimately resolved itself in the Mahdia.

The appointment of Gordon as governor-general placed at the head of the Sudanese administration a man devoted to his duties and possessed of daemonic energies. In the course of a few months he attempted to reach a settlement with Abyssinia, pacified Darfur, and appointed as governor of the Bahr al-Ghazal the one man who might possibly have served as an instrument of Egyptian rule—Sulayman, the son of Zubayr. But Gordon's successes were superficial, and his later years of office were to show the complexity of the problems which he struggled to solve. His difficulties were partly personal, partly the result of circumstances. He was inexperienced in the routine of administration and contemptuous of bureaucracy. He was impulsive and relied on intuition, while his deeply personal religion tended to invest his decisions and his vacillations with a divine sanction in his own eyes. He was a fanatical Christian. He was illiterate in Arabic, and his command of the spoken language seems to have been meagre in the extreme. Yet far less honest and far less able men have succeeded in building and administering empires. Gordon was unfortunate in that he assumed power at a time when Isma'il, the one man whom he could trust, was declining in authority. He had neither sound finances nor effective forces to back him. He mistrusted his Egyptian subordinates, often with reason, but the caprice of his appointments and dismissals indicates a lack of judgement, while his reliance on inexperienced Sudanese and Europeans, often ill-equipped for their tasks, weakened an administration already defective in tradition and *esprit de corps*.

From July 1878 the tide turned against him. He was now solely responsible for the suppression of the slave-trade, a policy difficult in any circumstances and impossible in the conditions of those years. Sulayman, who had been superseded by a rival, revolted in the Bahr al-Ghazal, and risings broke out in Darfur and Kordofan. Gordon, acting in concert with two Italian subordinates, Gessi in the Bahr al-Ghazal and Messedaglia in Darfur, succeeded in restoring order, but the southwest was sullen and unreconciled to the rule of the khedive's officials. To cut off supplies from Sulayman, Gordon had authorized the Baqqara chiefs to harry the *jallaba* who traded in their districts. El Obeid and the other towns of Kordofan and Darfur were filled with the survivors and kinsmen of these traders, thus abruptly deprived of their stake in Egyptian rule.

In June 1879, as a result of European pressure, Isma'il was desposed by Sultan 'Abd al-Hamid II. Realizing that his one support was gone, Gordon sought to resign. Effectively his administration ended with Isma'il's reign, although his formal resignation did not come until 1880, after a further unsuccessful attempt to reach a settlement with Abyssinia. His successor as governor-general was Muhammad Ra'uf Pasha, a man of mixed Nubian and Abyssinian parentage, who had served under both Baker and Gordon. During his administration, in June 1881, the storm broke.

In economic matters, the reign of Isma'il was a period of unfulfilled promise. The story of the Sudan railway project is typical. His predecessor, Muhammad Sa'id, had, as mentioned earlier, planned the construction of a railway to link Upper Egypt with the Sudanese provinces, but the scheme was abandoned.[3] Isma'il took it up with new enthusiasm as a means of assisting administrative centralization. A British engineer, Sir John Fowler, made plans for opening the First Cataract to shipping, and for constructing a railway from Wadi Halfa to Metemma. Work was begun on both schemes in 1873, but progress was delayed by the khedive's financial difficulties. However, in February 1875 work was resumed at Wadi Halfa. Labour difficulties and the deepening financial crisis again intervened. The line reached only thirty-three miles south of Wadi Halfa when the work was suspended. The project was finally abandoned after the British occupation of Egypt. Thereafter, apart from the abortive attempt to construct a line from Suakin to Berber in connection with the campaign against 'Uthman Diqna in 1885, there was no further railway-building in the Sudan until Kitchener's campaign in Dongola during 1896.

Two other grandiose schemes of Isma'il's time were equally unfortunate. At the beginning of his reign, he encouraged the formation of a private organization, the *Compagnie du Soudan*, to develop rail and river transport and assist the export trade. After an initial buying spree, the company got into difficulties, and in 1868 went into liquidation. His other great scheme has still left memories in the Sudan. The American Civil War caused a boom in Egyptian cotton, much to the khedive's profit. His governor in Suakin, Ahmad Mumtaz Pasha, rightly perceived that the Sudan also had areas eminently suitable for cotton-growing, and started an experimental plantation in the Tokar district. This was a success. Isma'il's interest was aroused and Mumtaz put 2,500 acres of the Gash delta under cotton. He had selected his areas well; under the Condominium, as we shall see, they became centres of cotton production; but by this time the Civil War was over and the boom was ending. Neither

Mumtaz nor his master had good heads for business, so although in 1871 the pasha was put over the combined provinces of Khartoum, Sennar and the White Nile, in which he found wider scope for his cotton projects, his financial situation crumbled and he was dismissed from office after less than a year. Among the Sudanese country-people until quite recent times, the name of Mumtaz was used as a synonym for cotton.

Against these failures must be set some developments in the communications of the Sudan. The first steamers had appeared on the Sudanese Nile before Isma'il's time, but the creation of a fleet of government steamers took place in his reign. Most of them were sent upstream from Egypt, and had difficulty in passing the cataracts that lay between Aswan and Khartoum. They were serviced at a dockyard west of Khartoum, near the junction of the Niles. The surviving steamers and the dockyard were subsequently part of the physical legacy of the Egyptian administration to the Mahdist state.

The steamers played an important part in strengthening the hold of the administration over the country, particularly over the outlying provinces of the south. It was aided also by the development of the electric telegraph system. In 1866, Wadi Halfa was linked with Upper Egypt, and by 1874 the line had been extended to Khartoum. Another section, completed in 1875, linked this line with the Red Sea coast, by way of Berber, Kasala and Suakin. A third section connected Khartoum with the west, running by El Obeid to the borders of Darfur. This system was a casualty of the Mahdist revolutionary war, since the long stretches of unprotected line were easily cut by the rebels. Under the Mahdist government, a fragmentary system, linking the treasury in Omdurman with the dockyard at Khartoum, survived and was operated by telegraph-clerks of the old administration.

PART 2
THE MAHDIST STATE
1881–98

'*A Mahdi who since he arose never betrayed or deceived, who guided the blind and codified religious knowledge: who penetrated into the inmost secrets of the divine presence; who every day is revealed in the colour of a new light; who strives not after created things but after the Creator.*'

> From a verse panegyric by Ahmad Sa'd, translated by S. Hillelson.

'*The woe which befell us has now befallen the Ansar; English gunfire, and slaughter, and wretchedness. The Sirdar takes up his quarters in the Khalifa's courtyard. Shaykh al-Din is a prisoner, and Ya'qub carries firewood.*'

> From anonymous verses circulating after the defeat of the Khalifa, translated by S. Hillelson.

CHAPTER VI

THE MAHDIST REVOLUTION
1881-85

IT IS frequently asserted that the Mahdia was due to the oppression and misgovernment of the Egyptians in the Sudan. This hypothesis has been too easily and uncritically accepted, since it fails to explain why the revolution began precisely when and where it did. Examples of oppression and corruption could be found in the Turco-Egyptian administration, although it may be queried whether these were as universal and offensive as is sometimes suggested. The savage pacification by the *defterdar* was a regrettable but abnormal incident of the conquest; thereafter there was, as we have seen, a good deal of association of the Sudanese notables and men of religion with the administration. Corruption shocked the nineteenth-century European visitors, but it had long been endemic in Ottoman and Egyptian administration. To judge Turco-Egyptian administration by the standards of twentieth-century colonial rule, instead of seeing it as part of the pattern of late Ottoman provincial government, is unwarranted and unhistorical.

The accepted explanation would be more tenable if, on the declaration of the Mahdia, the revolt had flared out throughout the length and breadth of the Egyptian Sudan. But this was not the case. For two years it was practically confined to the southern fringe of the Arab provinces, centring in Kordofan, the conquest of which was the first major achievement of the Mahdi's followers. It spread only gradually to the other parts of the Sudan, last of all to those northern riverain provinces which had had the longest experience of Turco-Egyptian rule. This is a fairly clear indication that at the outset the reasons for the success of the Mahdia lay in local conditions.

The ascription of the Mahdia to the faults of Turco-Egyptian rule also fails to explain why it should have broken out in 1881. Why not sooner? The Sudanese had borne alien rule for sixty years; why did it suddenly become intolerable? There is no reason to assume that the burden had suddenly become heavier under the feeble rule of Muhammad Ra'uf. It had, however, become easier to throw off.

To explain the timing of the outbreak, one must look beyond the Sudan to events in Egypt, which followed to some extent a similar pattern. The khedivial autocracy had virtually ended with the deposition of Isma'il in 1879. His son and successor, Muhammad Tawfiq, was a puppet of the great powers. The change of rulers swept away the prestige which had surrounded the viceregal dynasty from the time of Muhammad 'Ali. In Egypt, the forces of opposition gathered around the army leader, 'Urabi Pasha, and effected by gradual stages a change in the centre of power; a genuine revolution which was abruptly nullified in September 1882 by the British occupation. The collapse of the khedivate in 1879 was as obvious to the Sudanese as to the Egyptians, and, by a turn of the screw, the revolutionary changes within Egypt made metropolitan control over Sudanese provinces weak and hesitant. There appears to have been no direct communication between the supporters of 'Urabi in Egypt and those of the Mahdi in the Sudan,[1] but both movements found their opportunity in the power-vacuum caused by the disappearance of Isma'il's autocracy.

The timing of the Sudanese outbreak may further be linked with the resignation of Gordon. Like Isma'il, Gordon was far from being an ideal ruler, but with all his faults of ignorance, caprice and misjudgement he was, like the khedive, a dynamic and masterful personality. His withdrawal from the Sudan after the deposition of Isma'il produced the classical situation for the outbreak of a revolution. Muhammad Ra'uf was the mild and gentle ruler who reaped the whirlwind sown by his energetic predecessor.

The Mahdia takes its name from its leader, Muhammad Ahmad ibn 'Abdallah, a man of Dunqulawi origin, who in June 1881 despatched letters from the island of Aba in the White Nile, informing the notables of the Sudan that he was the Expected Mahdi, the divine leader chosen by God at the end of time to fill the earth with justice and equity, even as it had been filled with oppression and wrong. He was then a man about forty years of age. From childhood he had been deeply religious and, although he had never been outside the Sudan, he had studied at the feet of more than one Sudanese teacher, and had been initiated into a Sufi order. His rigorous asceticism had led him to quarrel with one of his teachers, but for some years past he had lived at Aba, gaining among the surrounding tribes an increasing reputation for holiness and supernatural powers. He was attended by a small company of devout men like himself, and had been joined within the previous two or three years by a disciple who was to eclipse them all.

This was a certain 'Abdallahi ibn Muhammad, the son of the soothsayer of the Ta'aisha, a tribe of Baqqara living in the south of Darfur. 'Abdallahi shared the expectation of the coming of the *mahdi*, which was current in the Sudan in this period, and he had on one occasion hailed Zubayr with this title. But Zubayr refused to accept the rôle, and passed out of Sudanese history. 'Abdallahi's coming to Muhammad Ahmad may well have been the decisive event in turning the Dunqulawi teacher's thoughts towards assuming the Mahdiship. In these years also Muhammad Ahmad made two visits to Kordofan, and stayed a while in El Obeid, where political intrigue and resentment against the local administration were rife.

What were the motives that drove Muhammad Ahmad to lead a revolt against the Egyptian administration in the Sudan? To many modern Sudanese, he is *Abu'l-Istiqlal*, 'The Father of Independence', a nationalist leader who united the tribes of the Sudan by an Islamic ideology, drove out the alien rulers, and laid the foundations of a nation-state. This is an interpretation of the consequences of his revolt, rather than an appreciation of his motives. Another modern Sudanese view of Muhammad Ahmad sees in him a *mujaddid*, a renewer of the Muslim Faith, come to purge Islam of faults and accretions. Much in Muhammad Ahmad's own statements about his mission supports this opinion. A theme which occurs frequently in his pronouncements is that he was sent to establish the Faith and the Custom of the Prophet—the normative ideals of Islam. Seen from this point of view, Muhammad Ahmad is comparable to the Muslim reformers of the eighteenth and nineteenth centuries, such as Muhammad ibn 'Abd al-Wahhab, the founder of the Wahhabi movement in Arabia.

But Muhammad Ahmad went further than this. His mission as reformer developed eschatological overtones. He claimed for himself unique status, reflected in the three titles which he associated with his name—the Imam, the Successor of the Apostle of God, the Expected Mahdi. As Imam, he asserted his headship of the community of true Muslims. As Successor of the Apostle of God, he envisaged himself recapitulating the rôle of the Prophet, by restoring the community which Muhammad had established. As the Expected Mahdi, he was an eschatological figure whose advent foreshadowed the end of the age.

At times of crisis in the Islamic world, the appearance of a *mahdi*, claiming divine sanction to overthrow the old order and set up a new theocracy, is a not uncommon development. Two medieval *mahdis* had established durable political regimes, 'Ubaydallah, the founder of the Fatimid dynasty in North Africa and Egypt in the tenth century, and Muhammad ibn Tumart, whose followers, the Almohads, had conquered and ruled north-west Africa and Moorish Spain in the twelfth century. There had been others more recently, including one who assailed, and was defeated by, Bonaparte's French troops in Egypt at the end of the eighteenth century.

To an established government, the appearance of a *mahdi* is therefore a dangerous symptom. Muhammad Ra'uf apprehended the danger, but did not act with sufficient force to suppress it. An expedition sent to Aba in August 1881, to seize Muhammad Ahmad, miscarried, and the troops were beaten off with some casualties by the Mahdi's followers. This victory of spears and clubs over firearms was hailed as a miracle and, as soon as the government steamers had withdrawn, the Mahdi and his little group of followers crossed the White Nile and made their way to Qadir, a remote hill in the south of Kordofan, on the fringe between Arab and Negro territory. Here the malcontents began to assemble. In this period three main groups may be distinguished among the *Ansar*,[2] as the Mahdi called his supporters.

There were, first, the genuinely pious men who were his disciples in a religious sense and, in some cases, had been with him for years. These men accepted him as the Expected Mahdi. They deplored the state of the Sudan because they were puritans and wished the conduct of its people to be governed by the Holy Law of Islam in its full rigour. The administration was odious, not so much because of oppression and corruption in the usual sense, but because any government not patterned on the primitive Islamic theocracy was inherently depraved. When the Mahdi and these men spoke of misgovernment and purification, they were thinking in theological rather than political terms.

A second group of the Ansar had more practical grievances. These were the Ja'aliyin and Danaqla of the dispersion, who had settled on the southern fringe of the Arab Sudan, penetrated the White Nile and Bahr al-Ghazal, and worked as boatmen, traders and soldiers of fortune in the great opening-up of the south. Directly or indirectly, the livelihood of many of them was connected with the slave-trade, and Gordon's policy, culminating in the harrying of the *jallaba*, had struck at the roots of their prosperity. Now that Gordon and Isma'il were gone, the opportunity had come to resume their old ways of life. These men were neither theologians nor devotees, but they could cover their political and economic interests with a veil of religion, since the institution of slavery was not as such repugnant to Islam, and the wholesale employment of Christians by a Muslim government derogated from the prestige of their religion.

The third group consisted of the Baqqara nomads, who shared neither the religious ideals of the Mahdi's disciples nor the political grievances of the northerners of the dispersion. To them the Mahdia made its appeal in simple and elementary terms: 'Kill the Turks and cease to pay taxes.' To the nomad, control by any settled government is hateful, and the firmer its control, the more hateful it becomes. The nomads of the southern fringe had in the previous ten years become increasingly conscious of government. The Rizayqat had suffered from the superior armament and forces of Zubayr. Then came the conquest of Darfur, and the substitution of thoroughgoing Egyptian administration for the easy yoke of Sultan Ibrahim.

79

It was the fickle, light-hearted Baqqara who formed the army of this puritan revolution, and their importance is reflected in the unique status of their kinsman, 'Abdallahi, in the Mahdi's councils.

Qadir was still more difficult of access than Aba. An attempt to intercept the Ansar while crossing Kordofan failed, and an expedition organized by the governor of Fashoda against the orders of Ra'uf Pasha was annihilated in December 1881. Ra'uf was recalled in the following March, and the 'Urabist government in Egypt appointed as his successor an energetic soldier with long experience in the Sudan, 'Abd al-Qadir Hilmi Pasha. Meanwhile a much more serious attempt to crush the Mahdi had been organized by the acting governor-general, a German telegraph official named Giegler. In spite of its superior forces, this expedition also was overwhelmed in May 1882 by the Ansar. Each of these victories raised the prestige of the Mahdi, while the booty acquired augmented his meagre resources. The Baqqara began to turn increasingly to the new leader of revolt, among them the Rizayqat, who welcomed the prospect of a clash with the provincial authorities of Darfur.

Hitherto the Mahdi, in his refuge at Qadir, had been on the defensive. He now turned to the offensive and led his followers in a holy war against Kordofan. He knew that in the provincial capital, El Obeid, he could count on a fifth column of sympathizers. The operations in Kordofan followed a pattern which was to be characteristic of the Mahdi's wars. Sporadic local tribal risings first occurred, and were dealt with, usually effectively, by the forces of the administration, but as fast as one was suppressed, another broke out. The immense distances and difficult circumstances of these petty engagements laid a heavy burden on the provincial troops. The second phase opened with the arrival of a Mahdist army in the province. This, combined with more general tribal risings, tried the Turco-Egyptian provincial forces to the utmost. In pitched battles they were still usually victorious, but they were unable to consolidate their successes and had to withdraw to their fortified bases, which, in the third phase, were gradually reduced by the Ansar. In Kordofan, by the autumn of 1882, only two garrisons still held out, at Bara and El Obeid.

The governor at El Obeid, Muhammad Sa'id Pasha, had taken early precautions by fortifying the administrative cantonment which, then as now, was separate from the commercial town. At the beginning of September 1882, the Mahdi with the main body of his supporters, augmented by large tribal levies, encamped near El Obeid. A general assault on the town, delivered in the Friday Battle of 8 September, was a failure: as so often in history, a tribal army found itself checked by a fortified garrison. But Muhammad Sa'id failed to press his advantage, and kept his troops in the cantonment. In the Mahdi's camp there were divided counsels. 'Abdallahi himself advised a retreat to Qadir, but was overruled. Instead the Mahdi moved his camp closer to El Obeid and the Ansar settled down to besiege the town. At the same time a new Mahdist force was organized, of what were in effect regular soldiers, neither fanatical devotees nor tribal warriors. These soldiers were mainly Sudanese originating from the south, who had served in the Turco-Egyptian forces, and had been captured in battle. Their status was interesting; they were commanded by Hamdan Abu 'Anja, who belonged to a servile tribe, clients of the Ta'aisha; they were known, not as Ansar, like the other troops, but by their former Turco-Egyptian designation of *Jihadiyya*; and they alone, it seems, were officially equipped with firearms.

As the year moved to its close, the situation of both Bara and El Obeid deteriorated. A relieving force sent by 'Abd al-Qadir Hilmi from Khartoum was intercepted in October. After negotiations, the garrison of Bara surrendered on terms in January 1883, and swore allegiance to the Mahdi. A few days later, the determination of Muhammad Sa'id to resist was overborne by a council of his officers. On 19 January El Obeid capitulated and the Mahdi led the prayer of victory in the mosque. This was the first considerable town to fall into the hands of the Ansar, and its capture was followed by a ruthless search for treasure. The former governor and his chief officers had been granted their lives, but the Mahdi learnt that they were attempting to communicate with Khartoum. They were handed over to tribal chiefs, who made away with them.

While these events were taking place at Qadir and in Kordofan, there were sporadic risings in the Gezira and riverain districts south of Khartoum. These areas were however easily accessible by land or steamer, and the vigorous actions of Giegler and 'Abd al-Qadir Hilmi succeeded in holding in check the rebels on the Blue and White Nile. 'Abd al-Qadir indeed planned a vigorous counter-offensive against the Mahdists. He concentrated troops in Khartoum, organized three additional battalions of black *Jihadiyya*, and strengthened the chief administrative centres. He tried to counter the Mahdi's propaganda, and dealt harshly with officials whose loyalty he suspected. He appealed to Cairo for reinforcements, but the 'Urabist government was preoccuped with the threat of British intervention. 'Abd al-Qadir continued to hold office for a few months after the occupation of Egypt in September 1882, but, as a nominee of the 'Urabists, he was not in good standing with the new regime. He was recalled in February 1883, after a successful campaign against forces threatening Sennar.

Turco-Egyptian rule in the Sudan during its last two years, from the fall of El Obeid to that of Khartoum, was dominated by British policy towards Egypt. The British occupation of Egypt was at first regarded by Gladstone's government as a temporary measure, which would be ended as soon as Khedive Muhammad Tawfiq had been firmly re-established on his throne. The revolt in the Sudan was regarded as something outside the sphere of British responsibilities. The serious financial state of Egypt was an argument against large-scale measures to suppress the rebels and regain the lost territory. There was also the point of view expressed by Gladstone, that the Sudanese were a people rightly struggling to be free; against whom, therefore, military operations would be morally unjustifiable. Thus an illogical assemblage of political, financial and moral considerations led the British government, not only to evade involvement in the Sudanese problem, but also to check the attempts of the khedivial government to promote resolute action in the threatened provinces.

A success in the Sudan was, however, badly needed by Muhammad Tawfiq's ministers to restore the prestige of the khedivate and give it at least some semblance of autonomy *vis-à-vis* the occupying power. The Egyptian government was permitted by Britain to raise an expeditionary force entirely on its own responsibility. Many of the troops were demoralized survivors of 'Urabi's armies. A former British officer of the Indian Army, William Hicks, was appointed commander-in-chief, but on his advance into Kordofan, he was accompanied by the governor-general, 'Ala' al-Din Siddiq Pasha.

The expedition, which marched out from Dueim on the White Nile on 27 September 1883, was doomed from the start. Hicks disagreed with his Egyptian colleagues, his men lacked hope, the route in its later stages ran through waterless scrub. As it advanced into Kordofan, the column was harassed by a reconnaissance force of Ansar, and proclamations from the Mahdi, scattered on the line of march, warned the troops that it was hopeless to fight against the soldiers of God. On 5 November, the expeditionary force was surrounded at Shaykan south of El Obeid, and cut to pieces by the Ansar and *Jihadiyya* of the Mahdi. Hicks and 'Ala' al-Din perished with all their chief officers. The last Egyptian attempt to hold the Sudan had failed.

The victory of Shaykan convinced the waverers all over the Sudan that Egyptian rule was doomed. The provinces neighbouring Kordofan were the first to fall. In Darfur an Austrian officer, Rudolf von Slatin, had been governor since 1881, and had struggled to repress the rebel Rizayqat in the south. After the fall of El Obeid his position became very precarious, although he publicly professed Islam in an attempt to secure the loyalty of his troops. One of his subordinates, a certain Muhammad Khalid, generally called Zuqal, was a kinsman of the Mahdi. After Shaykan the Mahdi invested him as governor of Darfur. On 23 December 1883, Slatin made his submission to Muhammad Khalid. For the next twelve years Slatin remained in the entourage of the Mahdi and his successor, sometimes an honoured councillor, sometimes a humiliated captive, always a secret enemy of the regime.

In the Bahr al-Ghazal, the authority of the khedive was upheld, to the limit of his feeble resources, by a young Englishman, F. M. Lupton, formerly an officer in the British mercantile marine. Like his colleagues in Kordofan and Darfur, he succeeded at first in suppressing local revolts in which both the

Dinka and the northerners of the dispersion took part. But the victory of the Mahdi at Shaykan doomed him, and he was cut off from Khartoum. A force sent by the Mahdi to invade the province reached the capital, Daym al-Zubayr, in April 1884, and Lupton had no choice but to surrender. He was sent to the Mahdi and died in Omdurman four years later.

The fall of El Obeid was followed by an extension of the revolt to a region hitherto untouched, one moreover of vital strategic importance, the hinterland of Suakin. The Beja tribes, isolated by their language and way of living from the Arab Sudanese, were unaffected at first by the Mahdia. Not until the summer of 1883 did an emissary reach them, to summon them to the holy war. The Mahdi's messenger and delegate was 'Uthman Diqna,[3] a Suakinese of partially Beja descent. He belonged to a mercantile family and had suffered arrest and imprisonment for slave-trading across the Red Sea. The Haden-dowa, the leading Beja tribe of the region, had a grievance against the administration, since they had been bilked of part of the dues promised them for transport work in connection with the Hicks expedition, but neither this nor the personality of 'Uthman Diqna seems to have been the real factor which incited them to revolt.

The decisive event was an alliance which 'Uthman made with Shaykh al-Tahir al-Tayyib al-Majdhub, the local head of the Sufi order which had its centre at El Damer.[4] By swearing allegiance to the Mahdi and recognizing 'Uthman as his duly accredited representative, Shaykh al-Tahir called from the soil a fanatical and devoted tribal army. Within a few months, the vital line of communication between Suakin and Berber had been cut, and two Egyptian forces had been defeated on the coast near Tokar. Sinkat, the nodal point on the route across the Red Sea Hills, and Tokar both fell in February 1884. Suakin itself was reinforced by British troops, and never fell, although it was frequently threatened by the Ansar under 'Uthman Diqna.

The battle of Shaykan inescapably confronted both the Egyptian and British governments with the problem of the future of the Sudan. Although the British government was prepared to send troops to Suakin, which was of some strategic importance as a Red Sea port, it was still determined to avoid involvement in the interior, and in January 1884 it insisted that the Egyptians should evacuate their troops and officials. Largely in consequence of a press-campaign in Britain, Gordon was sent out to fulfil a mission which was variously understood by the different parties concerned. The British government believed it had sent him to report on the best method of carrying out the evacuation. Baring,[5] the British agent and consul-general in Cairo, who was the effective ruler of Egypt, thought Gordon was authorized to execute the evacuation. On the way, and after his arrival in the Sudan, Gordon added to the confusions and misunderstandings by communicating the varied schemes which sprouted incessantly in his fertile mind.

He was commissioned by the khedive as governor-general, and provided with two sets of documents; one set speaking of the restoration of good government, the other announcing the policy of evacuation. By a fatal error, Gordon published the second set while passing through Berber on the way to Khartoum. Shortly before this he had written to the Mahdi, offering to recognize him as sultan of Kordofan—an offer which the Mahdi indignantly rejected. These two actions indicated to the Sudanese that the Egyptian government had abdicated its responsibilities. Gordon's authority was now effective only so long as he had physical force to maintain it.

He arrived in Khartoum on 18 February 1884. Having quickly realized that an accommodation with the Mahdi and a peaceful evacuation of the Egyptians were impossible, Gordon swung to the other extreme. He felt himself bound to establish a strong government to check the Mahdi, and demanded the appointment of Zubayr Pasha to succeed him. He went on to propose that Indian troops should be sent to the Sudan to 'smash the Mahdi'. To the inhabitants of Khartoum he announced that British troops would in a few days be at Khartoum—a dangerous piece of bluff. When on 13 March the British government overruled these proposals, which went far beyond the scope of their instructions and intentions, Gordon sombrely resigned himself to remaining at Khartoum until help came or the city fell.

The evacuation of the riverain garrisons was by this time

becoming impossible. The telegraph-line to Egypt was cut on
12 March. On 27 April a Mahdist emissary arrived to carry the
Holy War into the province of Berber. The provincial capital
fell in the middle of May. Khartoum was thus cut off, both from
the Egyptian frontier and from Suakin. Meanwhile the Mahdi
was preparing to advance on Khartoum. He had left El Obeid
in April, and the Mahdist vanguard took up its siege-positions
outside the capital in September. The Mahdi himself arrived on
23 October and established his headquarters on the western
bank of the White Nile. Khartoum, now strictly besieged, was
doomed unless help came.

Under the pressure of public opinion in Britain, Gladstone's
government at last agreed to send a relief expedition, but its
organization did not get under way until the autumn. The news
of its advance, in January 1885, placed the besiegers in a
dilemma. They failed to gauge its very limited strength, and
some of the Mahdi's advisers counselled a retreat to Kordofan.
Finally it was decided to assault the city before the relieving
force could arrive. The attack was delivered in the early hours
of 26 January 1885. The exhausted garrison was overwhelmed,
and Gordon was killed in the fighting. On 28 January the
relieving steamers arrived at the junction of the Niles, to learn
that they had come too late.

The capture of Khartoum completed the Mahdi's control over
a great part of the former Egyptian Sudan, although Suakin,
the far north and the equatorial regions were still held for the
khedive. The Mahdi disliked the former capital, and transferred
his headquarters to a village on the western bank near his old
camp. Here in Omdurman were his house, his mosque and,
in time, his tomb. The Mahdi and his Ansar had seen the taking
of Khartoum as but one in a series of conquests throughout the
Muslim world. Their expectations were to be disappointed,
for after a sudden and short illness, the Mahdi died on 22 June
1885.

He left to his successor a rudimentary administrative system,
which reflects both the religious ideology of his movement and
the wars which had brought it to power. The Mahdi and his
Ansar were dominated by the idea that they were re-enacting

the drama of primitive Islam. Hence the Mahdi equated his chief disciples with the Companions of the Prophet.

To three of them he gave titles linking them with three of the four Companions who had succeeded the Prophet as heads of the Muslim community. 'Abdallahi ibn Muhammad was designated *Khalifat al-Siddiq*, the Successor of the Caliph Abu Bakr. 'Ali ibn Muhammad Hilu, a man of great piety and a disciple of long standing, was entitled *Khalifat al-Faruq*, the Successor of the Caliph 'Umar. The title of Successor of 'Uthman, the third historical caliph, was offered to Muhammad al-Mahdi al-Sanusi, the contemporary head of the Sanusiyya order, but he ignored the proposal, and the place remained vacant. A young relative of the Mahdi, Muhammad Sharif ibn Hamid, was appointed *Khalifat al-Karrar*, the Successor of the Caliph 'Ali' the cousin of the Prophet.[6]

These were not empty titles, since each of the three *khalifas*, as they are usually called, commanded a division of the Mahdist army. The Khalifa 'Abdallahi, being of Baqqari origin, commanded the great, if fluctuating, tribal levies of the Baqqara. This division was known from its standard as the Black Flag. The Khalifa 'Ali had a comparatively small tribal force, drawn from his own kinsmen in the southern Gezira: it was called the Green Flag. The Khalifa Muhammad Sharif, being, like the Mahdi, of Dunqulawi origin, commanded the riverain tribes of the main Nile and of the dispersion. His division was probably entitled the Red Flag.

The position of 'Abdallahi was as superior to that of his colleagues as that of Bonaparte to the two other consuls in 1799. He was given the title of Commander of the Armies of the Mahdia, and from the outset controlled the administration as the vizier (although this title was not used) of the Mahdi. His paramountcy excited jealousy, and on various occasions the Mahdi affirmed their implicit mutual reliance. One lengthy proclamation of the Mahdi was in effect a diploma conferring plenary powers on 'Abdallahi. There was a deep significance in his nomination as *Khalifat al-Siddiq*, since his prototype, Abu Bakr, had been the closest to the Prophet of all the Companions, and had succeeded him on his death.

Subordinate to the khalifas were other officers who, in the

first place, had often been early adherents to the Mahdi and had raised their districts or tribes in his support. They had thus a dual rôle, as propagandists and, later, as military commanders. These officers are usually called by European, and even by Sudanese, writers the Mahdi's 'emirs', although the title *amir* (commander) was officially superseded in 1883 by that of '*amil* (agent). Such officers, who were commissioned in writing by the Mahdi, might be anything from petty local leaders to military governors of an extensive area, such as 'Uthman Diqna in the east or Muhammad Khalid in Darfur. The rank and file, called by the outside world 'dervishes', a term usually applied to the members of Sufi orders, were from a very early date designated by the Mahdi *Ansar*, 'Helpers'.

Two other great officers of state were appointed during the time of the Mahdi; the treasurer and the chief judge. The Mahdist treasury, which, again following a primitive Islamic precedent, was entitled *Bayt al-mal*, 'the house of wealth', was intended to contain all the material resources of the movement, in both cash and kind. For the elaborate tax-system of the Egyptians, lighter taxes authorized by the Holy Law of Islam were substituted. But throughout the period of the revolutionary war, the treasury was augmented chiefly from the booty acquired in battle. It was no easy task to induce the warriors to hand over their booty to the common treasury, as repeated proclamations by the Mahdi and the Khalifa 'Abdallahi make clear. The treasury was put under Ahmad Sulayman, a man of Nubian origin and a friend of the Mahdi.

The chief judge, entitled *qadi al-Islam*, 'the judge of Islam', was Ahmad 'Ali. He had been a judge under the Turco-Egyptian regime in Darfur. In theory the law of the Mahdist community was the Holy Law of Islam, but the Mahdi in practice exercised extensive powers of legislation. This he did by his proclamations and by his decisions on points of law submitted to him. Although Ahmad 'Ali was the special delegate of the Mahdi's judicial functions, legal cases were also heard and determined by the Mahdi himself, the khalifas and the other chief officers. The Mahdist theocracy was in form a state in which supreme power was held directly from God by the Mahdi, and exercised by other officials only by delegation from him. Yet it is clear that before the Mahdi's death a large part of the substance of power was already held by the Khalifa 'Abdallahi.

The Mahdi was the first Sudanese sovereign to exercise one of the traditional prerogatives of a Muslim ruler: that of striking money. After the sack of Khartoum, gold and silver acquired as booty by the treasury was minted by his orders. The gold pounds of the Mahdi were of an unusually high standard of fineness and, in accordance with Gresham's Law, rapidly vanished from circulation. Dollars, at first of silver, later (in the Khalifa's reign) of increasingly debased metal, continued to be struck throughout the Mahdist period. The coins were modelled on Ottoman currency circulating in Egypt, but with Omdurman as the mint-mark. At no time, however, did foreign specie cease to circulate in the Sudan. The Mahdi ordained that the various types of currency should all pass at their face value. This edict was confirmed by the Khalifa, early in his reign, and gave rise to frauds, practised on the treasury by its own officials. The foreign coins were preferred to the local *maqbul* (i.e. 'acceptable') currency, which was further held in low esteem owing to the prevalence of counterfeiting.

CHAPTER VII

THE REIGN OF THE
KHALIFA 'ABDALLAHI: 1885–98

THE DEATH of the Mahdi brought to a head the tensions underlying the revolutionary movement. Although the ideology and organization of the Mahdia reflected the outlook and aims of the pious devotees, and although its later victories would have been impossible without the help of the Baqqara, the fruits of conquest had fallen largely to the riverain tribesmen, especially to the Danaqla and Ja'aliyin of the dispersion. At the centre of this last group, who are called in the Mahdist documents *Awlad al-balad*, (i.e. villagers, sedentaries) were the Mahdi's own kinsmen, the *Ashraf*. Although many of them were late adherents to the movement, they had claimed a privileged position, and their actions had been disavowed by the Mahdi himself in the last few weeks of his life.

Each of the three groups, whom victory was turning from allies into rivals, had its representative in the upper grades of the Mahdist hierarchy. The leader of the devotees was the Khalifa 'Ali ibn Muhammad Hilu, a truly religious man without political ambitions, who constantly played the part of a mediator and conciliator in the crises which followed the Mahdi's death. The party formed by the *Awlad al-balad* had, as a figurehead rather than an active leader, the Mahdi's young kinsman, the Khalifa Muhammad Sharif ibn Hamid. Insofar as the Baqqara were prepared to recognize any authority, it was embodied in neither of these, but in the Khalifa 'Abdallahi ibn Muhammad, himself of Baqqari origin.

At the time of the Mahdi's death, 'Abdallahi headed a strong concentration of military power in Omdurman. A body of *Jihadiyya*, commanded by one of his clients, was garrisoned there, as were also Baqqari tribal levies of the Black Flag division. The forces of the *Awlad al-balad,* belonging to the Red Flag division, his only serious rivals, were, by contrast, scattered in various parts of the Sudan. The Green Flag troops were few in number, and could play no effective military rôle by themselves.

Thus, when the moment came for the *Ashraf* and *Awlad al-balad* to take control of the nascent Mahdist state, they were in no position to do so, lacking, as they did, both determined leadership and effective military force at the centre. At a council of notables, held immediately after the Mahdi's burial, the intention of the *Ashraf* to designate the Khalifa Muhammad Sharif as the new ruler was frustrated by the rest of the company. While the dispute raged, the Khalifa 'Abdallahi sat silent. His restraint was rewarded. One of the notables at last took him by the hand and swore allegiance to him. The other notables followed suit, last of all the *Ashraf* and Muhammad Sharif himself. Thereupon a public oath-taking followed in the open mosque outside the room in which the Mahdi lay dead. Proclamations were despatched to inform the provincial governors of the new sovereign, and to empower them to administer the oath of allegiance to their troops.

'Abdallahi now added to his style the new and unique title of *Khalifat al-Mahdi,* 'the Successor of the Mahdi': he was now 'the Khalifa' *par excellence.* He bolstered up his position by skilful propaganda, claiming the sanction of visions for his sovereignty. The *Ashraf* were not yet, however, prepared to abandon the struggle for power. Most of the great provincial commands as well as the chief offices of state were held by them or their sympathizers. A conspiracy was hatched, in accordance with which the military governor of Darfur, Muhammad Khalid, was to march on Omdurman with his very considerable forces. The Khalifa's handling of this crisis is typical of his astute and resourceful policy. He first removed the danger in the capital, by sending a Baqqari officer, Yunus al-Dikaym, to occupy the fertile Gezira, the granary of the capital, which the *Ashraf* intended to allot to the troops of Muhammad Khalid. Next he instructed his representative at Dueim to intercept the mails passing between Omdurman and the western provinces. Thirdly, in April or May of 1886, 'Abdallahi, supported by the

Khalifa 'Ali, proposed that the two junior khalifas should relinquish their personal bodyguards and armouries, and that these should be placed under the control of Ya'qub, 'Abdallahi's brother and successor as commander of the Black Flag division.

Meanwhile the army of Darfur had begun a leisurely advance towards the Nile. 'Abdallahi possessed two advantages. First, a large part of the Darfurian army consisted of Baqqari levies, who could not be relied on to support Muhammad Khalid. Secondly, in Kordofan was stationed a powerful Black Flag Army, commanded by Hamdan Abu 'Anja, whose loyalty to the Khalifa was beyond question. Acting on instructions, which became steadily more uncompromising as 'Abdallahi's position improved in Omdurman, Hamdan intercepted the Darfurian army in April 1886 at Bara. Muhammad Khalid allowed himself to be arrested and deprived of his command without resistance. His forces were incorporated in those loyal to the Khalifa.

For six years after the meeting at Bara, the *Ashraf* and *Awlad al-balad* relapsed into impotence. Chance or policy removed their sympathizers from the chief commands, which 'Abdallahi bestowed on his kinsmen and clients. A year after the Mahdi's death, only two of the great provincial governors whom he had appointed remained in office. One of these, in the Bahr al-Ghazal, was to fall from power in 1887; the other, 'Uthman Diqna, was an indispensable instrument for the control of the Beja, and remained in high office until the overthrow of the Mahdist state. Elsewhere the military governors and other high executive officers were clansmen or clients of 'Abdallahi. In subordinate offices, especially in the bureaucracy, the *Awlad al-balad* could not be superseded by the mostly illiterate and unsophisticated nomads, whom they wryly styled 'Our lords the Ta'aisha'.

After the ending of the internal threat to his rule, the Khalifa took up an aspect of the Mahdi's work left incomplete at his death—the promotion of the Holy War, to extend the Mahdia (equated by the Ansar with true Islam) throughout the world. There had already been fighting on the frontiers. In December 1885 the Ansar of Dongola had been defeated by Anglo-Egyptian forces, and for a while 'Abdallahi believed an invasion of his territories to be imminent, whereas in fact the battle preceded a withdrawal of Egyptian troops from all posts south of Wadi Halfa. The garrisons of Kasala and Sennar, which had held out with great fortitude and endurance even after the fall of Khartoum, surrendered in July and August 1885 respectively. An Egyptian officer, Saʿd Rifʿat, succeeded in evacuating the garrison of Gallabat and bringing the refugees through Abyssinia to safety at Massawa. The intrepidity and resource of this man passed unnoticed by a generation whose deepest emotions had been roused by the failure of Gordon's mission.

The Holy War was fought in three particular areas; in the west, on the Abyssinian marches, and on the Egyptian frontier. The war in the west was in its essential nature a pacification of Darfur. On withdrawing from that province, Muhammad Khalid had appointed as its governor a member of the old royal family, Yusuf Ibrahim. At first Yusuf had acted as a loyal vassal of the Khalifa, but by the summer of 1887 he was obviously aiming to restore the Fur sultanate. Operations against him were entrusted to a young kinsman of the Khalifa, ʿUthman Adam, called Janu, who was governor of Kordofan. ʿUthman advanced into Darfur, defeated the rebels and re-established the Mahdist administration of the province. Yusuf fled, but was shortly afterwards defeated. His brother, Abu'l-Khayrat, succeeded to his claims to be the legitimate sultan of Darfur.

The very success of the Mahdist movement led to the appearance of other messianic figures, aiming to subvert the rule of the Khalifa. One such, commonly known by his nickname of Abu Jummayza, gained a large number of militant adherents on the western frontiers of Darfur. Abu Jummayza sought to legitimatize his movement by claiming that he was the rightful third khalifa, the Successor of ʿUthman. Since it was known that the Mahdi had originally offered this title to Muhammad al-Mahdi al-Sanusi, the intelligence officers in Egypt at first gave credence to the market-rumour that the Sanusiyya were on the march, and that the Khalifa was trembling in Omdurman.

The revolt was indeed serious enough. Abu Jummayza advanced into Darfur, gathering supporters as he went, including the shadow-sultan, Abu'l-Khayrat, and his followers.

Two of 'Uthman Adam's subordinates were heavily defeated and the young governor was faced with revolt throughout his province. Yet he did not lose heart, but concentrated his forces in El Fasher. The danger passed away as suddenly as it had arisen. Abu Jummayza died of smallpox, and the heart went out of his followers, who were defeated in a pitched battle outside El Fasher in February 1889. Abu'l-Khayrat fled back to the hill-country of Jabal Marra, where he was murdered two years later. 'Uthman Adam had saved Darfur for the Khalifa, but after his premature death in 1891, his successor, Mahmud Ahmad, was to have considerable difficulty in holding the province.

On the Abyssinian frontier, the Holy War was simply a further phase of the hostilities which had frequently recurred throughout the Turco-Egyptian period, and indeed in earlier times. The absence of a defined frontier, the opportunities for raiding which local war-lords on both sides found irresistible, and the coincidence of bellicose rulers in both Abyssinia and the Mahdist Sudan, made a clash inevitable. Fighting began early in 1887 between the Mahdist commander at Gallabat and Ras 'Adar, the Abyssinian governor of the contiguous territory. The Ansar were worsted, and their chief killed. This led the Khalifa to send an expeditionary force to Gallabat under Yunus al-Dikaym, who followed a provocative policy. The Ansar were soon afterwards augmented by more troops under Hamdan Abu 'Anja, who was given the chief command.

Abu 'Anja had some difficulty in asserting his authority, not only over Yunus but also over many of the troops, who were on the verge of mutiny under a leader with messianic pretensions. He claimed to be the Prophet Jesus, whose Second Coming is to be expected, according to some Mahdist traditions, after the appearance of the Mahdi. The conspiracy was suppressed, Yunus was recalled to Omdurman, and Abu 'Anja seized the opportunity of his absence to make a large-scale raid into Abyssinia. Ras 'Adar was defeated, and the Mahdist army penetrated as far as Gondar, the ancient capital. Much booty fell into the hands of the Ansar, but the campaign as such was indecisive.

This campaign took place in January 1888. Abu 'Anja made

another raid in the summer, but it did not produce the successes of the earlier one. Abu 'Anja then returned to Omdurman, where he was welcomed by the Khalifa. By the end of the year he was back at Gallabat, where he died in January 1889.

The lull in hostilities was soon to end. King John of Abyssinia had sent offers of peace to the Khalifa, and had received a bellicose reply. He prepared for war, and was favoured by conditions in the Mahdist camp. Abu 'Anja's death was followed by a dispute over the command at Gallabat. Recognition was ultimately granted to al-Zaki Tamal, a member of the same servile tribe as Abu 'Anja. In March 1889 the Abyssinian army, commanded by the king in person, drew near to Gallabat. At the first onset, the Abyssinians were victorious, but a chance bullet fatally wounded their king. During the night, the Abyssinians began to withdraw, pursued by the exultant Ansar. Among the booty taken by the Sudanese was the crown of the dead king. It was sent with his head to Omdurman, whence the Khalifa issued lithographed copies of al-Zaki's despatch giving news of the victory. Abyssinia fell into anarchy, from which the Italians, who had occupied Massawa in 1885, profited by establishing control over Eritrea, thereby becoming neighbours to the Mahdist state.

In Darfur, and on the Abyssinian frontier, the Khalifa was grappling with problems of pacification and frontier-disputes such as had faced Gordon and the Turco-Egyptian administrators before him. The Holy War on the southern frontier of Egypt was something new, a legacy of the dream of universal conquest throughout the lands of Islam, which had been frustrated by the Mahdi's death. A campaign against Egypt had been planned by the Mahdi, under the command of 'Abd al-Rahman al-Nujumi, a general of Ja'ali origin who had served with distinction during the campaigns in Kordofan and against Khartoum.

When the Khalifa resumed the Mahdi's schemes, al-Nujumi remained as the designated commander of the expeditionary force. The campaign, however, was slow to get under way. Not until the Anglo-Egyptian forces had been withdrawn from Dongola, and 'Abdallahi had secured his position against his domestic rivals, did an expedition really become feasible. Even then, inordinate delays occurred. These were partly physical, arising from the difficulties of constituting and keeping together a force, mainly of tribal warriors, and provisioning it for an advance through the arid districts of Nubia. There were also difficulties of another kind. Al-Nujumi was the last of the great commanders originating from the *Awlad al-balad*. Although his loyalty appears to have been exemplary, he and his riverain troops were suspect to the Khalifa, who appointed a Baqqari officer, nominally as his lieutenant, but in fact as a standing check on his authority and actions.

The expeditionary force remained at its advance base in Dongola from November 1886 to May 1889. During this time its morale decayed, its predatory activities antagonized the local people, and its high command was paralysed by the Khalifa's mistrust of al-Nujumi. In February 1889, Yunus al-Dikaym arrived in Dongola to take over the administration. Already in April 1887 the Khalifa had sent messages to invite Khedive Muhammad Tawfiq, Queen Victoria and the Ottoman Sultan 'Abd al-Hamid II, to submit to the Mahdia. Two years later further messages of the same kind were sent, and the Ansar began their march northwards.

Unprovisioned and ill-armed, they struggled desperately on, down the western bank of the Nile. Once across the border, they hoped to receive a welcome and assistance from the Egyptians, whom they were coming to liberate from the English yoke. They were doomed to disappointment. Whatever the secret sympathies of the Nubian villagers, they were aware of the futility of resisting the Anglo-Egyptian military power concentrated around Wadi Halfa. In July, Grenfell, the British commander of these forces, sent al-Nujumi an arrogant demand for surrender. Al-Nujumi replied as arrogantly, asserting his loyalty to the Khalifa, and his trust in the help of God. On 3 August 1889, the two armies met near the village of Tushki.[1] The Mahdist expeditionary force was crushingly defeated, al-Nujumi himself being killed in the battle. The threat to Egypt from the Mahdist state had passed for ever away.

The year 1889 was highly critical for the Khalifa. Although the Anglo-Egyptian victory at Tushki was not, as he had feared, followed by an immediate invasion of his territories, his northern frontier was watched by a vigilant enemy, whose material resources he affected to despise, but whose strength he dimly yet forebodingly apprehended. Elsewhere, also, the expansion of the Mahdist state had attained its limits. The victories of 'Uthman Adam and al-Zaki Tamal had resulted in no acquisitions of territory, but had merely established a temporary and precarious Mahdist supremacy in disputed border-regions. The deaths of Hamdan Abu 'Anja and 'Abd al-Rahman al-Nujumi, both in 1889, soon to be followed in 1891 by that of 'Uthman Adam, deprived him of his ablest generals. 'Uthman Diqna was unable to capture Suakin, even though he remained master of the hinterland. In 1889 old tensions between the Beja and Arabic-speaking Ansar on the Suakin front developed into a quarrel characterized by the rivalry of their commanders, to suppress which the Khalifa had to intervene. The *élan* which had carried the Mahdi's followers to victory in the revolutionary war had passed away.

Besides these military and political difficulties the Khalifa was confronted in 1889 and 1890, with an age-old problem, a devastating sequence of bad harvest, famine and epidemic. These natural calamities had always taxed the resources of rulers in the Nile valley; for the Khalifa they were aggravated by his military dispositions. Three great armies were stationed in Darfur, at Gallabat, and, until the Tushki campaign, at Dongola, consuming unproductively the diminishing supplies of corn. Horrifying tales were told of famished beggars snatching bread in the market-places with the last remains of their strength, of silent villages whose people starved quietly to death behind shut doors. There was nothing new in such stories, which may be paralleled from the chronicles of Egypt in the previous centuries, but European opinion laid upon the Khalifa blame for a catastrophe which he was powerless to avert and could do little to alleviate.

By a fatal mischance, the great famine coincided with one of his major acts of policy, the enforced migration of his tribe, the Ta'aisha, and their Baqqara neighbours from their homelands in Darfur to Omdurman. This act has a dual aspect. From one point of view it was the successful consummation of the policy which the Mahdi and the Khalifa himself had endeavoured to follow from the start; that of attaching the nomads closely and permanently to the regime, and turning them from casual raiders into a standing tribal army. The Khalifa's experiences in the first year of his rule had shown him the desirability of surrounding himself with warriors on whose loyalty he could rely. From another point of view, however, the summons to the Ta'aisha was connected with 'Uthman Adam's pacification of Darfur.

The Baqqara did not respond willingly to their kinsman's call. They were attached to their tribal lands, and the Khalifa, after all, was not their hereditary chief but a parvenu. For long they resisted both threats and promises, until at last, in March 1888, the Khalifa's anger flared out in a proclamation, which is a superb piece of Arabic invective, commanding the Ta'aisha, under pain of destruction and dispersion, to place themselves under the orders of 'Uthman Adam. This command, backed by 'Uthman's military power, was at last effective. The great tribal migration began, and in the early months of 1889 the Ta'aisha contingents reached Omdurman.

The coming-in of the Ta'aisha profoundly affected the future of the Khalifa's rule. They must have depleted the corn-supplies of Kordofan as they made their way to the river. Once arrived in Omdurman, they were a privileged *élite*, who had to be fed at all costs. The effects of the famine were thus aggravated by this great tribal displacement. The migration also had its political consequences. The settled and sophisticated *Awlad al-balad* had as little liking for these romantic nomads as the lowland Scots had for the Highland clans in the 'Forty-five. The Khalifa's open reliance upon his tribal kin deepened the already existing rift between 'Abdallahi and the most advanced group of his subjects. The Ta'aisha, for their part, proved an ineffective instrument for the purposes of government. They tried to elude the Khalifa's vigilance and slip back to their homelands—on one such occasion their hereditary chief himself was pursued and killed. They were unproductive and over-bearing, and as little tolerant of discipline as ever. They rapidly became a liability to the Khalifa, and a stumbling-block in his way when he sought to establish a strong monarchy.

In the early days after Tushki, the Khalifa had sought to conciliate his Sudanese opponents. Muhammad Khalid, who had been brought out of prison some months previously, was sent as a commissioner to investigate the troubles in 'Uthman Diqna's command; then to inquire into conditions in Dongola, and to promote trade there. In April 1890 he actually superseded the Baqqari, Yunus al-Dikaym, as governor of Dongola. Other appointments at this time seemed to betoken a renewed participation of the *Awlad al-balad* in the high offices of state. Commerce was encouraged, both with Upper Egypt and with Suakin.

But there were other, less agreeable, indications. In April 1886 the Khalifa had dismissed from office Ahmad Sulayman, whom the Mahdi had appointed as commissioner of the state treasury, and had replaced him by a certain Ibrahim Muhammad 'Adlan, formerly a merchant. 'Adlan was a first-class administrator, and introduced into the haphazard arrangements for the receipt, storage and disbursement of state resources, both in cash and kind, methods based on Turco-Egyptian practice which survived until the end of the regime. The coming of the Ta'aisha was 'Adlan's downfall. He clashed with Ya'qub, the Khalifa's half-brother, who, as commander of the Black Flag division, had a special responsibility for the Ta'aisha. He toured the Gezira to find corn to provision the troops in Omdurman, but his methods were apparently too lenient to suit the Khalifa. Early in 1890, he was disgraced and executed.

The prospects of an improvement in the political status of the *Awlad al-balad* were soon to be dashed. In Dongola, relations between Muhammad Khalid and his Baqqara subordinates degenerated into an open quarrel and, a year after taking office, he was recalled to Omdurman. Once again, Yunus al-Dikaym took the command in the north. In Omdurman a new conspiracy against the Khalifa developed. As in 1886, its promoters were the *Ashraf*, and its principal supporters were the Danaqla sailors and settlers in the Gezira. Their ostensible complaint was the lack of respect shown towards the Khalifa Muhammad Sharif and the Mahdi's family, but they had also economic grievances of a kind which would affect the *Awlad al-balad* rather than the Baqqara. The revolt seems to have been brought to a head by the recall of Muhammad Khalid from Dongola, and his subsequent imprisonment.

Under the leadership of Muhammad Sharif, the conspirators made their headquarters around the Mahdi's tomb, thus threatening 'Abdallahi, whose house was only a few yards away. On 23 November 1891, the Khalifa assembled his own supporters and tried to cordon off the *Ashraf*. He was in a dilemma, since if fighting broke out the Ta'aisha might get out of control, sack the capital, and flee to Darfur. Hence he was anxious to open negotiations with the *Ashraf*, and in this he was ultimately successful. The Khalifa 'Ali ibn Muhammad Hilu strove for a settlement, and on 25 November the insurgents laid down their arms. They were promised a general pardon; the Khalifa Muhammad Sharif was to be given the full honours and authority due to his position, and the family of the Mahdi were to receive a monthly pension. Having disarmed his opponents, the Khalifa proceeded to reduce them to impotence. A few weeks later, seven notables including the former treasurer, Ahmad Sulayman, were seized and transported up the White Nile to Fashoda, where al-Zaki Tamal put them to death. The Danaqla in the Gezira were rounded up, detained and only released after the confiscation of a third of their goods. In March 1892 the Khalifa Muhammad Sharif was himself arrested and tried before a special body of commissioners. He was deprived of his dignities and flung into prison, where he remained until the eve of the Khalifa 'Abdallahi's own overthrow.

The power of the *Ashraf* and the *Awlad al-balad* was thus finally and completely broken. The next four years display 'Abdallahi as an autocratic monarch. Never had his authority over his subjects seemed to be so firmly established. Organized revolt against him had ceased, and even those Sudanese who disliked his rule were increasingly prepared to acquiesce in it. The transformation of the theocratic state of the early Mahdia into a secular despotism was becoming obvious. One sign of the change was the organization of a new armed force, immediately dependent on the Khalifa, the *Mulazimiyya*, which, from a small corps of orderlies (to which Slatin belonged), was expanded from 1892 onwards into a bodyguard of nine thousand men, commanded by the Khalifa's son, 'Uthman Shaykh al-Din. The *Mulazimiyya* thus superseded the Ta'aisha, as the Ta'aisha had the *Jihadiyya*, as the principal military support of the regime. The *Mulazimiyya* was composed half of slave-troops, half of free Sudanese, but Danaqla and Egyptians were strictly excluded from it. It had its own treasury, to which the Gezira contributed corn and cash.

In the tradition of oriental autocracy, the Khalifa began to withdraw himself from his people. It had been his custom to attend the weekly parade of the Ansar, held each Friday outside Omdurman. Now he appeared, surrounded by his bodyguard, only on the principal festivals. A great wall was constructed around the part of Omdurman containing his residence where he and his bodyguard were housed—a district which until today is known as the *Mulazimiyya* quarter. In his councils, two men were prominent, his half-brother Ya'qub, who from the first had acted as his vizier, and later his eldest son 'Uthman. Although the two junior khalifas were perhaps regarded as having a reversionary claim to the succession, on the analogy of the caliphs, whose 'successors' they were, 'Uthman was clearly regarded by his father as heir-apparent. He was groomed in state affairs and, apparently in 1891, married to Ya'qub's daughter, when he received the honorific title of *Shaykh al-Din*, indicating his senior standing in the Mahdist hierarchy. Ya'qub became increasingly jealous of 'Uthman, as the latter's influence grew, and the political marriage exacerbated their relations. As 'Abdallahi cultivated the manner of a despot, his suspicions of his servants showed themselves. In 1893, the victor of Gallabat, al-Zaki Tamal, was arrested and starved to death. The two following years saw the destitution and death in prison of two successive chief judges, the first of whom, Ahmad 'Ali, had held office since the time of the Mahdi.[2]

The Khalifa's temper in these years was no doubt affected by his growing awareness that the Mahdist state was no longer immune from the attacks of its external enemies. This was the heyday of the European scramble for Africa, and the Khalifa's military strength, which a century earlier would have been adequate to repulse any likely invader, was set against the superior might and organization of the European powers. It was ironical that, at the very period when his rule was least questioned by his subjects, and had been established internally on elaborate administrative foundations, the Khalifa was to be overthrown by a foreign invader.

For a time the remoteness of his dominions, the considerable geographical obstacles to a military conquest, and the very rivalries of the European powers themselves, deferred a development which in the circumstances of the time was almost inevitable. There were, however, ominous portents. In February 1891, an Anglo-Egyptian expedition from Suakin routed 'Uthman Diqna and captured his headquarters near Tokar. This was the first decisive defeat of the Ansar on the Red Sea littoral. In December 1893 a Mahdist expedition into Eritrea was heavily defeated by the Italians at the battle of Agordat. This was the prelude to an Italian offensive against Kasala, which fell in July 1894. Slatin has borne witness to the deep impression which this loss made upon the Khalifa. Yet a lethargy of false confidence seemed to overcome him, and he returned a cold reply to the overtures of friendship from Menelik II of Abyssinia, who was also threatened by the Italians.

Further threats to his power were now appearing in the south. The southern Sudan was not effectively part of the Mahdist state. The Bahr al-Ghazal had not had a Mahdist governor since 1886. Emin Pasha, the last khedivial governor of Equatoria, after withdrawing to the south of his province, had maintained a shadow of Egyptian authority on the Upper Nile until he was more or less compelled to evacuate the province by H. M. Stanley's relief expedition in 1889. A Mahdist garrison was established at Rejaf, but the river-line from Fashoda southwards was not permanently held, while away from the river Mahdism was but a name. In 1893 the Khalifa sent an expeditionary force under 'Arabi Dafa'allah to strengthen his hold over the far south, but steamer connections with Omdurman were even more infrequent and hazardous than they had been in the Turco-Egyptian period.

Meanwhile the Belgians had established Leopold II's power in the Congo, and expeditions were beginning to push across the Nile-Congo divide towards the former Egyptian provinces of the Bahr al-Ghazal and the Upper Nile. In 1894 there were clashes between the Belgians and 'Arabi Dafa'allah, while at the same time another Belgian force was contacting the tribal rulers in the Bahr al-Ghazal. In August 1894, however, a Franco-Congolese agreement opened the door to a French advance to the Bahr al-Ghazal and the Upper Nile. In consequence of this, an expedition under the command of Captain Marchand was approved in November 1895 by the French foreign minister.

In March 1896 the British government suddenly and unexpectedly authorized an advance by Egyptian forces into Dongola. The reason for this act is to be sought in the relations of the European great powers: it had no particular relevance to the situation in the Mahdist state, nor was it undertaken primarily for any advantages that might accrue to Egypt from a reconquest of the Sudan, which indeed was not contemplated at this stage. Neither was the advance intended to forestall Marchand's appearance on the Upper Nile, which was at that time regarded as a remote contingency, and in any case could not be affected by military action in Nubia. The event which precipitated the British government's decision was the defeat of the Italians by Menelik at Adowa on 1 March 1896. But the British desire to make a gesture of assistance to Italy, by a move which might distract the Mahdist forces from an attack on the Italian flank at Kasala, was further intended to conciliate Germany and to guard against the dissolution of the Triple Alliance, which at this time were objectives of Lord Salisbury's foreign policy.[3] The expedition was less agreeable to Cromer, Britain's proconsul in Egypt, than to the British officers, who had not forgotten the defeats which troops under their command had suffered at the hands of the Ansar. At home, the British public was allured by the prospect of a long-delayed vengeance for Gordon.

The reconquest took place in two stages. In the first a railway from Wadi Halfa was pushed up the main Nile to support an expeditionary force commanded by Sir Herbert Kitchener.[4] The Mahdist forces in Dongola were defeated in a series of actions, and by September 1896 the whole province had been occupied. Kitchener now began the construction of a new railway line across the Nubian Desert, from Wadi Halfa to Abu Hamad on the main Nile. Abu Hamad fell in July 1897, and the Anglo-Egyptian forces prepared to penetrate to the heart of the Mahdist state.

In this crisis the Khalifa was ill-served by the general to whom he committed the defence of his dominions. He summoned Mahmud Ahmad from Darfur, and put him in command. Mahmud made his headquarters at Metemma. Its Ja'aliyin inhabitants refused to obey the Khalifa's order to evacuate their town, vainly appealed to Kitchener for help, and were massacred after an unsuccessful resistance. There for months Mahmud remained, unwilling or unable to move, badgering the Khalifa with a constant flow of despatches, seeking advice on every contingency, and failing to act on the instructions he received. Like al-Nujumi earlier, he found great difficulty in provisioning his army, which began to melt away as the weeks passed.

Meanwhile the enemy was advancing. Berber was evacuated by the Mahdist garrison and fell without resistance to the Anglo-Egyptian forces at the end of August 1897. In February 1898, 'Uthman Diqna with his forces arrived in support of Mahmud, but the old fighter and the young general worked badly together. Soon afterwards the Mahdist army left Metemma and advanced to the river Atbara, where it encamped. The Ansar were starving, but, in the hour of their defeat, their old heroic courage returned to them. Kitchener delivered his attack on Good Friday, 8 April 1898. At the end of the day 3,000 Sudanese were dead and 4,000 wounded. 'Uthman Diqna had again escaped, while Mahmud Ahmad was a prisoner, humiliated by his captor. He was taken to Rosetta, where he died in 1906. On the Anglo-Egyptian side, the casualties were 81 killed and 487 wounded.

When the advance on Omdurman began, four months later, the last phase in the campaign opened. On 1 September, the Egyptian and British forces were encamped near an abrupt hill called Jabal Surkab,[5] on the left bank of the Nile, six miles north of Omdurman. The vicinity is known as Karari. Against them the Khalifa threw the considerable reserves he had kept in his capital. Once again, although not without difficulty,

Kitchener was victorious. It was estimated that 11,000 Sudanese were killed and 16,000 wounded. The Anglo-Egyptian
losses were 49 killed and 382 wounded. Ya'qub died on the
field. The Khalifa rode back to his deserted capital and led the
remnant of his forces to Kordofan. The battle of Omdurman,
more accurately called the battle of Karari, marked the end of
the Mahdist state in the Sudan.

The significance of the Khalifa's reign has not always been
appreciated either by his countrymen or by foreign observers.
A legend, fostered by war-propaganda, grew up around his
name, depicting him as a bloodthirsty and barbarous despot,
from whose tyranny the Sudanese were released by the Anglo-
Egyptian invasion. The reality is rather different. When he
came to power, the initial drive of the Mahdia was at an end.
The objects of the revolutionary war had largely been attained.
The greater part of the Muslim north was under Mahdist rule.
His primary problem was to restore order and make administration effective over a vast area in which four years of warfare
against the established government had broken down the habits
of obedience. His task was complicated by the uncertain loyalty
of the *Awlad al-balad*, from whom the Mahdi had drawn the
bulk of his ruling *élite*, and by the insubordination and backwardness of the Baqqara, on whom he himself chiefly relied.

He sought to establish his authority by developing an
increasingly elaborate and centralized administration. Although
the forms of the Mahdist theocracy were retained, the spirit had,
by the middle years of his reign, departed from them. The other
two khalifas were in no real sense his colleagues; his closest
associate in government was his brother, Ya'qub. The great
military commands were held almost exclusively by Baqqara.
The simple fiscal system of the Mahdi was abandoned. The
revenue was augmented by a whole range of new taxes, dues
and confiscations, closely resembling the Turco-Egyptian taxes,
which the Mahdi had come to destroy. The development of
specialized treasuries, notably the Khalifa's own privy treasury,
siphoned off from the original *Bayt al-mal* the cream of its
revenue. The judiciary similarly acquired an increasingly complex organization, although no greater independence of the
ruler in the performance of its functions.

The reign of the Khalifa, then, is characterized by the passing of the Mahdist theocracy and the creation of a personal rule exercised through a bureaucracy, largely composed of Sudanese civil servants inherited from the Turco-Egyptian regime. 'Abdallahi prevented the northern Sudan from relapsing into anarchy after the Mahdi's death. His success in establishing his control so firmly that it was broken ultimately only by a foreign invader with superior military resources, is a measure of his inherent strength of personality and his administrative talent. Yet the price was high. 'Abdallahi, permanently resident in Omdurman, was never fully in control of his provincial officials, although his system of constant communication with them destroyed their initiative in emergencies. His reliance on the Baqqara opened a rift between himself and the *Awlad al-balad* which weakened the foundations of the state. Finally, the sustained military character of the regime, derived from the revolutionary period, and continued at first in accordance with the policy of the Holy War, and later because of the growing threat from outside, prevented a genuine resettlement of the country. 'Abdallahi was much less a malevolent despot and much more the prisoner of his circumstances than contemporary European writers were willing to perceive.

PART 3

THE ANGLO–EGYPTIAN CONDOMINIUM: 1899–1955

'*The cannon which swept away the Dervish hordes at Omdurman proclaimed to the world that on England—or, to be more strictly correct, on Egypt under British guidance—had devolved the solemn and responsible duty of introducing the light of Western civilization amongst the sorely tried people of the Soudan.*'
Lord Cromer, *Modern Egypt*, 1908

'*At the end of time the English will come to you, whose soldiers are called police: they will measure the earth even to the blades of the sedge grass. There will be no deliverance except through the coming of Jesus.*'
Attributed to Shaykh Farah wad Taktuk (17th century), translated by S. Hillelson.

CHAPTER VIII

THE ERA OF KITCHENER AND
WINGATE: 1899–1918

THE OVERTHROW of the Mahdist state created a number of legal and diplomatic problems for the British government. Although the campaigns had been undertaken on British initiative, and with British financial and military aid, the regained territories were technically former possessions of the khedive. The simple restoration of Egyptian rule over the Sudan was, however, out of the question. Since the British occupation of 1882, Egypt had lost the great measure of autonomy which her rulers had possessed since the time of Muhammad 'Ali, and was in effect a protectorate. British opinion was convinced that the Mahdia was the direct consequence of sixty years of Egyptian oppression of the Sudanese. This belief supported a conviction that henceforward Britain had the mission in the Sudan of establishing an orderly and just government, embodying those ideas to which Gordon had devoted his services and his life.

But if the restoration of Egyptian rule was repugnant to the British, the apparent alternative, of creating an undisguised British colonial administration, was not feasible. Open annexation would do violence to Egypt's historical claims, which had served as the pretext for launching the reconquest from Egypt, employing Egyptian troops, and drawing on the Egyptian treasury to finance the fighting. Egyptian objections could perhaps at this time have been overridden, but the Egyptian claims were convenient. The Italians, Belgians and French had also, as we have seen, intentions of acquiring Sudanese territory. By espousing Egypt's claims to the whole of her former Sudanese provinces, the British government covered the extension of its power in Africa with a show of legality which its European competitors did not possess.

This *locus standi* was adopted at the outset in the Fashoda Incident. The French expedition commanded by Captain Marchand had reached and occupied the post of Fashoda on the Upper Nile on 10 July 1898. The fact was reported to Kitchener on 7 September by the crew of a Mahdist steamer, which had been sent by the Khalifa to bring grain from the Shilluk country, and had exchanged shots with the French. Kitchener immediately set out for Fashoda, where he informed Marchand that 'the presence of a French force at Fashoda and in the valley of the Nile was regarded as a direct infringement of the rights of the Egyptian government and of Great Britain'. Marchand was isolated and powerless in a military sense, but the crisis was now transferred to London and Paris, where for some time there was very grave tension. On 4 November, however, the French government acquiesced in the existing situation, and ordered the withdrawal of Marchand's party from Fashoda.

Considerations of a rather different kind preoccupied Lord Cromer, who, as British agent and consul-general, was the virtual ruler of Egypt. He was anxious to prevent Europeans acquiring in the Sudan the privileged status which was theirs in Egypt. Throughout his Egyptian career he had been hampered by the anomalies of the international status of the country—the nominal suzerainty of the Ottoman sultan, the control over Egyptian finances exerted by the European Commissioners of the Debt, the enclaves of privilege derived by the consular authorities from the Capitulations,[1] the juridical independence of the Mixed Tribunals.[2] All these he was anxious to exclude from the Sudan.

Cromer's solution, which was accepted by the British government and embodied in the Anglo-Egyptian Conventions of 1899[3] (usually known as the Condominium Agreement), was to confer on the Sudan a separate political status from that of Egypt. The link between the two countries was however formally preserved by associating the khedivial with the British government in a joint sovereignty, or condominium, over the Sudan. On Cromer's advice, the British claim to a share in the control was openly based on the rights of conquest which, he said, 'alone constitute the real justification for the creation of a political and administrative status in the Sudan different to that which exists in Egypt'.

The northern boundary of the newly acquired territory, described in the Agreement as 'certain provinces in the Sudan which were in rebellion against the authority of His Highness the khedive', was fixed at latitude 22° N.[4] The khedive's claims were further recognized by the provisions that 'the British and Egyptian flags shall be used together, both on land and water, throughout the Sudan', that the appointment and removal of the governor-general should be by khedivial decree (but only on the motion of the British government), and that proclamations of the governor-general, having the force of law, should be notified to the president of the Egyptian council of ministers, as well as to the British agent in Cairo.

These stipulations apart, the Agreement deliberately excluded both Egyptian and international authority from the Sudan. The shadowy claims of the Ottoman sultan as suzerain were tacitly ignored. Egyptian legislation was not to apply to the Sudan unless specifically proclaimed by the governor-general. No special privileges, such as had accrued to Europeans in Egypt under the Capitulations, were to be accorded in the Sudan. The jurisdiction of the Mixed Tribunals was excluded, and no consular representatives were to be allowed to reside in the Sudan without the previous consent of the British government.

Within the Sudan, the supreme military and civil command was to be vested in the governor-general, a nominee of the British government. Although the Agreement was silent on the point of nationality, all the governors-general from 1899 to 1955 were British subjects from the United Kingdom. With full executive powers, the governor-general combined, as we have seen, complete authority to legislate by proclamation. An article of the Agreement placed the Sudan under martial law for an indefinite period.

The Condominium Agreement was not a constitution for the Sudan: it was simply an instrument giving formal recognition to the existing situation on the morrow of the Reconquest. The name is misleading: the agreement did not in any real sense create a true condominium, a conjoint sovereignty over the Sudan, but merely gave a nominal recognition to the historical claims of the khedive, whilst reserving almost complete autonomy to an official nominated by the British government. It was not seriously questioned by the European powers. It never satisfied the Egyptians, who felt, with a sullen resentment, that they had been jockeyed out of their rights. Once Egypt had passed from under British control, the artificiality of the Condominium could no longer be concealed, and from the end of the First World War onwards, Cromer's clever device was increasingly an embarrassment, both to successive British cabinets and to the administration in the Sudan, which came to be called the Sudan Government.

The first governor-general to be appointed under the Condominium Agreement was Lord Kitchener in January 1899. He was recalled in the following December for service in the South African War, and was succeeded by Sir Reginald Wingate, who had been in control of Egyptian Military Intelligence since 1887 and played a notable part in the Reconquest. Wingate remained governor-general until 1916, and his long period of office saw the foundations of the new regime in the Sudan firmly laid.

Although the Mahdist state had collapsed at the battle of Karari, the pacification of the Sudan was still far from being complete. There were three main types of danger to be apprehended; from the remaining Mahdist elements, from local risings in the north (which might assume a Mahdist colouring), and from the enormous and still unsubdued tribal areas in the southern Sudan. The Khalifa 'Abdallahi was still, in 1899, at large in Kordofan with a considerable fighting force, accompanied by his son, 'Uthman Shaykh al-Din, the Khalifa 'Ali ibn Muhammad Hilu, 'Uthman Diqna and other Mahdist notables. He was joined by his general, Ahmad Fadil, with the remnant of an army from the eastern frontiers. The third khalifa, Muhammad Sharif, had submitted to the conquerors and was living with two of the Mahdi's sons at the village of al-Shukkaba, between Wad Medani and Sennar. In August 1899, the authorities learnt that they were trying to slip away and join 'Abdallahi. They were arrested, but an affray broke out between the government troops and their followers. The Khalifa Muhammad Sharif and the Mahdi's two sons were shot. Wingate, not yet governor-general, was, in November 1899, put in command of a flying column to track down the Khalifa 'Abdallahi. The final clash took place at Umm Diwaykarat, not very far from Aba Island, the cradle of the Mahdist revolution. The last organized force of Ansar was defeated. After the battle, the Khalifa was found dead on the field with his colleagues, the Khalifa 'Ali ibn Muhammad Hilu and Ahmad Fadil, on either side. 'Uthman Shaykh al-Din was wounded and captured: he died, a prisoner, at Rosetta in 1900. 'Uthman Diqna once again escaped and made his way back to the Red Sea Hills. There he was betrayed and captured in January 1900. He survived until 1926, when he died in the odour of sanctity at Wadi Halfa.[5]

There were in the early years of the Condominium several petty revolts against the new government. These, like the revolts during the Khalifa's reign, tended to assume a messianic form. Early in 1900 a party of Ansar in Omdurman who expected the coming of the Prophet Jesus, since the Khalifa of the Mahdi was dead, threatened public security. They were condemned as heretics by a council of religious notables, and exiled. Other rebels in the outlying provinces were less easily crushed, and military action was sometimes necessary. In 1903 a *mahdi* was captured and hanged in Kordofan. The following year saw the appearance and suppression of a Prophet Jesus at Sinja on the Blue Nile. The most serious incident of this kind occurred in 1908, when a former Mahdist notable in the Gezira, 'Abd al-Qadir Muhammad Imam, usually called Wad Habuba, his temper exacerbated by failure to recover possession of his ancestral lands, killed an Egyptian and a British official and raised a revolt. A small military operation followed, and 'Abd al-Qadir was brought in and hanged. One of his followers set himself up as the Prophet Jesus in Kordofan in 1912, and was put down in his turn. Trifling as these revolts seem in retrospect, they were taken very seriously by the Sudan Government, since the Mahdist revolution had developed from as petty beginnings. During these years a resurgence of Mahdism was still feared, the reading of the Mahdi's prayer-book was proscribed, and the Mahdi's surviving sons lay under a cloud.

The pacification of the non-Arab tribal areas of the south was a slow business, and its completion takes us beyond the chronological limits of this chapter. The Nuba Mountains formed a series of pockets of resistance to the Sudan Government as they had to the Mahdist and Turco-Egyptian regimes previously. In 1904 the outlying hill, Jabal al-Dayir, against which Hamdan Abu 'Anja had operated twenty years previously, was finally reduced to submission. Other patrols, amounting sometimes to minor campaigns, against refractory Nuba communities took place at intervals for the next twenty-five years. The marshes of the Upper Nile and Bahr al-Ghazal were obstacles to pacification which could only slowly be overcome. The first British governor on the Upper Nile had his headquarters at Fashoda (soon to be renamed Kodok), but penetration of the Bahr al-Ghazal and equatorial districts could not take place until a channel through the Sudd had been reopened. This task required enormous efforts, but by 1903 a way had been cleared, and provincial administrations were set up in the Bahr al-Ghazal and the far south. Gradually, over many years, the tribes were brought under control, but it was not until 1928 that the intractable Nuer were finally pacified.

The delimitation of Sudanese territory also extended over many years. Cromer in 1899 was careful not to define the Condominium as extending over all the territory which formerly belonged to Egypt. Apart from Khedive Isma'il's possessions in Somaliland and Abyssinia, which were geographically distinct, and had been lost after the Egyptian withdrawal from the Sudan, the European powers had nibbled away outlying portions of Sudanese territory proper. Italy had retroceded Kasala to the Anglo-Egyptian forces on Christmas Day 1897, but Massawa remained part of Eritrea. The southernmost portion of Isma'il's former dominions was now under British rule, as part of the Uganda Protectorate. North of this, territory on the west bank of the White Nile to Lado was leased for life by King Leopold II of the Belgians. The Khalifa 'Abdallahi himself had ceded the Beni Shangul district to Menelik of Abyssinia in 1897. The possibility of extensive French claims being asserted to the southern Sudan had ended with the Fashoda

Incident. The Nile-Congo watershed was accepted in March 1899 as the line of demarcation between French and British control. To the north of this line there was no immediate problem, since Darfur was once again a sultanate, autonomous but tributary to Khartoum, under 'Ali Dinar, a member of the old ruling house. Beyond Darfur, the sultanate of Wadai did not come under French control until 1909.

A series of agreements and treaties defined the other frontiers of the Sudan. The boundary with Eritrea was fixed between 1898 and 1902. A treaty between Abyssinia and Great Britain in 1902 determined a frontier which, as in the past, was to cause constant trouble to the authorities in the Sudan. The boundary with the Congo Free State was agreed in 1906. The Lado Enclave remained under the administration of the Free State until 1910, when, after the death of Leopold II, it reverted to the Sudan. The frontier with Uganda was not delimited until 1913, and in the following year the Sudan received a further stretch of the Upper Nile in exchange for part of the former Lado Enclave.

The development of an administrative system was another achievement of the years following the Reconquest. The old Turco-Egyptian administration had perished, and the tribal system had been disrupted in the Mahdist revolution. The Baqqara, who had ruled under the Khalifa, were either dead, prisoners or fugitives: they were in any case too backward to serve as suitable instruments for the new regime. The sophisticated and patient bureaucracy, which had served the *hükümdars* and had been reconstituted under 'Abdallahi, was literate only in Arabic; its records were a sealed book to the British officers who now ruled. It was simpler to dismiss the past comprehensively as a time of anarchy, oppression and misgovernment, and create a new, enlightened and alien administration.

At the head of the Sudan Government stood the governor-general, whose extensive powers have already been noted. His real responsibility was to the British agent and consul-general in Egypt, who formed the channel through which the policy of the British government was conveyed to him. The autonomy of the governor-general in financial matters was limited by regulations, originally drawn up in January 1899 by Cromer, Kitchener and Eldon Gorst, who was at that time financial adviser to the Egyptian government. Since Egypt between 1899 and 1913 made an annual subvention to the Sudan, the governor-general and his financial secretary were held responsible for seeing that its amount was not exceeded. The Egyptian Ministry of Finance had the right of supervision, audit and inspection of the finances of the Sudan. These functions of the Egyptian ministry were in fact exercised by its British financial adviser.

These formal paper arrangements were of far less importance than the personal relations of the men concerned. Cromer had a genuine interest in the settlement and progress of the Sudan and, until his retirement in 1907, collaborated closely first with Kitchener and then with Wingate. He and his successors abstained from interference with the routine of administration, so that to the Sudanese the governor-general appeared as an autocrat, backed by the khedive's appointment and the military power of Britain. Personal relations rather than regulations governed also the inner workings of the administration. Wingate's right-hand man was Rudolf von Slatin, whose knowledge of Sudanese affairs and personalities, gained during his service in Darfur under the Egyptian administration and his detention in Omdurman under the Mahdi and Khalifa, placed him in a unique position to advise and influence the new regime in internal affairs. Slatin Pasha, with the title of inspector-general, was the effective head of the Intelligence Department in Khartoum. With his enforced retirement, as an Austrian subject, on the outbreak of war in 1914, the post ceased to exist. Apart from Slatin, the three chief officers of the Sudan Government were the financial, legal and civil secretaries. In 1910 an ordinance substituted a formal Council, of which the inspector-general and the three secretaries were *ex-officio* members, for the previous informal consultations between the governor-general and his chief officials.

The country was divided into provinces which, in the north, originally corresponded closely to those of the Turco-Egyptian period. At the head of each province was a British governor. The provinces were divided into districts, each with an

Egyptian officer. But a deviation was made from Egyptian practice in introducing a new cadre of British inspectors between the governors and Egyptian district officers. In course of time these officials became the actual administrators of the districts, with the title of district commissioners, and the Egyptian (later Sudanese) district officers were relegated to a subordinate position. The administrative machine was thus British in its higher, and Egyptian in its lower ranks. It was not until about fifteen years later that Sudanese began to replace Egyptian officials. Valuable service was also rendered for many years by a group of Lebanese, who formed in some ways a bridge between the British ruling-group and the Sudanese. Arabic-speaking, but fluent in English, more western in outlook than the Egyptians, they had a unique rôle to play. One of the earliest Lebanese civil servants, Na'um Bey Shuqayr, was Wingate's right-hand man in the Intelligence Department. Shortly after the Reconquest he wrote an Arabic history of the Sudan, which, for its scope, impartiality and abundant documentation is a most impressive piece of work, and remains an indispensable source of information.

At the outset the administrative personnel was almost entirely military, being composed of British and Egyptian officers of the Egyptian army. Many of these were able men: they included one officer, Sir Edgar Bernard, who was for twenty years financial secretary, and two others who were in their turn governors-general, Sir Lee Stack and Sir Stewart Symes. Nevertheless an administrative service and technical departments could not be staffed indefinitely by army officers on secondment, and as early as 1900 the recruitment of civilians began in Britain.

From this recruitment developed the upper cadres of the Sudan Civil Service, particularly the administrative branch, which came to be known as the Political Service. These administrators were selected by a board, held annually in London, from young men who had just left the universities, endowed, as Cromer said, 'with good health, high character and fair abilities'. Their numbers were small; this, with their close personal relations with their superiors, and the scope left to them for initiative in their work, stimulated the growth of a strong *esprit de corps*. Frequent transfers from one province to another, and from the provinces to the Secretariat in Khartoum, gave them experience and adaptability. Many of them acquired a considerable knowledge of the spoken Arabic or the other languages of the Sudan; a few became proficient readers of Arabic. Since they normally passed the whole of their careers in the Sudan, they acquired a wide and intimate knowledge of the country, and a devotion to what they regarded as its best interests. The reverse of these qualities was a tendency towards parochialism of outlook, and an over-confidence in their understanding of the Sudanese. The Sudanese, for their part, respected their authority and applauded their justice, but were sensitively aware of an arrogance of bearing which resulted as much from a difference in manners as from deliberate intent.

The Condominium Agreement had conceded to the Sudan a legal system independent of that of Egypt. In the north the years of revolution, tribal migrations and war had shattered the old structure of land tenure, and a new settlement was urgently necessary. In 1899 Kitchener enacted two ordinances, dealing respectively with urban and rural property. The fundamental principle adopted was 'that five years' continuous possession at the date of claim [should] confer an absolute title as against all persons'. Questions of ownership were most acute in the riverain areas of the north where the cultivable land was limited, and where there was an ancient settled population. Here land commissions were appointed to investigate and register titles.

Other ordinances, published in the same year, enacted the system of taxation. Following precedents set by the Khalifa, three main taxes were recognized—on land, herds and date-palms—and the rates of assessment were fixed. Meanwhile, codes of law, based on the Indian model and thus widely different in inspiration from those in force in Egypt, were being devised. Their authors were (Sir) William Edward Brunyate, a British lawyer in the Egyptian service, who was responsible for drafting the land ordinances; and (Sir) Edgar Bonham-Carter, one of the first civilians recruited by the Sudan Government, who served as legal secretary until 1917. A penal code, a code of criminal procedure, and a civil justice ordinance were enacted in the first two years of the Condominium. A system of courts was developed.

The Condominium period witnessed some interesting developments in connection with Muslim law in the Sudan. The *Sudan Mohammedan Law Courts Ordinance* of 1902 set up a hierarchy of courts—a High Court in Khartoum, provincial courts and district courts. These administered the Holy Law in accordance with the doctrines of the Hanafi school, as in Egypt.[6] They dealt with cases between Muslims, and were principally concerned with marital and testamentary questions, and with charitable endowments. At the head of the system stood the grand *qadi*, who, until the last years of the Condominium, was invariably an Egyptian jurist.

Under the Ordinance of 1902, the grand *qadi* was empowered with the approval of the governor-general, to 'make regulations consistent with (the) ordinance regulating . . . the Mohammedan Law Courts and other matters concerned with such Courts'. This provision opened the way to new developments at a time when the reform of Muslim law was being eagerly debated in Egypt. Thus, the very important *Sudan Mohammedan Law Courts Organization and Procedure Regulations (1915)*, promulgated under this provision, are closely modelled on the Egyptian regulations of 1897 and 1910. Other reforms were introduced through the Circulars, which successive grand *qadis* issued under the Ordinance of 1902 and the Regulations of 1915. A provision of these Regulations enabled the grand *qadi* to issue directives based on legal doctrines other than those of the Hanafi school. The apparent rigidity of the system of Muslim law in the Sudan was thereby considerably modified. Some legal reforms in the Sudan have even anticipated those in Egypt.

The educational policy of the new regime was laid down by (Sir) James Currie, who was appointed director of Education in 1900. In this field, shortage of funds combined with misgivings as to the effects of unrestrained access to western learning tended to retard development. Currie's scheme was essentially limited and practical in its aims. He sought to provide vernacular elementary schools to enable the masses 'to understand the elements of the system of government'; a technical school 'to train a small class of competent artisans'; and primary (later called intermediate) schools, to train elementary schoolmasters and 'to produce a small administrative class for entry to the government service'. This was a scheme which would commend itself to administrators rather than to educationalists, and its implementation was slow. Its poverty of conception and meagreness in execution were partially concealed by the construction in Khartoum of the magnificent buildings of the Gordon Memorial College. Kitchener had appealed in 1898 for the foundation of a school to bear this title. There was a generous response, and Kitchener returned to open the college in 1902. In its early years it served as an intermediate and technical school but subsequently it attained secondary status.[7] During Currie's time, the basic pattern of the educational system was laid down, as it still survives: a four-year course at each of the elementary, intermediate and secondary levels. The age of entry to each level was (and is) theoretically 7, 11, and 15 years respectively. Only a minority in each grade pass on, after examination, to the next.

The period of Wingate's governor-generalship up to the outbreak of war in 1914 saw the steady growth of order and prosperity in the Sudan. In 1900 revenue had stood at £E156,888[8] and expenditure at £E331,918: in 1913, the first year in which revenue exceeded expenditure, the respective figures were £E1,654,149 and £E1,614,007. In that year the annual Egyptian subvention was discontinued, the Sudan instead being credited with the customs dues collected in Egypt on goods in transit to and from the Sudan.

The military railway which Kitchener had constructed was adapted after the Reconquest to civilian purposes and became the first portion of a railway system linking the provinces of the northern Sudan. In December 1899, railhead was brought to the Blue Nile opposite Khartoum, and around it the present town of Khartoum North sprang up. The construction of a railway to link the Nile and the Red Sea coast, attempted and abandoned in the fighting against 'Uthman Diqna, was successfully accomplished in 1905. This resulted in the creation of two new towns, Atbara, on the Nile, supplanting Berber as the junction of the riverain and coastal routes; and Port Sudan, superseding Suakin. The old harbour was found to be inadequate for modern shipping, and in 1906 the construction of Port Sudan began. Although the new railway and port were the successors of the old caravan-track and of Suakin, their construction was not without political significance, since they made the trade of the Sudan largely independent of the route through Egypt. In the following years the railway was brought into Khartoum, and then pushed southwards through the Gezira to Sennar, whence it swung westwards and across the White Nile to reach El Obeid in 1911. At the river-crossing a new town, called Kosti, arose, while the old river-port of Dueim fell into decline. On the White Nile a steamer-service supplied the absence of railway-transport in the western Gezira and, as in Turco-Egyptian and Mahdist times, linked the southern Sudan with the north. Throughout the Condominium period, railway construction in the south remained technically difficult and economically prohibitive, but the geology of parts of the southern Sudan enabled roads to be constructed which were far superior to the unmade tracks of the north. The telegraph-system of the Turco-Egyptian period, which had been almost completely destroyed in the Mahdist revolution, was restored and extended.

The opening up of the Sudan by modern communications, the prestige and veiled power of the government, and the existence of a disciplined, loyal and incorruptible administrative service all contributed to the solution of the problem of the slave-trade, which, more than any other, had destroyed the old Turco-Egyptian regime. An article of the Condominium Agreement had declared the trade to be absolutely prohibited, but the practical execution of this policy took several years. In one respect the new government was more fortunately placed than Khedive Isma'il and Gordon had been: contrary to assertions which are still sometimes uncritically retailed, the trade seems to have declined sharply during the Mahdia. Its previous expansion had been, as we have seen, a corollary of the penetration of the Upper Nile and the Bahr al-Ghazal, but these areas which, with the Nuba Mountains, had been the principal hunting-grounds for slaves in the Turco-Egyptian period, had been virtually outside the range of Mahdist control during the reign of the Khalifa. The slaves occasionally mentioned in

Mahdist archives seem to have been almost entirely members of the existing slave-population in the north. The closing of slave-markets in areas under Ottoman or British control was another factor in the decline of the slave-trade. When the south was reopened under the Condominium administration vigorous precautions, amounting to a virtual exclusion of the northern Sudanese, were taken to prevent a recurrence of the trade. In 1912 Kitchener, then British agent and consul-general in Egypt, reported that 'slave-trading on a large scale is clearly a thing of the past'. It remained however an inveterate problem in the difficult areas bordering on Abyssinia. Domestic slavery, widespread throughout the northern Sudan, was a different matter. It was not mentioned in the Condominium Agreement, and although officially it was not recognized, there was no unnecessary interference by the administration while service was willingly rendered. By the suppression of the slave-trade and the improvement of economic conditions, it was hoped that slavery as an institution would wither away.

Wingate's governor-generalship saw the beginning of a revolution in the economics of the Sudan—the production of long-staple cotton for the world market. Experimental planting began as early as 1900, and by 1905 there were nearly 24,000 acres under cotton, 16,000 of which were watered by flood. But the future of cotton-production depended upon irrigation. A small concession for cotton-growing by pump-irrigation was held near Berber by the Sudan Plantations Syndicate, a company originally formed by an American, S. J. Leigh Hunt. The potentialities of the Gezira as an area for irrigation were being considered by the government, which arranged for the Syndicate to open an experimental farm near Wad Medani. The successful results obtained between 1911 and 1914 led to the next step; a project to dam the Blue Nile near Sennar and irrigate a portion of the eastern Gezira by a canal. The British government in 1913 guaranteed a Sudan Government loan of £63,000,000, while a commission worked from 1906 to 1912 on the problems of titles to land and boundaries of the holdings which would be affected. The outbreak of war interrupted further progress on the scheme.

The First World War affected the Sudan in several ways. The

administrative service was weakened by the withdrawal of British army officers, the release of civilians who wished to join the forces (although officials were as far as possible kept at their posts), and the suspension of new recruitment from England. From 1916 onwards, Sudanese products enjoyed a wartime boom: revenue rose from £E1,857,856 in that year to a post-war peak of £E4,425,340 in 1920. This meant prosperity for producers but also high prices for consumers. The entry of the Ottoman Empire into the war on the side of Germany in November 1914, followed by the deposition of Khedive 'Abbas II[9] and the proclamation of a British protectorate over Egypt, aroused apprehensions that the authority of the Sudan Government over its Muslim subjects would be undermined. Wingate addressed the religious notables in Khartoum, calling on them to set an example of loyalty, and the provinces under his administration remained quiescent.

The war afforded the Sudan Government the opportunity of extinguishing the autonomous sultanate of Darfur. On the downfall of the Khalifa, Sultan 'Ali Dinar had established himself as an autocratic ruler in his ancestral kingdom, which he governed on principles learnt from his forefathers and from the administrators of the Mahdist period. He had created a slave-army, which he equipped with rifles. Officials of the Sudan Government, the nominal suzerain, were excluded from Darfur.

As his reign proceeded, 'Ali Dinar felt the growing difficulties of his position, pressed as he was between the directly-administered provinces of the Anglo-Egyptian Sudan and the expanding power of the French. In 1909 the sultanate of Wadai fell under French rule, and the petty buffer-states on the western frontier of Darfur (Dar Masalit, Dar Tama, Dar Sila and Dar Qimr) were next threatened. Sila was occupied by the French, Tama by 'Ali Dinar, while Masalit maintained a precarious independence. This situation was also unsatisfactory for the Sudan Government, since the French advance was making a final frontier settlement increasingly urgent, and no delimitation could be attempted while 'Ali Dinar controlled Darfur.

Over many years there had been friction between 'Ali Dinar and the Sudan Government. The deposition of Khedive

'Abbas II by the British turned the Sultan of Darfur's smouldering resentment into open anger. There was some exchange of letters between 'Ali Dinar and the Young Turk leaders, Enver Pasha and Nuri Bey, but these had little to do with the course of events, although they featured largely in the Condominium government's presentation of its case.

Wingate had in fact decided in August 1915 to conquer Darfur at the first favourable opportunity. When 'Ali Dinar sent a small reinforcement to a frontier garrison the following February, this was seized on as the pretext for launching an invasion. Wingate declared that 'Ali Dinar was at least going to raid the Sudan, if not to invade it, and that action was necessary to forestall him.[10]

A force of between two and three thousand troops, supported by three aeroplanes, was concentrated in Kordofan, ninety miles from the frontier. The expedition advanced with some difficulty, caused by the heat and shortage of water, to a point about twelve miles from 'Ali Dinar's capital at El Fasher. The sultan was incapable of advancing to meet the invaders, but here he made a last-ditch stand. After a battle the Fur army withdrew. El Fasher was entered next day, 23 May 1916, and the sultan fled. He was surprised and killed on 6 November 1916 in a dawn attack, led by Major Huddleston, later to be governor-general of the Sudan. The settlement of the boundary between French and British controlled territory was made in a convention concluded in 1919. Masalit was left as a part of Darfur, while Tama and Sila passed under French administration. The actual delimitation of the frontier on the ground was not completed until 1924.

The annexation of Darfur was Wingate's last major act as governor-general. In November 1916 he was appointed high commissioner in Egypt, the title held by the British representative in Cairo after the declaration of the protectorate. He took up his duties in the new year, and held this office until February 1919, being succeeded as governor-general of the Sudan and sirdar of the Egyptian army by the civil secretary, Sir Lee Stack.

CHAPTER IX

REVOLT AND REACTION

1919–33

THE GOVERNOR-GENERALSHIP of Sir Lee Stack coincided with a period of growing tension in Anglo-Egyptian relations, a tension which was partly caused by the problem of the Sudan, and which in turn had disturbing repercussions in that country. The assassination of Stack in Cairo on 19 November 1924 brought to a head a crisis in both Egypt and the Sudan, which profoundly affected the relations of Britain with the Egyptians and the Sudanese throughout the remaining years of the Condominium.

Egyptian nationalism had found little opportunity for overt political action under the strong rule of Cromer and his successors until the end of the First World War. It then emerged, under the leadership of Sa'd Zaghul Pasha, with explosive force. Wingate, who had attempted to warn the British government of the approaching storm, was recalled early in 1919, and Allenby, the victor over the Ottomans in Palestine, was appointed as high commissioner in Egypt. He was regarded as a strong man who would restore the British position. But it was impossible to put the clock back, and after various fruitless negotiations with the nationalist leaders, the British government authorized Allenby to issue a declaration recognizing Egyptian independence. In the declaration, published on 28 February 1922, four matters were 'absolutely reserved to the discretion of His Majesty's Government', until agreements concerning them could be freely negotiated. The fourth of these matters was the Sudan. On the following day the Egyptian sultan, Fu'ad, took the title of king, and in April a commission was formed to draft a constitution for the monarchy.

*

The reservation of the Sudan in the British declaration brought to a head Egyptian fears and resentments which had been felt since the Condominium Agreement. These had become more acute in recent years. It was very clear that the so-called Condominium was British rule in all but name. The Egyptians were excluded from the higher administrative cadres, and had no share in the determination of policy. The legal and educational systems were based on British models and were widely different from their French-influenced counterparts in Egypt. Since 1913, the Sudan had been financially independent. Thus the Egyptians had reason to fear that the Sudan, which had been given a separate political status from that of Egypt in 1899, would in course of time lose even the tenuous formal connections maintained in the Condominium Agreement. Their anxieties were the greater since the prosperity and very existence of Egypt depended on the Nile waters. The development of irrigation in the Gezira, planned before the War, had been resumed in 1919. Egypt was faced, as never before in her history, with the prospect of a territory under the protection of a great power exploiting the Nile waters which were a necessity of life to her.

For very different reasons the situation recognized by the Condominium Agreement had now become unsatisfactory to the British. The Conventions of 1899 had been concluded with a deferential Egyptian government in the heyday of Cromer's power. Cromer recognized its anomalies, but in his time they did not matter in practice: in different forms Britain ruled Egypt and the Sudan alike, and the precise formulation of legal rights was an academic exercise. By 1919, however, the British claim to rule Egypt was threatened, and in 1922 it had ceased to exist. Whatever control Britain might henceforward seek to exert, whether by open reservations or by hidden influence, Egypt was now *de jure* an independent power. The nationalists, organized in the Wafd party, would not admit any derogation from Egypt's historical and legal rights in the Sudan. Even if they were not in power, their influence in the country was so great that neither the king nor his supporters could afford openly to flout the nationalist thesis.

The British mistrust of Egyptian intentions and capabilities in the Sudan, which had been a factor in the drafting of the Condominium Agreement, had developed with years of successful rule into a sense of unique moral responsibility; a feeling that, legal niceties apart, the British administrators and the British government stood in a position of trusteeship towards the Sudanese. The explosion of Egyptian nationalism at the end of the war had shocked the British, who were conscious of the benefits they had conferred on Egypt rather than of the resentment that had been simmering since the occupation. There was therefore less likelihood than ever that the British would transfer to independent Egypt their responsibilities in the Sudan, or even consent to any serious diminution of their power there. A head-on clash of the two co-domini was inevitable.

That the Sudanese themselves might become a party to the dispute was a possibility totally ignored by the British, but realized by the Egyptians. Although the Egyptians in the Sudan were confined to the lower and middle ranks of the army and civil service, they could influence Sudanese opinion where the British officials could only dominate it. Their community of language and religion with the northern Sudanese were priceless assets. The British governors and district commissioners had learned how to deal with the Sudanese notables, and a degree of confidence, albeit with profound if unspoken reservations on both sides, existed between them. Towards the country people and nomads they behaved with the paternal benevolence of a squirearchy. But the urban middle-class, especially the Sudanese who had acquired a westernized education in the intermediate schools and Gordon College, they viewed with little sympathy or respect. These, however, were the Sudanese with whom the Egyptians came most closely into contact—in the urban areas, especially the capital; in the army units, where British officers commanded both Sudanese and Egyptian subordinates; and in the government offices, where the first generation of western-educated Sudanese was now employed side by side with Egyptian officials.

It would be wrong to depict the Sudanese malcontents of this period as mere deluded instruments of Egyptian nationalist ambitions. As the 'Urabist revolution in Egypt had synchronized with the spontaneous Mahdist movement in the Sudan, so the revival of militant Egyptian nationalism after the First World War coincided with, and stimulated, the beginning of Sudanese nationalism. It found a leader in 'Ali 'Abd al-Latif, a young man of Dinka origin, who had been an army officer. His personal crisis had come in a clash with a high British official, whom he felt to have treated him arrogantly and unjustly. His first political organization, the Sudanese United Tribes Society, founded in 1921, spoke of the Sudanese nation and demanded independence, but looked to the religious notables and tribal chiefs as the natural governors of the country. He was arrested and imprisoned in 1922.

When he resumed political activities and founded a second organization in May 1924, his ideas had undergone a significant change. He was now ready to work with the Egyptians to overthrow British rule. The White Flag League, as his new society was called, aimed not at an independent Sudan, separate from Egypt, but at a state of the Nile Valley, freed from the British and united under the Egyptian monarchy. Henceforward, Sudanese nationalism as it developed was to be divided between these two alternative aims, of an independent nation-state or unity of the Nile Valley. From the first, however, the programme of a unified Nile Valley seems to have been adopted by most of its Sudanese partisans rather as a weapon against Britain, a tactical scheme, than as a serious political commitment. The White Flag League received more or less concealed support from Egyptian political circles within and outside the Sudan: this and its slogan of unity have led some British writers to dismiss it as a mere agency of Egyptian agitators. Branches of the League were founded in the principal towns of the north: the southern Sudan was too isolated, divided and backward to share in any political movement at this stage.

After demonstrations in Omdurman and Khartoum in June, 'Ali 'Abd al-Latif was again arrested and imprisoned. More serious symptoms of disaffection appeared in August, when the cadets of the Military School made an armed demonstration through the streets of the capital, which coincided with a mutiny of the Egyptian railway battalion stationed in Atbara.

These disturbances were suppressed. It was, however, both significant and alarming that the alliance of Egyptian and Sudanese nationalism should be affecting the loyalty of the army. The system of command in the Egyptian army indeed typified the anomalous relationship between Egypt and Britain of which the Condominium Agreement had been another expression. The historical accident that Kitchener, the *sirdar* (or commander-in-chief) of the Egyptian forces, had been appointed governor-general of the Sudan had become a precedent for the continued combination of these two offices. But in Sir Lee Stack's time, Egypt had become independent. The Egyptian and Sudanese officers were bound by an oath of allegiance to the king of Egypt, but at the same time they were commanded by a British subject who, as governor-general, embodied and symbolized the British paramountcy in the Sudan. It was not surprising that a clash of loyalties should be most acutely felt by some officers.

On 19 November 1924, the *sirdar* and governor-general was mortally wounded by an Egyptian in the streets of Cairo. His death provided Allenby with an opportunity to seek to end a situation which had become intolerable to all parties. Acting without waiting for the approval of the British government, he presented to Sa'd Zaghlul Pasha, then prime minister, two communications which demanded, *inter alia*, that the Egyptian government should 'order within twenty-four hours the withdrawal from the Sudan of all Egyptian officers and the purely Egyptian units of the Egyptian army, with such resulting changes as [should] be hereafter specified', and sanction an increase in the area to be irrigated in the Gezira 'to an unlimited figure as need [might] arise'.

This ultimatum produced a crisis in Egypt and repercussions in the Sudan. The Egyptian units were with difficulty induced to evacuate. Troops of the 11th Sudanese battalion mutinied and established themselves in the military hospital in Khartoum. The building was surrounded and ultimately destroyed by artillery, the mutineers fighting to the last man.

The events of 1924 were a turning-point in the history of the Condominium. One anomaly ceased to exist: subsequent governors-general were no longer *sirdars* of the Egyptian army, and the military forces of the Sudan, henceforward recruited in the Sudan and commanded by a British officer, were given a separate organization from those of Egypt and were known as the Sudan Defence Force. This further step in the separation of Egyptian and Sudanese institutions might logically have been accompanied by the termination of the Condominium, which had become unworkable. But the wishes of the British administrators in the Sudan were overborne by the government in London. The name of the Condominium was retained, the Egyptian flag continued to be flown together with the Union Jack, the king of Egypt confirmed the appointments and withdrawals of the British governors-general. But the actual participation of Egypt in the Condominium shrank to vanishing point with the evacuation of Egyptian troops, who were soon followed by the Egyptian civilian officials. To establish a lien on its lost dominion, the Egyptian government offered an annual financial contribution for military purposes, which was accepted by the Sudan Government without specification of object.

In one important respect, however, Egyptian interests were safeguarded. Allenby's demand for the unlimited irrigation of the Gezira was dropped by the British government. In 1925 a committee representing Britain and Egypt, with an independent chairman, was appointed to propose a basis for the allocation of the Nile waters as between Egypt and the Sudan. Their recommendations, subsequently embodied in the Anglo-Egyptian Nile Waters Agreement of 7 May 1929, abandoned the principle of a fixed area to be irrigated in the Gezira, and substituted a quota of the waters, to be used as seemed best to the authorities in the Sudan. Sudanese opinion later showed itself hostile to the Agreement, both because it was concluded between Britain and Egypt alone, and because the fixed quota, under one twenty-second part of Egypt's share, was inadequate to the growing needs of the Sudan.

Superficially, the fifteen years that elapsed between the troubles of 1924 and the outbreak of the Second World War resembled the halcyon days of Wingate's governor-generalship. Yet there were significant differences between the two periods. In the earlier one, a small band of devoted men had worked

in the full confidence of their mission to bring order and prosperity to a ravaged land. By 1924 the fundamental tasks of
pacification and administration had been accomplished, while
the Sudan was enjoying the real, if temporary, fruits of a post-
war boom. The passing of the Egyptians had violently removed
a discordant element from the ruling *élite*. But the events of
1924 had produced a crisis of confidence between the rulers and
an important section of the ruled. The recent troubles might be
ascribed to Egyptian intrigues; the Sudanese nationalists might
be contemptuously described as 'partly recruited from ex-
officials with an incomplete or ill-assimilated Western education, who had been dismissed for corruption or other miscon-
duct'.[1] Nevertheless, while the administration rightly perceived
that active opposition was confined to a small minority, mainly
of middle-class officials and officers, it proceeded to act in the
following years as if the western-educated class as a whole was
its inveterate enemy, to be checked and circumscribed in the
interests of political stability. Thereby it stimulated the very
opposition it feared, and antagonized the class on which the
political evolution of the Sudan depended.

The reaction which followed Stack's death can be seen in two
fields: education and administrative policy. Education had
always been tied to administrative requirements; it now came
to be dominated by the political outlook of the administration.
The expulsion of Egyptian teachers deprived the Education
Department of some of its best trained men, without whose
work the early developments under Currie would have been
impossible. The Military School at Khartoum was closed:
henceforward commissions were granted only to men who had
served in the ranks. In 1918 and the following years, courses
had been organized to train as junior administrative officers
Sudanese who had shown promise in any branch of government service. These were shut down in 1927. The Gordon
College, the head of the educational system, stagnated: it was
viewed with suspicion as a breeding-ground of discontented
youths. During the years of prosperity, from 1925 to 1929,
there were no significant educational developments in the
Sudan. The Kitchener School of Medicine, which produced its
first doctors at this time, had been opened by Stack as his last

public act in the Sudan, and marks the end of the first phase of educational development that began with the building of Gordon College. A decade of utter stagnation ensued until the middle thirties.

The illiberal attitude of the Sudan Government towards education in these years was accompanied by, and connected with, a new dogmatism in administrative policy. In the early Condominium, shortage of staff and the overriding need for economy had encouraged two developments: the appointment of Sudanese to the lower cadres of government service, and, where circumstances permitted, the recognition of chiefs as agents of government over their tribes. Such recognition was, of course, nothing new: it had been practised by the Mahdist state and the Turco-Egyptian administration in the Sudan, and it was an obvious expedient to adopt in the circumstances. Like the recruitment of Sudanese as government officials, it was a measure originally adopted under the Condominium for purely practical reasons.

These two methods of employing Sudanese in administrative functions were equally accepted by the Sudan Government until the death of Sir Lee Stack. In his annual report for 1921, Stack himself enunciated the principle lying behind the practice as 'the policy of admitting the native to a share in the management of affairs and helping him to fit himself for the increased responsibilities involved'. Stack's statement is important because it is the first explicit reference to the conception of the Sudan Government as a mandatory for the Sudanese people, rather than a mere agent of the co-domini. It is important also because Stack went on to speak of his policy as being implemented in two ways.

'In the first place natives of the Sudan have been selected and appointed to certain governmental posts carrying direct administrative duties.

In the second place legislation has been passed regularizing the exercise by native chiefs of certain powers over the members of their own tribes.'

The legislation referred to was *The Power of Nomad Sheikhs*

Ordinance, passed early in 1922, which recognized and regularized judicial powers which had from time immemorial been exercised by the chiefs of certain nomad tribes. By 1923 some three hundred shaykhs had received recognition for these purposes.

The loss of confidence by the British administrators in the educated Sudanese was reflected after 1924 in a one-sided development of the policy which Stack had enunciated. This change of attitude is reflected in a passage of the annual report for 1926:

'By the judicious and progressive application of devolutionary measures in districts where conditions are suitable, and by ensuring that the native agencies which are to be responsible for administering these measures are remunerated on a scale sufficient to give them their requisite measure of status and dignity, it should be possible not only to strengthen the fabric of the native organization, but, while maintaining our supervisory staff at proper strength, gradually to reduce the number of sub-*mamurs*,[2] clerks, accountants and similar bureaucratic adjuncts in the out-districts.'

In other words, under the guise of continuity, the policy of Stack and his predecessors was being abandoned. Provincial administration was to be committed as far as possible to tribal authorities supervised by British officials, while the rôle of the educated Sudanese in the administration was to be progressively reduced. The exponents of this policy of 'native administration' or 'indirect administration' by the British would have been shocked to hear it compared to the Khalifa 'Abdallahi's calling-in of the Baqqara, forty years previously, yet both were the consequences of a failure of confidence. In both cases the ruler turned from the more advanced of his subjects, who nevertheless remained essential to the working of his bureaucratic machine, and sought to use the less sophisticated elements as the instrument and support of his authority. But the predicament of the British in 1926 was in one respect more serious than that of the Khalifa. The wars of the Mahdia, the Khalifa's own policy, and the migrations of the tribes had shattered the tribal system. Many ruling houses had been divided, many tribes had been fragmented. Where traditional authority still existed, Stack's ordinance had already recognized it. Now, however, more tribal authorities were to receive recognition.

The situation that ensued was described by the former director of Education, Sir James Currie, who revisited the Sudan, after some years' absence, in 1926, and again in 1932. Aghast at the abandonment of the traditions of Wingate's time, he wrote:

'After the troubles that culminated in Stack's murder, the British local administration took fright, and in spite of the loyalty of the educated Sudanese to the Government that had given them opportunity, the spectacle could be beheld of young administrators diligently searching for lost tribes and vanished chiefs, and trying to resurrect a social system that had vanished for ever.'[3]

The new policy was embodied in *The Powers of Sheikhs Ordinance* of 1927, which no longer restricted recognition to nomad chiefs and which deliberately sought to extend the powers committed to tribal authorities. Even in the Gezira, where the development of the irrigation scheme had impinged with profound social effects on a tribal system far gone in decay, efforts were made to resuscitate tribalism.

The prosperity of this period was followed by the great depression of the early thirties. The impact of this on the Sudan cannot be understood without reference to the economic development of the preceding decade. The scheme for the establishment of an irrigated, cotton-producing area in the eastern Gezira had been shelved on the outbreak of the First World War. In 1919 the project was revived, but the financial provision made before the war was no longer adequate. The amount of the loan guaranteed by Britain was raised from £3,000,000 to £6,000,000 in 1919, and, in subsequent stages between 1921 and 1924, to £13,000,000. In October 1919 an agreement was reached with the Sudan Plantations Syndicate which laid down the organization of the scheme as it was to remain for thirty years. Three parties shared in the work of production: the Sudan Government was responsible for the building and maintenance of the Sennar Dam and the major canals on which irrigation depended; the Syndicate managed the scheme and handled the crop; the tenants, about 26,000 in number, provided the labour.

Most of the tenants were the original owners of the land and, as such, received a small rent representing its undeveloped value. The profits of the cotton crop were divided in the proportion of forty per cent each to the Government and tenants, and twenty per cent to the Syndicate. Each tenancy was of forty *feddans*,[4] the cultivation of which was strictly controlled. Ten acres were devoted to cotton, five each to millet (the staple food grain) and fodder, twenty were left fallow. The grain and fodder were, like the cotton, irrigated free of charge, but remained at the sole disposal of the tenants and tax-free. Much of the labour was recruited, by the tenants themselves, from immigrants from the west who passed through the Anglo-Egyptian Sudan on pilgrimage to the Holy Cities. From this development a social and political problem has arisen. The Gezira Scheme was an admirable piece of social planning, designed to combine the advantages of state ownership and technical control with the maintenance of a prosperous landed peasantry.

The physical organization of the scheme was completed in its essentials by 1925. Its inception aroused fears that Egyptian interests in the Nile waters would be sacrificed. These Allenby sought to allay by a declaration in February 1920 that the amount of land to be irrigated in the Gezira should not exceed 300,000 acres without reference to the Egyptian government. A Nile Projects Commission, appointed by the Egyptian government, visited the Sudan and pronounced, in August 1920, that the projected scheme would utilize only water which would otherwise go to waste, and therefore could not adversely affect Egypt. Egyptian opinion, however, remained suspicious, and the worst fears seemed to be justified by Allenby's ultimatum in 1924. The subsequent Nile Waters Agreement (1929) did something to allay Egyptian apprehensions. Construction of the Sennar Dam had begun in 1921 and was completed in 1925. It became clear that a considerably larger area could be irrigated from the available supply of water, and extensions of the original scheme, completed in 1929, brought the total irrigated area up to over 500,000 acres.

Other cotton-growing schemes had been begun before the First World War in the Gash and Baraka deltas, where streams arising in Eritrea finally lose themselves in the deserts of the eastern Sudan. These also were developed after the war, the Gash scheme (organized on a tripartite basis similar to that in the Gezira) being conceded to the Kassala Cotton Company, which was linked financially with the Sudan Plantations Syndicate. A consequence of the rise of cotton production in the Gash region was the construction in 1924 of a railway between Kasala and Port Sudan. This was subsequently extended to Sennar, so that by 1929 the Gezira was directly linked with the Red Sea coast.

In 1929 local conditions in the Sudan combined with the onset of the great depression to cloud the earlier promise. The stagnation of international trade meant lower prices for cotton, now the Sudan's principal export. Excessively heavy rain in 1929 brought disease to crops and cultivators alike, and in the following season the cotton was again diseased. Meanwhile the perennial threat to the grain-crops from locusts had been increasing from 1927, and in the first years of the new decade their depredations were increasingly severe. The deterioration in the economic situation was reflected in the financial statistics. In 1929, revenue stood at £E6,981,590; expenditure at £E6,610,274. By 1932, when the lowest point had been reached, the comparable figures were £E3,653,394 and £E3,853,758. Subsequently the position improved to a revenue of £E5,053,765 and expenditure of £E4,890,871 in 1939.

An inevitable consequence of the depression was financial retrenchment. In 1931 the Sudan Government set up a special committee to advise on economics, and shortly afterwards a British Treasury official was appointed financial secretary. The loans which had been contracted in connection with the Gezira Scheme had raised the public debt of the Sudan to over £15,000,000, the annual service of which required over £900,000. Cuts were made of from five per cent to ten per cent in official pay and allowances. Departmental staffs and services were reduced. The number of British officials, which had shown a tendency to increase in the recent years of prosperity, had to be reduced, and the government was compelled by force of economic circumstances to adopt a policy of sudanization. Although the implications were not for many years clear either to the Sudanese or to many British administrators, the years of depression had struck a mortal blow at the romantic imperialism which lay behind the unbalanced development of 'native administration'.

The suspicion which had been building up between the Sudan Government and the educated class since 1924 was revealed in 1931 in an apparently trivial yet significant incident. Among its economies, the government had reduced the starting salaries of Sudanese officials, newly appointed from Gordon College, by about thirty per cent. Although British salaries had also been reduced, the cuts had not been so heavy, nor had they been imposed on starting rates. Since the College had from the beginning been used as a feeder for government service, and its intake had been regulated by the prospective requirements of the departments, the whole body of pupils felt threatened. They went on strike, regardless of the attempts of parents and religious notables to intervene. The 'graduates' (i.e. former pupils of the College) elected a committee to mediate with the government. Ultimately the reduction was fixed at twenty per cent, and the pupils returned to work. Currie, who revisited the Sudan in the following year, showed an understanding of the deeper motives underlying the strike. Since 1924, he stated:

'the sphere of employment open to educated natives of the country [had been] materially reduced. The terrific economic crisis of 1930 aggravated the situation, and rendered considerable quantitative reduction a necessity for reasons of economy. If all the inhabitants had been persuaded that there was no change of policy, all would have been well. Curtailment of opportunity was the real grievance.'[5]

Currie went on to give a prophetic warning of the dangers ahead:

'Unless all responsible are made to understand that the employment of educated Sudanese is a cardinal plank in Government policy, no real progress will be made before a narrow nationalism comes triumphantly into existence, and western advisers—good and bad alike—are swept away together.'[6]

CHAPTER X

THE RISE OF SUDANESE
NATIONALISM: 1934–52

THE MIDDLE and late thirties saw some indications of
impending changes in the Sudan. By 1934 the country was
showing signs of recovery from the economic depression. In
the following years new men and methods brought fresh life to
the educational service, with results that will be described later.[1]
The excesses of 'native administration' gave way to a more
balanced policy of the development of local government institutions, democratically constituted on a territorial rather than a
tribal basis. From 1941 onwards local government councils
were set up in the larger municipalities, the smaller towns and
the rural areas. The rural district councils were particularly
significant, since they marked a deliberate reversal of the older
policy. Henceforward the tribal leaders would work in association with local representatives. Ten years of development and
experiment followed, after which the institutions were systema-
tized in the comprehensive *Local Government Ordinance* of 1951.

In the years before the Second World War there were signs
that the period of unquestioned British authority was ending.
The conclusion of the Anglo-Egyptian Treaty of 1936[2] was a
critical event. After fourteen years of unsuccessful negotiations,
terms were at last agreed upon, in consequence of the Italian
conquest of Abyssinia, which had altered the balance of power
in north-east Africa. Over the question of the Sudan, the
standpoints of Britain and Egypt were still, as in 1922 and 1899,
fundamentally irreconcilable, and the treaty attempted no
settlement of the problem. The question of sovereignty over the
Sudan was shelved; the administration resulting from the
Condominium Agreement was left intact. The two states agreed
upon a vaguely benevolent formula 'that the primary aim of

their administration in the Sudan must be the welfare of the Sudanese'. There were, however, some more practical stipulations. The virtual exclusion of the Egyptians from the Sudan was ended. Egyptian as well as Sudanese and British troops were to be placed at the disposal of the governor-general. Egyptian immigration into the Sudan was to be unrestricted 'except for reasons of public order or health'. There was to be no discrimination in the Sudan between British and Egyptians 'in matters of commerce, immigration or the possession of property'. But it was impossible to restore to the Egyptians the share in government service which they had held in 1924. In spite of the doubts and hesitations of the administration in educational matters, there was by this time a large and increasing body of Sudanese in the lower and middle cadres of the public service. The principle of sudanization could no longer be avoided, and it was agreed that British and Egyptian candidates would only be selected for appointment to posts for which qualified Sudanese were not available. In the event, the only substantial appointments of Egyptians were as teachers in the post-war period.

The repercussions of this treaty upon the Sudanese were not long in showing themselves. As in 1929, when the Nile Waters Agreement was reached, important decisions had been made concerning the Sudan without any reference to its people. The educated Sudanese considered themselves the section of the community best entitled to speak for their nation as a whole. This consciousness found expression in an organization, the Graduates' General Congress, founded in February 1938. Its original members were 1,180 'graduates', meaning in this context Sudanese who had completed the course of study at either Gordon College or an intermediate school. Since 'graduates' were almost invariably appointed to posts in government service, the Congress was largely, if not ostensibly, an organization of Sudanese civil servants. Its secretary was Isma'il al-Azhari, the descendant of a family of religious notables, who was himself a mathematics teacher in the Gordon College. He belonged to a small group of Sudanese who had been sent in 1924 and the following years to the American University of Beirut.

Congress announced its formation to the Sudan Government in a letter written by Azhari. This stated that the duties of the organization would lie in two spheres: outside the field of government, in matters such as social reform and charities; and 'matters of public interest involving the Government or lying within the scope of its policy and concern'. With regard to the last, the letter stated:

'It is not our intention in any way to embarrass the Government, nor is it to pursue lines of activity incompatible with the Government policy. Most of us are Government officials and are fully conscious of our obligations as such, but we feel that the Government is aware of our peculiar position as the only educated element in this country, and of the duties which we, in this peculiar position, feel to be ours.'

The civil secretary, in replying on behalf of the government, formally welcomed the formation of Congress, in so far as its purposes were the service of the country and philanthropic activity. He stressed that it was not recognized as a political body, and could not claim to represent the views of any but its own members.

Both these limitations were to be contested by Congress in the future. For the time being, however, it concentrated on educational activities, particularly the establishment of private intermediate schools to meet the growing demand for places, especially in the towns. These supplemented the ten schools (four of which had been built since 1920) provided by the Education Department. With the outbreak of the war, however, the strength of political feeling increased, and two incidents produced a change in the relations between Congress and the Sudan Government. In February 1940, 'Ali Mahir Pasha, then prime minister of Egypt, was invited by the governor-general to visit the Sudan. During his stay, he attended a tea-party held in his honour by Congress. Previously the Egyptians had suspected that Congress was an organization secretly promoted by the Sudan Government to oppose Egyptian penetration. 'Ali Mahir was now convinced that this was not the case, and that indeed Congress was potentially an organ of opposition to the British administration. Congress for its part appealed to 'Ali Mahir for financial help to carry out its social schemes.

By 1942 Congress was determined to assert its claim to act as the spokesman of Sudanese nationalism. The moment seemed favourable. The governor-general, Sir Hubert Huddleston, appointed in 1940, was a man of long experience in the Sudan. His civil secretary, Sir Douglas Newbold, who had held office since 1939, was an able and far-sighted administrator. He realized that the old regime of unquestioned British control was doomed, and that the political ferment, stimulated by the war, would hasten its departure. Yet his position was not free from difficulties. The Sudan was much more directly involved in the Second World War than it had been in the First, since Italy was an enemy power. Kasala had been occupied by the Italians for a few months in 1940, and afterwards an army of British, Indian and Sudanese troops, under General Platt, invaded Eritrea, and won the decisive battle of Keren on 15 March 1941. This ended the danger on the Sudanese border, but a greater danger remained in the north, until Montgomery's victory at El Alamein in November 1942 destroyed the prospect of a German occupation of the Nile valley. Newbold was inevitably preoccupied with the administrative and economic problems which war had brought to the Sudan. He was working with a depleted staff. Even in the most favourable circumstances, he could expect opposition from the more conservative members of the Political Service, who were still imbued with the ideas of the previous decade, and continued to view the educated Sudanese with suspicion and mistrust.

It was therefore unfortunate that, at a time of external crisis and internal strain, Congress should have decided to put forward a political manifesto in which it claimed to speak for the Sudanese people as a whole. A letter addressed to the civil secretary on 3 April 1942 and signed by the president of Congress, Ibrahim Ahmad,[3] put forward twelve demands with clear political and constitutional implications. The first of these was basic: it asked for:

'The issue, on the first possible opportunity, by the British and Egyptian governments, of a joint declaration granting the Sudan, in its geographical boundaries, the right of self-determination, directly after this war; this right to be safe-guarded by guarantees assuring full liberty of expression in connection therewith; as well as guarantees assuring the Sudanese the right of determining their natural rights with Egypt in a special agreement between the Egyptian and Sudanese nations.'

Whatever Newbold's personal sympathies, he had no power to reopen the thorny question of the future status of the Sudan, nor was the spring of 1942 a suitable time for raising so delicate an international problem. A firm answer was to be expected, but his reply to the memorandum was brusque in the extreme. The claim of Congress to represent the Sudanese was rejected. By submitting the memorandum it had forfeited the confidence of the Sudan Government. Although Newbold toned down his snub to the educated Sudanese in private exchanges, his formal reply represented the official policy of the Sudan Government. A new crisis of confidence was the inevitable result.

A further result, which had serious political consequences in the ensuing years, was a split in Congress itself. While one group was prepared to accept the good faith of the Sudan Government, the other, headed by Azhari, was suspicious of British motives in the Sudan, and turned, as 'Ali 'Abd al-Latif had done before, to Egypt as an ally. Once again, the unity of the Nile Valley became the watchword of a Sudanese nationalist group. Among the educated youths, the townspeople and the extremists, Azhari's influence was very great. At this stage he seemed little more than a shrewd demagogue, but an able politician was in the making. His supporters captured the organization of Congress, which henceforward became a partisan body, with little claim to speak for the educated class as a whole. In October 1942, the Egyptian Ministry of Education accepted Congress as the channel for Sudanese applications for admission to Egyptian educational institutions; a useful instrument of patronage was thereby placed in its hands. In 1943 Azhari organized the first genuine political party in the Sudan, the *Ashiqqa'* or 'Brothers' (literally, 'Brothers by the same father and mother').

The moderate nationalists saw the initiative passing to Azhari and the unity group. Their response was to organize a party demanding the complete independence of a Sudanese national state. This party became known as the *Umma*, a word which in modern Arabic means 'nation', but which still carries overtones of its original significance; i.e. the community of Islam in the time of the Prophet and subsequently. It might seem that a party claiming complete independence for the Sudan would have a wider popular appeal than one advocating union with Egypt, but two considerations militated against the general acceptance of nationalism of the Umma type. First, its leaders were known to be prepared, as the Ashiqqa' were not, to co-operate with the existing administration in the progressive realization of independence: hence it was easy to represent them as tools of British imperialism. Secondly, the party placed itself under the patronage of Sayyid 'Abd al-Rahman al-Mahdi, the posthumous son of the Mahdi, who had become one of the two great religious leaders of the Sudan.

The implications of this alliance reached far back into the history of the Condominium and beyond. At the outbreak of the Mahdia, the most influential Muslim sect in the Sudan was, as we have seen, the Khatmiyya, whose leaders, the Mirghani family, descendants of the founder, co-operated with the Turco-Egyptian administration in the Sudan and supported it with their religious authority. With the Mahdi's triumph, the Khatmiyya went into eclipse; it would not recognize Muhammad Ahmad's claim to be the Mahdi, and it was associated with Turco-Egyptian rule. After the Reconquest, the Mirghani family returned to the Sudan and the Khatmiyya revived with un-diminished vigour in its old areas of influence, chiefly in the north and east of the country. It supported the Condominium administration as it had supported its Turco-Egyptian pre-decessor, and hence was an important factor in the years of pacification and organization following the Reconquest. The head of the sect, Sayyid 'Ali al-Mirghani, was treated with deference by the Sudan Government, and received a knight-hood in 1916.

In the early years of the Condominium, Mahdism seemed a spent force. The religious impulse behind it had dwindled after the Mahdi's death; the military defeat of the Mahdist state had discredited it politically. It was proscribed by the new regime and lacked a potential leader. After the death of the two elder sons of the Mahdi in the Shukkaba incident, the heir to the tattered remnants of Mahdist loyalty was his posthumous son, 'Abd al-Rahman. For many years he lived obscurely under surveillance in Omdurman, drawing, like the last Jacobite pretender, a pension from the government which had supplanted his family.

The turn in his fortunes came with the First World War. Wingate invited him to use his influence among his followers in the Gezira to counteract the pan-Islamic propaganda of the Ottomans. He agreed with alacrity. In 1919 he was a member of a delegation of Sudanese notables sent to London to congratulate George V on the British victory. There he offered the reputed sword of his father to the king in token of loyalty. In 1926 he too received a knighthood. Meanwhile he had been allowed to acquire estates on Aba, the cradle of his family's fortunes, where he planted cotton and became a wealthy landowner. The events of the twenties increased his political standing. As the influence of Egypt declined, the Sudan Government came to see in Sayyid 'Abd al-Rahman al-Mahdi, rather than Sayyid 'Ali al-Mirgani, an authentic spokesman for Sudanese.

The head of the Khatmiyya, whose dynastic history was so closely bound up with that of Egyptian influence in the Sudan, was naturally perturbed at the rapid rise of a rival whose family had in the past triumphed at the expense of his own. He feared that 'Abd al-Rahman would succeed in establishing, with British support, a Mahdist monarchy in the Sudan. Although he himself stood ostentatiously aloof from politics, his followers were less restrained. Only in an alliance with Egypt could they see a safeguard against a revival of the Mahdist state.

There was thus a basic similarity of outlook between the Ashiqqa' and Khatmiyya on the one hand, between the Umma Party and the Ansar on the other. To the party-politicians on both sides, furthermore, the alliance with a religious sect offered certain advantages. The number of politically conscious

Sudanese was still small. By linking their parties with one or other of the two great sects, they would acquire a semblance of mass-support from great bodies of simple, unsophisticated Sudanese, who were moved really by traditional religious loyalties to personal leaders, and stirred by inveterate sectarian rivalries. Hence the Umma obtained Sayyid 'Abd al-Rahman as their patron, and his son, Sayyid Siddiq, as their titular head. Sayyid 'Ali al-Mirghani was, as ever, unwilling to commit himself openly in politics, but there was a broad identification of the Khatmiyya as a sect with the party headed by Azhari.

The split in the ranks of the nationalist politicians, and the identification of political parties with religious sects, were disturbing developments. They marked a polarization of the northern Sudanese into two groups, more deeply divided than is compatible with sound political growth. Ancient religious and dynastic rivalries, dying out in the younger generation which had received a western education, and thought and spoke in western political terms, were given a new lease of life. The hatreds and suspicions aroused were to sour Sudanese politics for ten years, and then, after a brief intermission, were to strangle parliamentary government in the independent Republic.

Newbold's clash with Congress coincided ironically with preparations that he was making to associate the Sudanese with the government as makers of policy, not merely as civil servants. The outcome of his study of the problem was a note which he presented to Council in September 1942. In the following January a committee of Council was set up to consider the formation of a new advisory body. On 15 May 1944, Sir Hubert Huddleston inaugurated the Advisory Council of the Northern Sudan. It consisted of the governor-general as president, the civil, financial and legal secretaries, and twenty-eight Sudanese members. Of these, eighteen were elected or nominated from councils which had already been established in the six northern provinces.[4] The governor-general appointed eight other members, to secure the representation of social and economic interests, including agriculture, education and health. The remaining two members were elected by the Chamber of Commerce.

The establishment of the Advisory Council represented a

major development in government policy, a serious attempt to come to terms with Sudanese nationalism. Nevertheless, it provoked criticism both within and outside the Sudan. Although the intention of setting up the Advisory Council had been announced in September 1943, the formal approval of Egypt, which might have been difficult to obtain, had not been sought. Its inauguration aroused angry comments in the Egyptian press, that the Sudan Government was endeavouring to separate the two countries. In August 1944 the Egyptian prime minister, Mustafa al-Nahhas Pasha, who had succeeded Zaghlul as head of the Wafd, asserted that he considered Egypt and the Sudan to be one nation. A spokesman in Khartoum replied that the Sudan Government was 'attempting to train the peoples of the Sudan for local self-government and the management of their own affairs. This intention [constituted] no attempt to alter the legal and constitutional relationship of the Sudan with Egypt or Britain.'

Within the Sudan, the Advisory Council was criticized on three grounds: its functions, its composition, and its limitation to the northern provinces. The Advisory Council did not supersede the governor-general's Council which, since its inception in 1910, had remained the supreme organ of government, combining both executive and legislative powers. Although the Advisory Council discussed a number of important political and social issues, such as Sudanese nationality and the future of the Gezira Scheme, its deliberations were not binding on the government, and its opponents could represent it as a mere debating society, meeting under the supervision of the British administrative heads. Its composition was criticized since tribal chiefs composed a large proportion of the Sudanese members. Although the unbalanced enthusiasm of the administration for this social group had declined in the previous decade, they were still regarded as influential, and as a useful counterweight to the nationalist politicians. The latter continued to view them, with the antagonism born in the days of 'native administration', as ignorant and backward representatives of an obsolescent social order, and tools of the British.

The exclusion of the southern Sudan[5] from the representation and scope of discussion of the Advisory Council brought to the surface misgivings which had long been felt by the northern Sudanese. For historical and administrative reasons, the southern provinces had been dealt with separately from the north ever since the Reconquest. The unifying influences of Islam and Arabic speech, which made for a broad cultural unity throughout the north, were lacking in the southern Sudan. The pacification and establishment of administration in the south were, as we have seen, much more slowly accomplished than in the north, where the Sudan Government was heir to a well-rooted tradition of centralized government derived from its Turco-Egyptian and Mahdist predecessors. The backwardness of the southern tribes, as compared with the sophistication of the riverain and urban Sudanese, was an impediment to the rapid integration of the two regions. Finally, the economic stringency which beset the government until the end of the First World War made impossible any costly schemes for the development of the south and its peoples.

These were all genuine reasons, at least during the first two decades of the Condominium, for regarding the southern Sudan as constituting a region with problems distinct from those of the north. Other considerations were also alleged which had less validity. It was suggested that the share of the northerners in the slave-trade had left odious memories, and that to allow them free entry into the south would expose the southern tribes to exploitation. This was a specious argument. The slave-trade in Equatoria and the Bahr al-Ghazal had resulted from Turco-Egyptian and European penetration of those regions. The northern Sudanese had been the assistants and successors of the alien traders, not initiators. During the Mahdia, there had been an almost complete withdrawal of the northerners from the south; except on the southern fringes of Baqqara territory the Nilotic slave-trade was almost dead at the time of the Reconquest. It was absurd to suggest that a trade which had flourished at a time when administrative control was either weak or totally absent could revive under the strong and honest rule established by the Condominium. Neither was it reasonable to assume that every northern merchant in the south would be an unscrupulous shark, or that the southerners would be so lacking in native wit as to be unable to deal with them.

Two important groups were particularly associated with the policy of excluding the Muslim northern Sudanese from the south. The first of these was the administration itself. The work of the British administrators in opening up and pacifying the southern Sudan, their devotion to duty at the cost of health and life, cannot be too highly praised. Yet there was an insidious danger in their position. Their isolation, the great burden of their individual responsibilities, and their immunity from criticism by the people they ruled, tended to confirm the idea that the system of administration they represented was the only possible system, and must endure indefinitely. The personal rule of the British administrators was in its origin beneficent; the mistake was that it went on too long. The integration of the south with the north began too late, and the result was the cataclysm of 1955.

The Christian missionaries had also a special place in the southern Sudan. Proselytization had, from the outset, been forbidden in the Muslim north, although missionaries found scope for medical and educational activities, while Anglican, Roman Catholic, Greek and Coptic cathedrals in Khartoum, and churches in other urban centres, ministered to the spiritual needs of the various expatriate and immigrant Christian communities. The pagan south, on the other hand, was opened to the missionaries. To prevent sectarian clashes, spheres of activity were demarcated for the various organizations. The missionaries were entrusted with the development of education in the south. This made possible the early, if limited, organization of schools at a time when the government's meagre resources were needed for the north. As time went on, however, the defects of missionary education began to appear. The sectarian differences of Europe and America were incongruously transported to the marshes and forests of central Africa. The language of instruction at the higher levels was English; Arabic, except in a debased pidgin form, was unknown. A new barrier of language and religion seemed to have been added to those already existing between north and south. The missionaries, for their part, had reason to fear that the admission of northern Muslims into the region would endanger the permanence of their work.

F

Just as the Egyptians suspected the British of intending to separate the Sudan from Egypt, the northern Sudanese feared that the Sudan Government meant to amputate the three southern provinces, and cede them to Uganda. Their apprehensions, stimulated by the composition of the Advisory Council, were not allayed by an official publication, issued in 1947, which spoke of 'a policy which aims at giving the south the same chances of ultimate self-determination as have been promised to the north'.

Sir Douglas Newbold died in office in March 1945. He had been a great civil secretary, not so much because of his creation of the Advisory Council, which was to be a transient organization, as because of his profound influence on the outlook of the Political Service and, indirectly, on the whole British official community in the Sudan. Under him, the administration came to accept the rapidly changing political situation in the Sudan, realized that nationalism could no longer be suppressed or ignored, and undertook the duty of training the Sudanese to manage the whole complicated machine of modern government.

The years from 1946 to 1952 are an unhappy period in the history of the modern Sudan. Two matters dominated the politics of the time: the dispute between Egypt and Britain, in which the status and future of the Sudan formed, as on previous occasions, an important element; and the development of self-governing institutions in the Sudan. The Anglo-Egyptian dispute produced a frustrating deadlock between the two co-domini. Constitutional developments exacerbated relations between the two groups of nationalists, and between the unionist group and the Sudan Government.

The opening of negotiations between Britain and Egypt, early in 1946, for a treaty to supersede that of 1936, found Sudanese nationalists of all parties determined to assert their right to be consulted by the co-domini. The governor-general had already, in November 1945, given the Advisory Council an assurance, backed by Britain, of 'the Government's firm intention to consult the people of the Sudan regarding the future of their country'. Meanwhile some independent members of Congress were working out a formula to reconcile the two nationalist groups, and in March 1946 an all-party Sudanese delegation went to Cairo to contact the negotiators. There the delegation rapidly broke up, since the Egyptians would accept only a constitutional settlement by which Egypt and the Sudan were permanently united. The Umma and their allies withdrew, while Azhari and his followers remained in Cairo, claiming and receiving from the Egyptians sole recognition as the spokesmen of the Sudanese.

In the same month of March 1946, Ernest Bevin, as foreign secretary, announced the position the British government had taken up in regard to the Sudan. It envisaged ultimate self-determination, the existing administration being maintained while self-governing institutions were established and the sudanization of the higher civil service proceeded. There should in the meantime be no change in the status of the Sudan 'until the Sudanese have been consulted through constitutional channels'. This statement, which amplified the governor-general's earlier assurances, was repeated by him to the Advisory Council. The policy was acceptable to the Advisory Council, since it agreed closely with the programme of the Umma Party, to which most of its Sudanese members belonged. It could not, however, satisfy the Egyptians, nor the unionist group among the Sudanese nationalists. In the course of negotiations with the Egyptian prime minister, Sidqi Pasha, Bevin therefore tried to devise a formula which would satisfy Egyptian pride while permitting the British policy to be implemented. The result, in October 1946, was a 'draft Sudan protocol' which assured the Sudanese of self-government and self-determination, but which contained the words 'within the framework of the unity between the Sudan and Egypt'. This phrase, which was naturally stressed by Sidqi to win over Egyptian opinion, was abhorrent to the Umma nationalists, who felt that they had been betrayed. The British prime minister explained the phrase away in the House of Commons, the governor-general and civil secretary did the same in the Advisory Council. The draft treaty perished in the controversy.

The speed of political advance now began to increase. The co-domini were in a sense bidding against each other for Sudanese support. Had the nationalists been united, they would have been in a position to control events, but the old division persisted. Britain and the Sudan Government, with the general support of the Umma Party, were able to take the initiative in proposing and implementing constitutional changes. The Egyptian government could criticize or oppose developments, but not prevent them; while the unionist parties refused their co-operation, and stirred up demonstrations in the towns and schools.

The feverish events and repetitive arguments of these years may be briefly summarized. An administrative conference of British and Sudanese members (but boycotted by the Ashiqqa') was held in 1946 and proposed the creation of a Legislative Assembly and Executive Council. In August 1947, the new governor-general, Sir Robert Howe, submitted these recommendations to Britain and Egypt. At the time, Egypt was bringing the dispute with Britain before the Security Council of the United Nations. There, after prolonged debate, the problem was shelved in September. The British government then accepted the constitutional proposals for the Sudan. The Egyptian government accepted the principle of Sudanese self-government without prejudice to a future settlement of the Anglo-Egyptian dispute (which would involve a solution of the problem of sovereignty), but criticized the actual proposals as not going far enough, and as excluding Egypt from participation in the new regime. Agreement on the points at issue was reached by an Anglo-Egyptian committee, but their suggestions were thrown out by the Egyptian Senate. Meanwhile the Advisory Council had debated and approved a draft ordinance implementing the constitutional proposals. When it became clear that the deadlock with Egypt would continue indefinitely, the British government on 14 June 1948 unilaterally authorized the governor-general to promulgate the ordinance. Elections to the Legislative Assembly were held in November: they were boycotted by the unionist parties, which promoted demonstrations against the government. The new Assembly met on 15 December: its opening was accompanied by further demonstrations in Omdurman and the arrest of Azhari.

Unlike the Advisory Council, the Legislative Assembly represented the Sudan as a whole. This notable abandonment by the government of its traditional 'southern policy' had been preceded by a conference held at Juba in June 1947 by the civil secretary, Sir James Robertson,[6] at which leading southerners accepted the idea of a united Sudan. The first steps towards the educational integration of the south with the north were taken in 1950, when the teaching of Arabic was introduced into all schools above elementary level, and students were sent to the Gordon College for higher education, instead of to Makerere College in Uganda as previously. The Legislative Assembly contained thirteen members elected by the southern provincial councils. Fifty-two other members were directly or indirectly elected to represent the north. Not more than ten members might be nominated by the governor-general, and there were some *ex-officio* members representing the executive.

The governor-general's Council ceased to exist, and was superseded by an Executive Council of twelve to eighteen members at least half of whom were to be Sudanese. The chief Sudanese member, in effect the prime minister, was the leader of the Assembly. He was elected by that body, and advised the governor-general on the appointment of Sudanese to ministerial posts. The three British secretaries and commander-in-chief remained members of the Council. The governor-general retained extensive powers, including a veto on the decisions of the Executive Council as well as competence to legislate by ordinance, and to define reserved matters on which the Assembly could not legislate. These reserved matters were the constitution, the Condominium, foreign relations and Sudanese nationality. The leader of the Assembly, who held office during the whole term of its existence, was 'Abdallah Bey Khalil, a former officer of the Sudan Defence Force who had become secretary-general of the Umma Party.

Abortive negotiations took place between Britain and Egypt in 1950, and on 16 November a speech from the throne announced the intention of the Egyptian government to abrogate both the treaty of 1936 and the Condominium Agreement of 1899, and demanded 'the unification of the Nile Valley under the Egyptian crown'. Bevin in the House of Commons reiterated the British position. In the Sudan, the Umma, who dominated the Legislative Assembly, were alarmed at the Egyptian announcement. In the Assembly a motion demanding from the co-domini a joint declaration of Sudanese self-government was carried in December 1950 by a margin of one vote. The opponents of the motion favoured a slower advance to self-government. In March 1951, in response to another motion of the Assembly, the governor-general appointed an Anglo-Sudanese Constitutional Amendment Commission to recommend the next stages in the advance to self-government.

These developments in the Sudan alarmed the Egyptians in their turn. Further negotiations failed, and on 8 October 1951 the Egyptian prime minister, Mustafa al-Nahhas Pasha, brought matters to a head by announcing the abrogation of the 1936 treaty and Condominium Agreement, and introducing into the Egyptian Parliament bills which proclaimed Faruq 'King of Egypt and the Sudan' and enacted a constitution for the Sudan. Supported by the British government, the Sudan Government denied the validity of this unilateral abrogation. But the question of sovereignty in the Sudan was now a matter of public debate. The Constitutional Amendment Commission, which had been sitting since April, was dissolved in November, when six of its thirteen members voted in favour of an international commission to take the place of the governor-general. It had nevertheless completed a substantial part of its work in drafting a new constitution. Its recommendations, published in January 1952, formed the basis of the *Self-Government Statute*, enacted by the Legislative Assembly on 23 April. This provided for a Council of Ministers, composed entirely of Sudanese, and responsible to a bicameral Parliament. The governor-general would act in domestic matters on the advice of the prime minister, but would be exclusively responsible for external relations, and have special responsibilities for the southern Sudan and the public services. He would also have emergency powers in the event of a breakdown of government. The new constitution was for an unspecified transitional period, after which the Sudanese would exercise the right of self-determination. To obtain Egyptian consent to this statute, after the repeated failures of negotiations in the previous six years, seemed impossible when in July 1952, the unpredictable happened. The *coup d'état* of the Egyptian army deposed Faruq and shattered the old structure of Egyptian politics.

The rapid acceleration of the pace towards Sudanese self-government in the post-war period was accompanied by economic and social developments. The war-years had enhanced the prosperity of the country, and this was reflected in the preparation of a special 'development budget', to cover works of reconstruction and development over the five-year period 1946-51. The resources of the first development budget were augmented by a grant of £2,000,000 made by the British government. Of this sum, £1,275,000 were allotted to education. In all, nearly £14,000,000 were appropriated in the end to this five-year scheme, of which £3,000,000 went to agriculture, and £3,500,000 to the improvement and development of communications. A second development budget, financed out of current revenue, was drawn up to cover the years 1951-56. By 1953, estimated expenditure under this budget had risen from £E24,000,000 to £E34,000,000, and some of the schemes included in it had to be dropped. During this second period the Condominium ended, and the later years of the development budgets belong to the history of the independent Sudan.

Meanwhile the prosperity of the Sudan continued to rest upon its agriculture, while its foreign trade depended largely on the production and sale of cotton. The concession to the Sudan Plantations Syndicate ended in 1950. Under an ordinance of the Legislative Assembly, the Syndicate's functions of management were taken over by a statutory body, the Gezira Board, responsible to the Executive Council (and its successors), while the twenty per cent share of profits, which formerly went to the Syndicate, was henceforth devoted to research, social development within the area of the Scheme, and the costs of management. The sudanization of the inspecting and engineering staff, hitherto British, had already been recommended by the Legislative Assembly in 1948, and proceeded rapidly after the nationalization of the Scheme.

Another agricultural development was the attempt to exploit more fully the rain-lands of the central Sudan, by the introduction of modern methods of cultivation and the better conservation of water-supplies. After some unsuccessful attempts in the previous years, experimental work on mechanized grain production was begun in 1945 on the Ghadam-baliyya plains, near Gedaref. Cotton production gave less satis-factory results. The scheme did not achieve its original large-scale objectives, and was expensive to initiate. Nevertheless the financial return has steadily improved, a stimulus has been given to the mechanization of private farming, and a useful body of knowledge and experience has been acquired. A further project of this type is being set on foot in the south of the Blue Nile Province, where rainfall is heavier than in the Gedaref region.

The post-war period saw the development of a labour move-ment in the Sudan. Owing to the fact that the government is the largest single employer in the country, and that the move-ment came into being at the time when Sudanese nationalism was acquiring a new militancy, Sudanese trade unionism, almost from the first, had a markedly political character. Its place of origin was the town of Atbara, the headquarters of the Sudan Railways, a department which formed almost an *imperium in imperio* within the administrative structure of the Sudan Government. Atbara owed its existence to the railways; nine-tenths of its people were railwaymen and their dependants. Thus alone amongst the towns of the Sudan it contained a large, homogeneous class of skilled artisans, many of them the products of the railway technical school.

It was these artisans who inaugurated, in June 1946, a Workers' Affairs Association, broadly with the functions of a trade union but without any overtly political character. The Association's request to the management for recognition was rejected, since the government was at this time encouraging the formation of works committees, with much more limited functions than those envisaged by the WAA. A struggle developed, culminating in a demonstration at Atbara and a railway strike throughout the Sudan in July 1947. A committee composed of representatives of both the unionist and inde-pendence political groups mediated between the Association and the government. Recognition was granted, an alliance was forged between the politicians and organized labour, and strikes came to be regarded as the first and only weapon in industrial disputes. The following year saw another clash between the WAA and the government over wage demands. Once again a strike took place.

By obtaining recognition, the WAA had forced the pace, and the Sudan Government drafted a body of labour legislation on which it had been working since early 1946. An enlightened group of laws, enacted from 1948 onwards, dealt with conditions of employment. These were favourably received, but the *Trade Union Ordinance* of 1948, which established the legal status and powers of trade unions and required their compulsory registration, was at first viewed with deep suspicion by the WAA. At a conference, held in April 1949 and composed of six workers' representatives and three members of the Legislative Assembly, some modifications in the ordinance were agreed upon. For nearly ten years, the ordinance remained the charter of trade union activity in the Sudan. This enactment was followed by a spate of registration of unions. Many of them were small bodies with brief and spasmodic existences. The sectarian division into Khatmiyya and Ansar was reflected in the unions as in other aspects of Sudanese life. Trade unionism remained strongest at its point of origin: the Sudan Railway Workers' Union (the reconstituted WAA) with 25,000 members, contained perhaps one-quarter of all the trade unionists in the country.

The WAA also pioneered attempts to link together all trade unions through a central body. In August 1949 it held a conference with other organizations which set up a Workers' Congress. This was reconstituted in the following year as the Sudan Workers' Trade Union Federation, and moved its headquarters from Atbara to Khartoum. Although the Sudan Government had on several occasions negotiated with the Congress and Federation, and treated them as representative of Sudanese labour, the formal application of the Federation for registration, and hence recognition, was rejected in April 1951, on the grounds that the *Trade Union Ordinance* applied only to individual unions. The Federation's leaders felt that the government was attempting to deprive them of established rights. Relations between the two parties, always strained, became tenser, and the Federation became increasingly associated with extremist opposition to the government. In

December 1951, it amended its constitution to admit political action. Stimulated by the unilateral abrogation of the Condominium Agreement by Egypt in the previous October, it urged complete non-co-operation with the Sudan Government, and, in alliance with the Ashiqqa', it formed the United Front for the liberation of the Sudan. During the following year it played a leading part in nationalist politics, but in 1953 its prestige abruptly declined, owing to its opposition to the Anglo-Egyptian Agreement of that year.

CHAPTER XI

SELF-GOVERNMENT AND SELF-DETERMINATION: 1953–55

THE PASSING of the Egyptian monarchy in consequence of the *coup d'état* of July 1952 appeared at first sight advantageous to British policy in the Sudan. With the departure of Faruq, the provocative Egyptian assertion of sovereignty over the Sudan ceased. Further, in August 1952, the new military government announced its willingness to separate the question of the Sudan from that of the Suez Canal Zone in its negotiations with the British government. The combination of these two problems had bedevilled all previous Anglo-Egyptian negotiations, and their separation was criticized as a tactical error by 'Ali Mahir, whose ministry had bridged the transition from the old regime to the new. Nevertheless the military junta in Egypt was convinced that by a more flexible handling of the situation it could obtain better results than had been obtained by the monarchy.

Proceeding with this policy, the Egyptian government began conversations with Sudanese political leaders of the independence group and accepted the proposition of immediate self-government for the Sudan, to be followed in due course by self-determination. Neither of these steps was completely new: in November 1951, before the *coup d'état*, the Egyptian delegation to the United Nations had declared itself not to be opposed to the principle of Sudanese self-determination, while representatives of the Umma Party had been invited by the Egyptian prime minister to Cairo in June 1952. But what had been half-hearted tactical moves in the twilight of the monarchy became a vigorous policy under the junta. Its adoption placed the initiative in their hands. Groups which mistrusted self-government and self-determination when these were advocated by Britain, were more favourably disposed when Egypt espoused these aims, and the British administration in the Sudan found its own weapons turned against it. The popularity of the new Egyptian policy was personified in General Neguib, the ostensible leader of the junta. Half-Sudanese by birth and educated partly in the Sudan, he won the trust and affection of thousands of Sudanese.

So it came about that in the autumn and winter of 1952–53 understandings were reached between the Egyptians and their old opponents among the Sudanese which made possible the Anglo-Egyptian Agreement of 12 February 1953. In October 1952 the British government had accepted the draft *Self-Government Statute*, passed earlier in the year by the Legislative Assembly. On 2 November, however, the Egyptian government proposed, not only to accept self-government on the basis of the statute, leading to self-determination, but suggested a number of amendments, more acceptable to Sudanese than to official British opinion. The bidding for Sudanese support was now on, and the Egyptians had the lead. Their success appeared when, on 10 January 1953, the four main Sudanese political parties signed a pact of agreement with the Egyptian proposals.

The division of Sudanese nationalists into a group seeking independence, but prepared in the meantime to co-operate with the Sudan Government, and another with Egyptian political allies, aiming at the unity of the Nile Valley, had persisted as the basic theme of Sudanese politics, but the party-pattern was now more complex, partly for ideological, but more for personal reasons. Essentially the Umma was and always remained the political expression of the Ansar religious group and was associated with the dynastic ambitions of Sayyid 'Abd al-Rahman al-Mahdi. The alliance between Azhari and the Khatmiyya sect was less intimate, since Sayyid 'Ali al-Mirghani publicly dissociated himself from party politics. This allowed Azhari more scope for development as a purely nationalist political leader, although for mass-support he remained dependent on the connections between the Ashiqqa' and the Khatmiyya. In 1949, he lost this mass-support. Jealousy of his claims to speak for Sudanese nationalism, of his close relations with the Egyptian government, and dislike of his extreme unionist views, led in August 1949 to the formation of a new party, the National Front, supported by many of the Khatmiyya. This too was unionist but less extremely so than the Ashiqqa', since it sought for the Sudan dominion status under the Egyptian crown, rather than incorporation with Egypt. Its formation was approved by Sayyid 'Ali al-Mirghani, and one of its leading members, an engineer named Mirghani Hamza, was to play an important part in politics in the following decade. Like the Ashiqqa', the National Front boycotted the elections to the Legislative Assembly but, on the other hand, it was represented on the Constitutional Amendment Commission of 1951. Azhari sank further into eclipse when in 1951, the Ashiqqa' themselves split into two factions, one supporting a rival leader, Muhammad Nur al-Din. The schism was later healed by Egyptian intervention and Azhari's following was reincarnated as the National Unionist Party (NUP). In July 1952 the National Front collapsed on the illness of its founder.

The close association of Sayyid 'Abd al-Rahman al-Mahdi with the Umma Party was an embarrassment to those who wished for independence without ties with Egypt, but who were not religiously committed to the Ansar. In December 1951 it seemed as if an effective alternative independence group was being formed. This was the so-called Socialist Republican Party, the nucleus of which was the group of members of the Legislative Assembly who, in December 1950, had opposed the motion requesting the grant of self-government. The party itself was formed a year later. It was composed mainly of the tribal notables of the northern Sudan, whose influence had grown during the period of 'native administration', and who had been strongly represented in the Advisory Council and Legislative Assembly. In changing conditions, they saw their position threatened by the nationalist politicians such as Azhari, with his large following among the educated youth and the urban working-class. They mistrusted Sayyid 'Abd al-Rahman al-Mahdi, because of his wealth as a cotton-capitalist and his dynastic ambitions; hence, and for no deeper ideological reasons, they denominated themselves Socialist Republicans. The party was viewed benevolently by the British administration, which saw in it a counterweight, not only to the unionist parties but also to the Umma, whose leaders began in 1952 to talk with Egypt. Its political significance was, however, over-estimated.

The pact between the Egyptians and the Sudanese parties in January 1953 created an alliance which could not be resisted. By the Anglo-Egyptian Agreement of 1953, the amendments proposed by Egypt to the *Self-Government Statute* were accepted. Essentially the Egyptians wished to modify those provisions which they, and many Sudanese, feared might be utilized to maintain British control behind a façade of self-government and self-determination. Hence the governor-general's residual powers under the *Self-Government Statute* were to be exercised with the concurrence of an international commission, consisting of two Sudanese, one British, one Egyptian and one Pakistani. The original statute had revived old suspicions by conferring on the governor-general special responsibilities for the southern provinces. In the modified statute this was trans-muted into 'a special responsibility to ensure fair and equitable treatment to all the inhabitants of the various provinces of the Sudan'. The Agreement itself spoke of the maintenance of the unity of the Sudan as a single territory as 'a fundamental principle' of policy.

The transitional period of self-government, preceding self-determination, was limited in the Agreement to a maximum of three years from 'the appointed day', when the self-governing institutions should be certified by the governor-general as having been created. An elaborate scheme for the termination of the transitional period and the process of self-determination was laid down in the Agreement, but this was not followed in practice. It was intended that a specially elected constituent assembly should opt either 'to link the Sudan with Egypt in any form' or for complete independence.

The first of the self-governing institutions to be created was the Parliament. The Agreement set up an international Electoral Commission, composed of three Sudanese, one Egyptian, one British and one American, with wide terms of reference to prepare and organize the general election. The Electoral Commission made important modifications in the electoral rules. In the original statute, direct elections were to be held in only thirty-five of the ninety-two constituencies, while in tribal areas and the south indirect elections were to take place. This system, which favoured the candidature of tribal notables, followed the precedent of the Legislative Assembly, and was suspect to the educated class. The Electoral Commission increased the number of direct-election constituencies to sixty-eight. The postal 'graduates' constituency', for Sudanese who had completed an educational course of secondary standard, had its representation increased from three to five members. Both these modifications showed how the tide was now flowing for the urban politicians against the old tribal authorities.

The elections, delayed by the onset of the rainy season, were not held until November and December 1953. The intervening months saw a high-pressure campaign, conducted by Egyptian officials and the Cairo radio, to spread propaganda and more material inducements among the voters. The result of the general election came as a shock to many British officials. Azhari's NUP won fifty-one out of ninety-seven seats in the House of Representatives, and twenty-two out of thirty elected seats in the Senate. The Umma Party was the largest single opposition group, with twenty-two seats in the House, three in the Senate. The hollowness of the Socialist Republican Party was unkindly exposed: it won three seats in the House, none in the Senate. The victory of the unionists was generally misunderstood by foreign opinion, not least in Egypt and Britain. The electors were expressing a negative, not a positive emotion. They wished for freedom from British control; hence the Umma and Socialist Republican parties, which were generally regarded as tools of the administration, lacked support. Events were soon to show that there was little desire for any form of unity with Egypt. The effect of Egyptian propaganda and inducements was probably marginal in winning votes: it certainly failed to gain support for the idea of unity with Egypt. The Sudanese nationalists were in fact repeating more subtly and far more successfully the tactics which had been crude and ineffective in 1924, of allying with Egypt to break the British hold on the Sudan.

The Sudanese Parliament held its first meeting on New

Year's Day 1954. On 6 January, Azhari was elected prime minister. He selected his colleagues, as was his right, entirely from the members of his own NUP. Two delicate problems of political and personal relationship were thereby created; on the one hand between the new government and the British officials, who still occupied the chief posts in the administration and were very numerous in the other departments of government; on the other, between the now dominant unionist politicians and the Umma Party, which had controlled the Legislative Assembly but was now completely excluded from executive power.

In spite of the latent tension between the Sudanese ministers and the British officials, no breakdown of relations occurred. This was partly because of the correct attitude of the British, in conformity with civil service traditions. The anti-British attitude of the ruling party in public was not usually carried over into departmental life. The new ministers were themselves former officials of the government service and instinctively felt that its work must continue as it had done for the past fifty years. Furthermore the British were on their way out. The sudanization of the civil service, which had proceeded gradually since the expulsion of the Egyptians in 1924, had been accelerated since 1946, when an Anglo-Sudanese committee was appointed to consider the problem. Reporting in 1948, the committee recommended that 62.2% of the posts held by non-Sudanese should be sudanized by the end of 1962. In 1947 the recruitment of expatriate officials on pensionable terms ceased, although long-term contracts continued to be offered, and these seemed likely to preserve the mainly British composition of the Political Service in particular for another twenty years.

The signing of the Anglo-Egyptian Agreement of 1953, however, hastened the process of sudanization. The maintenance of efficiency, hitherto a leading consideration, was now subordinated to political expediency. A Sudanization Committee was established under the Agreement 'to provide the free and neutral atmosphere requisite for Self-Determination'. It consisted of one British, one Egyptian and three Sudanese members. Its duties were primarily to complete the sudanization of the administration (i.e. the Political Service), the police and the Sudan Defence Force. Under the pressure of its Sudanese majority, the terms of reference were sweepingly interpreted. There were at this time about 140 British administrative officials, eight police officers, and some thirty officers in the Sudan Defence Force. All were dismissed, with compensation, in the course of 1954. The sudanization of the technical departments was sharply accelerated, while many British officials, foreseeing that their careers were endangered, sought to resign. Their way was facilitated by an ordinance enacted by the Sudanese Parliament in July 1954 which provided generous compensation for expatriate officials. Thus during 1955 the number of British in government service was heavily reduced. The need for officials with special professional or technical qualifications, however, remained; British staff for the educational and other services continued to be appointed, but recruitment of expatriates was no longer virtually confined, as in the past, to British and Egyptians.

Meanwhile the Umma Party, which had tasted power in the Advisory Council and Legislative Assembly, remained sullen and suspicious of the new regime. The co-operation of the British officials with the NUP government, and the constitutional requirement that the governor-general should now deal exclusively with the prime minister, seemed to the Umma an abandonment. Although defeated in the elections, the Umma, through its links with the Ansar, was still a power in many parts of the country, particularly in the regions adjoining Aba and the western provinces. The temptation to demonstrate its power proved irresistible.

The first session of Parliament had been opened quietly so that essential business might be concluded as quickly as possible. The second session was to have a ceremonial opening on 1 March 1954, and representatives of Britain, Egypt and other states were invited to attend. The Egyptian delegation was headed by President Neguib and Colonel Nasser. The Umma and other opponents of union with Egypt planned a great demonstration at Khartoum airport on their arrival. This was foreseen; the demonstrators were evaded and the Egyptian delegation was conveyed to the governor-general's palace by a roundabout route. Balked of their demonstration, the mob swarmed into Khartoum and clashed with the police. In the riot, several persons including a British and a Sudanese police-officer were killed. The opening of Parliament was postponed and a state of emergency was declared.

The riot of 1 March brought to a head the irresponsible factionalism which had been developing, and shocked the politically conscious Sudanese into a sober awareness of the speed with which a dangerous situation might develop. It revealed to Azhari and his ministry the limits of their power to manœuvre. Although the NUP had a majority of seats in Parliament, a large and powerful section of the people were bitterly opposed to its ostensible policy of union with Egypt, an objective which could only be achieved at the risk of civil war.

Nor were the Sudanese ministers deeply attached to the old slogan of unity of the Nile Valley. Having held power, they were perhaps uneasily aware that union with Egypt would inevitably diminish their own standing in whatever political organization was set up. The Sudanese as a whole were disenchanted with Egypt. The methods used by the Egyptians to acquire influence in the election campaigns had lost rather than gained them prestige. The ousting of Neguib by Nasser, attempted in February and consummated in November 1954, removed from the scene the one Egyptian leader who was a popular hero in the Sudan. Nasser's repression of the Egyptian Communists on the one hand, and of the Muslim Brotherhood on the other, antagonized the young educated Sudanese, who were attracted to these extremist groups. Azhari began to accommodate his tactics to the changing public opinion.

The smooth development of his policy was rudely interrupted in August 1955 by a revolt in the south. The troubles there were the inevitable result of over-hasty political change. The British administrators who, if alien, were at least familiar to the unsophisticated southerners, had gone and their places had been taken by the no less alien northern, Arabic-speaking, Muslim Sudanese. For the most part new to the higher responsibilities of administration, the northerners were particularly at a disadvantage in dealing with the south, from which they had been virtually excluded until less than ten years previously. The southern political leaders, conscious of their weakness under the new regime, adopted Azhari's own former tactics and began to seek Egyptian support. They announced that they were aiming to establish an autonomous South, linked only in a federation with the North. When mutiny broke out in the Equatoria Corps of the Sudan Defence Force, the mutineers were buoyed up by the impossible hope of receiving British help. The governor-general, Sir Knox Helm, who had succeeded Sir Robert Howe in March 1955, could only order the mutineers to lay down their arms. They surrendered on 27 August, but by this time disorder had spread through the southern provinces and many northerners lost their lives. The restoration of order was a long and difficult business, but the new rulers acted on the whole wisely and temperately in this very dangerous crisis. Like the riot of 1 March 1954 it was a sharp lesson in the responsibilities and problems of political power.

In spite of this interruption, Azhari was determined to achieve independence without delay and to bypass the procedure laid down in the Agreement of 1953. In August 1955, the Parliament passed a resolution demanding the evacuation of British and Egyptian forces, as a preliminary to self-determination. The evacuation was completed by the middle of November. Later in August, the Parliament, acting upon a suggestion of Sayyid 'Ali al-Mirghani, resolved to ask the co-domini to hold a plebiscite to decide the future of the Sudan. Egypt agreed in October, Britain in November. The Parliament next suggested that the plebiscite should be held simultaneously with the election of a Constituent Assembly. This proposal also was accepted by the co-domini. A parliamentary crisis involving Azhari then occurred.[1] The final phase in the ending of the Condominium opened on 19 December, when the House of Representatives passed a resolution declaring the independence of the Sudan. The Senate followed suit three days later. A Transitional Constitution was adopted, based on the existing parliamentary regime, but with the governor-general's powers transferred to a Supreme Commission of five Sudanese members, including one southerner. The formal end of the old order came on New Year's Day, 1956, when, in the presence of the representatives of Britain and Egypt, the Union Jack and the stars and crescent of Egypt were hauled down, and the blue, yellow and green flag of the new Republic was flown for the first time over the former palace of the governor-general.

PART 4

THE REPUBLIC OF THE SUDAN

'My mind recalls successively our struggle, endeavour, solidarity and persistence that enabled us to attain our hopes and to realize our complete independence in a smooth and easy manner; an independence not realized through blood and destruction of human lives, but through the consistence, solidarity and courage of all classes of the people and the leaders of the parties and organizations.'

> Broadcast by the prime minister, 'Abdallah Khalil, on the first anniversary of independence: 1 January 1957.

'Thanks be to God, your loyal Army has today, the 17th November, 1958, carried out a peaceful move which is hoped to be a turning point towards stability and clean administration.'

> Broadcast by General Ibrahim 'Abbud, President of the Supreme Council of the Armed Forces, Prime Minister and Minister of Defence.

CHAPTER XII

THE PARLIAMENTARY REGIME
1956–58

THE INCEPTION of the Republic could not fail to remind many Sudanese of the foundation, over seventy years before, of the Mahdist state. Yet there was little real similarity between the two. The ideology of the Mahdia was purely religious: any compromise between it and the khedivial administration in the Sudan was out of the question. The Mahdist state was born out of the devastation of a revolutionary war, in which the established administrative system had been subverted, and the precarious economic development of the Turco-Egyptian period arrested. The nationalists who had founded the Republic, on the other hand, were deeply affected by Western culture and political ideas. They sought, not to destroy, but to control the administration which had been built up since the Reconquest. They professed, with varying degrees of sincerity and understanding, attachment to parliamentary democracy. Hence the Republic was essentially not the supplanter but the successor of the Condominium government. New Year's Day, 1956, marks only in a formal and conventional sense a new era in Sudanese history. The real line of demarcation must be placed either earlier, on the 'appointed day' of 9 January 1954, when the essential transfer of power from British to Sudanese hands took place; or later, on 17 November 1958, when the Army *coup d'état* ended the brief period of parliamentary government.

The political history of the parliamentary period after independence was a development of that of the preceding years. Azhari's failure to monopolize the support of the Khatmiyya and to present himself as the political agent of Sayyid 'Ali al-Mirghani had several interesting results. He was forced to

171

become a secular politician, relying on the attractiveness of his programme and his own adroit manœuvres to win and keep popular support. Hence before the coming of self-government he appeared as an extremist both in his support of unity with Egypt, and in his refusal to collaborate with the Condominium administration. He was thus able to attract the emotional nationalism of the Sudanese, especially the students and younger educated men, while receiving the backing of successive Egyptian governments as their most reliable ally in the Sudan. On attaining office in January 1954, however, there was a gradual and subtle change in the sources of his influence. It became increasingly clear that, if he were to retain support, he would have to capture the direction of the movement towards independence. This he did, with considerable skill, and acquired new prestige as the champion of an independent Sudan; a paradox which baffled and chagrined his former Egyptian allies.

Yet when Azhari's National Unionist Party ceased to support the cause of unity with Egypt, it lost its ideological content and dissolved into personal factions. Azhari's tactical triumph in 1955 was thus the cause of his political eclipse in the following year. His personal ambitions were too clearly revealed, and his political opponents, united on no other issue, contrived to oust him from power—a political manœuvre hardly less paradoxical than Azhari's own conversion to the cause of Sudanese independence. Parliamentary life from 1954 to 1958 was characterized by factionalism rather than party politics, and its debased quality was to be used as a justification of their action by the soldiers who ended it.

It remains to survey in more detail the political history of the parliamentary period. In December 1954, Azhari dismissed Mirghani Hamza (who had been Minister of Education, Agriculture and Irrigation), together with two other ministers from his cabinet. The three men straightway formed the Republican Independence Party, which included amongst its aims the establishment of an independent Sudanese republic, co-operating with Egypt but maintaining its own sovereignty. It is unlikely that there was at this time any serious ideological difference between Mirghani Hamza and Isma'il al-Azhari: the events should be seen rather as a conflict of personalities. It is significant that Mirghani Hamza had been a leading member of the old National Front, which from 1949 to 1952 had been unionist in principle but independent of Azhari and very closely allied to the Khatmiyya. On 19 June 1955 another leading minister, Muhammad Nur al-Din (minister of Public Works), was dismissed. Shortly afterwards Azhari also dismissed Muhammad Nur al-Din from the vice-presidency of the NUP. Muhammad Nur al-Din and his associates promptly retorted by declaring Azhari himself expelled. Although Muhammad Nur al-Din attacked Azhari for abandoning the programme of unity with Egypt, this incident may also probably be ascribed to personal rather than ideological motives. It was indeed a repetition of the situation in 1951, when a schism had developed in the Ashiqqa', and both Azhari and Muhammad Nur al-Din claimed that their faction was the true party.

Up to this point, Azhari had enjoyed considerable success. Without tying himself closely to the Khatmiyya, he had achieved great personal popularity and influence, and was the undoubted master of his government, from which his rivals had been eliminated. Nevertheless the power of the Khatmiyya remained great behind the scenes. The mutiny in the south was a blow to his prestige, although this was counterbalanced by the accelerated movement towards independence in the summer and autumn of 1955. His hold over Parliament was, however, becoming weaker. On 10 November he lost a vote of confidence by four votes and resigned. Five days later he was reinstated in power by a majority of two votes.

Meanwhile the Umma and other opposition parties were pressing for a coalition government, so that they could be associated with the achievement of independence. Significant of the growing concentration of forces against Azhari was an unprecedented meeting of 'Ali al-Mirghani and 'Abd al-Rahman al-Mahdi. On 6 December, Azhari agreed to form a coalition, but on terms which would confirm his own tenure of power: that the existing Parliament should act both as the means of self-determination and as a constituent assembly. He clearly had no hope of securing a majority at another general election. Pushing ahead with the final measures for dissolving the Condominium, Azhari snatched at the claim to have brought independence to the Sudan. But it was a hollow triumph. At the end of January 1956 he could no longer resist the demand for a coalition government. The new government, sworn in on 2 February, not only included Mirghani Hamza and Muhammad Nur al-Din, but also two leading members of the Umma Party, 'Abdallah Khalil and Ibrahim Ahmad. Azhari could not hope to dominate men of this calibre and it was only a matter of time before he was edged out of the premiership. His divorce from the Khatmiyya was shown in June, when, with the support of Sayyid 'Ali al-Mirghani, some former members of the NUP formed the People's Democratic Party, (PDP), one of the founders of which was Mirghani Hamza. On 5 July 'Abdallah Khalil was elected prime minister against Azhari, with a majority of twenty-eight votes in the House of Representatives. Two days later a new coalition government, from which Azhari was excluded, took office.

The coalition of the Umma Party and PDP was artificial and opportunist in character. It was united only to exclude from power Azhari and the rump of the NUP, which had followed him into opposition. On every vital point of policy, the two parties had different and opposed objectives. The Umma, traditionally the party most friendly to Britain, wanted to strengthen ties with the West: the PDP looked to Egypt, where Nasser's policy was oriented towards the Soviet bloc. The permanent constitution had yet to be made law: the Umma Party wished to see Sayyid 'Abd al-Rahman al-Mahdi as life-president of the Republic, while the PDP rejected this as an attempt to derogate from the status of Sayyid 'Ali al-Mirghani. The internal disputes within the coalition continued after the general election of February-March 1958, and came to a head over the issue of the acceptance of economic aid from the USA.

'Abdallah Khalil remained in office until the army *coup* of November 1958. His period of power saw the assumption by the Sudan of the chief attributes of sovereignty and independence. Amongst these was the creation of a Diplomatic Service and the enunciation of a foreign policy. The first members of the diplomatic corps, many of them former teachers, were sworn in on 24 July 1956. The conduct of foreign policy was in the hands of Muhammad Ahmad Mahjub, a former lawyer who had played a prominent part in politics over the previous ten years, but now held ministerial office for the first time. The Sudan had already joined the Arab League, and applied for admission to the United Nations Organization, which it entered on 12 November 1956.

The basic principle of Sudanese foreign policy is neutrality between the two great power-blocs. This is not incompatible with friendly relations with both sides, or with the acceptance of foreign aid which does not involve military commitments. Within UNO, the Sudan works with the Afro-Asian group of countries. By joining the Arab League, the Sudan became a member of an organization no less deeply divided than UNO itself, chiefly by the rivalry between Egypt and Iraq for the hegemony of the Arab world. Here too Sudanese policy aims at neutrality between the competing groups and endeavours to reconcile their divergent interests. This purpose was symbolized by the tour of a goodwill delegation to Arab countries, headed by the prime minister in March 1957. Although the Sudan adopted the stand of the Arab League on relations with Israel and the Algerian problem, its geographical remoteness from these conflicts was reflected in a comparatively detached and moderate tone. Sudanese foreign policy is also influenced by the geographical situation of the country as a link between Arab and Negro Africa. Good relations with the non-Arab countries are assiduously cultivated; typical of this was a state visit of Kwame Nkrumah, as premier of Ghana, to the Sudan in June 1958.

Sudanese relations with Egypt form a special problem of foreign policy, in which the Republic is very clearly the successor to the previous Sudan Government. Professions of mutual goodwill and of fraternal Arab solidarity, although expressed in emotional terms, are on a level with the formal courtesies of the Condominium period, and do not conceal the determination of the government in Khartoum to pursue its own ends rather than to subordinate them to Egyptian interests. The most serious conflict between the two states was over the Nile waters. Even before the establishment of self-government,

some Sudanese were complaining of the quota of water accru-
ing to the Sudan under the Agreement of 1929. The problem
has become more acute in the last decade. Since 1952 successive
Egyptian governments have interested themselves in a project
for improving the water supply of their country by the construction of a High Dam, south of the present dam at Aswan.
This dam will flood a considerable area of the northern Sudan,
and from September 1954 onwards there were intermittent
negotiations between the Sudanese and Egyptian governments.

The concealed tension in Sudanese-Egyptian relations was
overlaid for a time in the winter of 1956 as a consequence of
the Suez Incident. The Anglo-French intervention against
Nasser shook British prestige in the Sudan as elsewhere in the
Middle East. It produced a brief outburst of anti-British feeling, the more regrettable since the old nationalist animosity
against Britain had practically vanished with the transfer of
power. In December 1956 the prime minister and minister of
the Interior paid a three-day visit to Cairo to congratulate the
Egyptian government and nation on their stand, and to seek
to further the mutual understanding and co-operation of the
two countries.

While these events demonstrated that the Sudan would
make common cause with Egypt against the outside world,
they did not indicate any solution of their fundamental conflicts. The ineptness of the Egyptian approach to the Sudan
appeared again in February 1958. At that time a general election
was about to take place in the Sudan, and Egypt was about to
hold a plebiscite and presidential election. The Egyptian
government sent troops into two areas to which it laid claim,
one on the Nile, the other in the Red Sea coastal region, on the
grounds that they lay north of Latitude 22°, which had been
specified as the northern boundary of the Sudan in the Condominium Agreement. In return, Egypt offered to cede a strip
of territory to the Sudan. The disputed areas had in fact been
administered from Khartoum since the Reconquest, and their
status had not previously been challenged. The Sudanese
government resisted the Egyptian claim and on 20 February
raised the matter to the Security Council of UNO. The storm
died down as abruptly as it had risen. The Egyptians agreed to

postpone the dispute and blamed it on 'imperialists'. The Sudan was left in possession of the two areas.

Before the general election was held, the parliamentary constituencies were increased and redistributed in the light of the recent census. Their number was increased from 97 to 173, each constituency having 50,000 to 70,000 inhabitants. The special 'graduates' constituency' with its postal vote was abolished. More constituencies were formed in the central area of the Sudan, while the number of those in the north was diminished. The effect of this was to strengthen the voting power of the Umma Party as against the NUP. Azhari, however, continued to find much support in the towns.

When the new Parliament, which was also intended to function as a constituent assembly, assembled in March, the Umma Party held sixty-three seats and the PDP twenty-six. A new coalition was therefore formed by 'Abdallah Khalil from these two parties. As was customary, three southern ministers were appointed, but these were not the men nominated by the Liberal Party, the political group which included the majority of southern deputies. The result of this was to antagonize the southerners, forty of whom combined in an alliance known as the Federal Bloc, which was prepared to vote with the NUP opposition, especially on questions concerning the south.

This development seriously undermined the stability of 'Abdallah Khalil's government, since he was dependent on southern support to obtain parliamentary ratification for an economic and technical aid agreement with the USA. Such aid had first been mooted early in 1957, when the American government was seeking to launch the Eisenhower Doctrine in the Middle East. The Sudanese government rejected the military and political implications of the Eisenhower Doctrine, but discussions over the possibility of aid to assist the Sudan's development programme began in May 1957. An Economic and Technical Aid Agreement was concluded on 31 March 1958.

Meanwhile the Sudan was entering an economic crisis. The 1958 cotton crop was poor; furthermore the world demand for cotton was declining, and prices were falling. A budget deficit of nearly £S3,000,000,[1] the first since 1932, was forecast for 1959. A third development budget for the period 1956–61 amounted to £S137,000,000, and could clearly not be financed out of revenue. The ratification of the American Aid Agreement was thus urgently necessary, but this and other aspects of 'Abdallah Khalil's policy in regard to the West were opposed by the PDP. The support of the southerners had therefore to be sought. They, however, had threatened to boycott the Parliament, in its rôle as a constituent assembly, because the government would not allow the discussion of a federal constitution. 'Abdallah Khalil was forced to compromise on this point which had been the principal southern demand since 1955. In July the bill ratifying the American Aid Agreement was passed, and shortly afterwards, to avert a vote of no-confidence, the Parliament was adjourned until November.

In the sphere of economic development, two important works were undertaken during this period. A great increase was planned in the amount of irrigated land in the Gezira Scheme, known as the Manaqil extension. The first phase of the development was opened in May 1957, while the whole was expected to be completed by 1961–62. On completion, it would almost double the area under irrigation. The filling of the main canal of this extension without the prior consent of the United Arab Republic, in June 1958, led to a protest from the UAR. The first major extension of the railway-system for over a quarter of a century was set in hand with a line branching off from the existing line in Kordofan and running south-westwards to Nyala in Darfur. This was officially opened along its full length on 30 April 1959. Work is now proceeding on a further branch which will run south to Wau in the western Bahr al-Ghazal.

A major educational problem in recent years has been that of the southern Sudan. The integration of the southern educational system, the product of missionary endeavour, with English, not Arabic, as the basic language of instruction, began in 1950, and during the following decade has been pushed on with ever-increasing speed. The southern revolt of August 1955 led to the temporary closure of schools there, but they were reopened in the following year. With the accession to power of a predominantly Muslim government, determined to obliterate as far as possible the cultural and educational differences between the north and the south (a policy which in the circumstances could only mean assimilation to northern practice) the missionary schools as such were clearly doomed. In February 1957, the minister of Education announced that it was the government's intention 'to take direct and full charge of education in the Southern Provinces', and laid down a timetable for taking over the various classes of schools. The absorption of the missionary schools by the government was one of the causes of southern resentment in the second Parliament, and hence contributed to the situation which brought about the Army's *coup d'état*.

CHAPTER XIII

THE ARMY *COUP* AND MILITARY GOVERNMENT

In the Sudan, as in other Middle Eastern countries, the nationalists had at first highly esteemed parliamentary institutions. The Parliament was a token of political maturity, of equality with the former co-domini. Its inception marked the end of the period of foreign authoritarian government. The adoption of parliamentary forms was, however, superficial. In the Sudan, more than in other states of the region, they were a recent importation of alien origin. Even the Advisory Council, with its limited powers, had been created less than a decade before self-government. The mass of the people were swayed in elections by broad general issues, such as union with Egypt or independence, or voted to assert their adherence to personalities rather than programmes. Hence the political parties were groups attached to leaders, or temporary alliances, rather than stable, well-organized groups with definite and distinct objectives. Azhari's skilful opportunism in 1954–55 was a bad introduction to parliamentary government. Under 'Abdallah Khalil in 1958 the tactics of party management were exhausted, and the bankruptcy of the parliamentary system itself stood revealed. In 1954 the control of the administrative machine, which was the traditional and essential institution of government in the Sudan, had passed from a small group of British officials to a small group of Sudanese politicians. In November 1958, a further transfer took place, from the parliamentary politicians to a small group of Army officers.

This was a development which had parallels in other Middle Eastern states which had emerged from foreign rule. It was accelerated in the Sudan by various factors. Parliamentary government was established in the Sudan at the very time when it was crumbling elsewhere in the Middle East; indeed the way had been prepared for it by the Army *coup* of 1952 in Egypt. The period during which the Sudanese regarded it as a panacea and a talisman was correspondingly shortened. It soon lost its appeal, except to those politicians who benefited from the power and patronage it conferred, and they were accordingly isolated from the mass of their countrymen, who regarded their manœuvres with impatience, cynicism or indifference.

The complex political situation, which developed against a background of economic crisis in the summer and autumn of 1958, has been described. The ruling coalition of Umma Party and PDP was clearly about to break up. Two mutually incompatible developments took place. In August it became known that Umma politicians were contacting their former opponents of the NUP over the formation of a new coalition. These negotiations continued during the next two months, and were watched benevolently by Sayyid 'Abd al-Rahman. On the other hand, contacts in Cairo, during October, between the leader of the PDP, President Nasser and Azhari, caused 'Abdallah Khalil to fear that a *rapprochement* was being prepared which would strengthen Egyptian political influence in the Sudan. His mistrust was shared by a small group of senior Army officers, headed by Major-General Ahmad 'Abd al-Wahhab and Brigadier Hasan Bashir Nasr. The possibility of a seizure of power by the Army began to be considered.

Nevertheless, the final agreement to form a coalition between the Umma Party and NUP was concluded on 16 November 1958. It would have been a very powerful combination, since both Sayyid 'Abd al-Rahman and Azhari were in their different ways men of high standing in the nationalist movement and endowed with great popular prestige. But it was never allowed to function. During the following night the government buildings in Khartoum and the radio station in Omdurman were occupied by soldiers, and the ministers were placed under house arrest. Four thousand troops had been moved into the capital on the authority of the commander-in-chief, General Ibrahim 'Abbud. By a completely bloodless *coup d'état* power passed to the soldiers.[1]

It is impossible at present to ascertain the degree of 'Abdallah

Khalil's complicity in, or foreknowledge of, this *coup d'état*. On 10 November he is reported to have had a conversation with 'Abbud in which he deplored the manner in which events seemed to be working for Nasser, and expressed his belief that only the Sudanese Army could stand up to Egypt. After the event, on 26 November, he publicly asserted that he was aware of what was going on in military circles. 'Abbud for his part denied that 'Abdallah Khalil had prior knowledge of the *coup* itself. The two statements are perhaps not incompatible.

On 17 November 'Abbud made a broadcast in which he spoke of 'the state of degeneration, chaos and instability of the country', which he ascribed solely to 'the bitter political strife between parties trying to secure personal gain by all ways and means'. He announced the dissolution of all political parties, the prohibition of assemblies and demonstrations, and the temporary suspension of all newspapers. The new regime would strive to improve relations with the United Arab Republic, 'to resolve all outstanding problems and put an end to the artificial strain which has hitherto subsisted between the two countries'. A series of decrees set up a Supreme Council of the Armed Forces, proclaimed a state of emergency throughout the Sudan, suspended the Transitional Constitution, and dissolved Parliament.

Sudanese parliamentary government, on its extinction, found no defenders, and required no martyrs. Politics since independence had been a private game for the players, rather than a civic education for the people. The new military regime met with no opposition from the religious leaders, nor, with one possible exception, from the political parties. The *coup* was welcomed warmly by Sayyid 'Ali al-Mirghani, with more reservations by Sayyid 'Abd al-Rahman al-Mahdi. Afterwards Sayyid 'Ali again withdrew from politics, while the death of Sayyid 'Abd al-Rahman on 24 March 1959 deprived his followers of the mainspring of their political action. The former ruling group were gently handled; both Azhari and 'Abdallah Khalil were awarded life-pensions of £S1,200 per annum. All in all, the politicians may not have been unwilling to pass to others a situation that was getting beyond their control. The assets of the dissolved political parties were liquidated in May 1959, and the surplus remaining after the payment of claims and the costs of administration was seized by the new government.

The one political group in the Sudan which was organized around a coherent ideology, and was not merely a nexus of personal interests and sectarian loyalties, was the Communist Party. This was in origin a by-product of Egyptian cultural influence, since it was first organized in 1944 among Sudanese students in Cairo. Although the party as such was illegal under both the Condominium and the Republic, it was very active in a number of cover organizations, which were tolerated until the army *coup*. Its supporters were to be found chiefly among the western-educated Sudanese, particularly the students, including those in the schools. It might be said, with some exaggeration, that, outside the lecture-rooms, student life was polarized between the rival ideologies of the Muslim Brotherhood[2] and Communism.[3] The second important area of Communist infiltration was the trade union movement, especially the oldest and most powerful organization, the Railway Workers' Union, and the Sudan Workers' Trade Union Federation founded in 1950.[4] The opposition of both the Federation and the Communists to the Anglo-Egyptian Agreement of February 1953 ran clean against the prevailing national sentiment, and left the Communists isolated. They regained influence with the coming of independence; their appeal to youth was as potent in the conditions of political life under the Republic as during the time of British rule. After the military *coup*, the new government suspended the trade unions and imprisoned the leaders of the Federation. Known Communist sympathizers were rounded up, and their leaders brought before the courts. Investigations to discover Communists among the young Army officers were also set on foot.

The military apparatus for controlling the administration of the Sudan consisted of a Supreme Council of the Armed Forces, composed of twelve officers under Ibrahim 'Abbud as president. This was decreed to be 'the supreme constitutional authority in the Sudan'. It formally delegated to 'Abbud all its legislative, judicial and executive powers, as well as the command of the armed forces. The regime also nominated a Council of Ministers. Of these, seven (including 'Abbud himself as prime minister and minister of Defence) were also members of the Supreme Council, while five (including one southerner) were civilians. Two of the ministers had held office under the parliamentary system. The ministers as such are little more than heads of departments: the formulation of policy takes place within the purely military Supreme Council. The prominent position of 'Abbud in the new regime is misleading. He fulfils the ceremonial functions of a head of state, and his signature is appended to all decrees. If Constitutional Order No. 1 of 17 November 1958 is to be accepted at its face value, he holds by delegation from the Supreme Council the plenary powers of a military dictator. Yet in the events of the succeeding months he has shown himself to be curiously inert, while a struggle for the reality of power has gone on within the Supreme Council itself.

This struggle of competing military factions and personalities occupied the new regime during the first twelve months of its existence. The eleven senior Army officers who, with the president, composed the first Supreme Council were much younger men than 'Abbud, who was commissioned in 1918. They, on the other hand, were close contemporaries, having all been commissioned between 1937 and 1942. During the first months of army rule, the most prominent amongst them was Major-General Ahmad 'Abd al-Wahhab, who had commanded in the operations against the southern mutineers in 1955, and, at the time of the *coup*, was second in command of the Army to 'Abbud. He was appointed to the key security post of minister of the Interior and Local Government. The only officer of equal rank in the Supreme Council was Major-General Muhammad Tal'at Farid, who had been commander of the Southern Area since February 1957, and now took another key post, that of minister of Information and Labour.

The prominence of Ahmad 'Abd al-Wahhab was challenged early in the following year. A senior officer who had not been appointed to the Council was Brigadier Muhyi al-Din Ahmad 'Abdallah, the commander of the Eastern Area. Resenting his exclusion and the predominance of Ahmad 'Abd al-Wahhab, he conspired with the commander of the Northern Area, Brigadier

'Abd al-Rahim Shannan, to bring troops to Khartoum on 2 March 1959. Ahmad 'Abd al-Wahhab was arrested with two supporters, colonels who had been appointed to the Council in spite of their lack of seniority. On the Council's agreeing to consider Muhyi al-Din's demands, the arrested officers were released, and the troops withdrew.

Two days later they were back in somewhat greater strength, since their commanders believed that action was about to be taken against them. Muhyi al-Din and Shannan demanded the resignation of the Supreme Council, on the grounds that the people and Army were dissatisfied with the situation and the policy of the government. Faced with this, the Council resigned and on 5 March an order appeared, over 'Abbud's signature, appointing a new Supreme Council of ten members. This included three new names, the two leaders of the pronunciamento and Brigadier Maqbul al-Amin al-Hajj, the commander of the Central Area. Ahmad 'Abd al-Wahhab was in fact reappointed to the Supreme Council, but on 9 May he was relieved of all his posts. No further action was taken against him, and he retired on pension with a grant of 3,000 acres of state land. Shannan subsequently asserted that 'Abd al-Wahhab had been seeking to make himself president; and that the object of the March incident had been to make 'Abbud a real leader, to solve outstanding problems with the United Arab Republic, and to stop 'foreign interference', which, he claimed, had been encouraged by 'Abd al-Wahhab and 'Abdallah Khalil.

Shannan and Muhyi al-Din had not, however, secured their own predominance. The newcomers to the Supreme Council were a minority faction who failed to make good their standing. On 22 May an obscure incident occurred when two platoons of troops from the Eastern Area arrived outside Khartoum. It was alleged that they had come in response to a telegram from Army Headquarters, and another pronunciamento seemed imminent. Muhyi al-Din at this juncture sent them peaceably back to their stations. It appears that he and Shannan had intended to make a further demonstration of their power, but had disagreed at the last minute, wavered, and lost the initiative.

The opportunity was seized by the rival faction. On 1 June

Muhyi al-Din and Shannan were arrested. Three weeks later they were brought before a court-martial, of which the president was Muhammad Tal'at Farid. They were accused of inciting to mutiny by launching an armed attack on Khartoum on 22 May, with the object of overthrowing the regime. The trial was held in public, and was fully reported in the press. No attempt seems to have been made to gag the accused, who spoke as if they were on the hustings rather than in the dock. They were condemned to death, but on 22 September the sentences were commuted to life imprisonment. Several other officers were dismissed from the Army, while a member of the Supreme Council lost his place and was put on trial for failing to report his knowledge of the mutinous movements.

One further abortive military *coup* took place in 1959. This, which took place on 9 November, originated in the Infantry School at Omdurman, and was headed by a number of young officers. The rising was suppressed without difficulty, and the leaders of the mutiny were brought to trial within a week. Five of them were sentenced to death, and were hanged on 2 December. The executions came as a shock to the Sudanese, who had prided themselves on the bloodless manner in which the army leaders had seized power and settled their internal differences. There have been no further challenges to the regime, and the internal faction struggles seem to have ceased. The most powerful member of the ruling junta seems to be Brigadier Hasan Bashir Nasr, who is the effective head of the Army. The ordinary life of the country appears to be proceeding normally, although observers have perceived signs of suppressed tension and the development of nuclei of opposition among the students and railway workers, and in the circles around the old political leaders. 'Abbud has promised a new constitution, and a committee has been set up to devise one.

It is still too early to hazard any prophecies as to the stability of the military regime or the structure of the future political organization of the Sudan. Perhaps the most that one can say is that the tradition of an authoritarian administration, which was in different forms embodied in the Turco-Egyptian system, the Mahdist state and the Condominium government, is likely to be perpetuated. Again, if past history is anything of a guide, the power of the government, so vast in appearance, will be greatly checked in practice by the geographical and social circumstances in which it has to work. The inherent complexity and ancient traditions of Sudanese society, rather than the paper safeguards of any constitution, are its best safeguards against oppression.

In the meantime, the military regime has brought some apparent benefits. Since the Army assumed power, the economic situation of the Sudan has remarkably improved. This was partly due to a general improvement in world trade since the autumn of 1958, but credit must also be given to a more realistic policy towards the selling of cotton, the principal export crop. Previous governments had insisted on maintaining a fixed stated reserve price, with the result that nearly a quarter of a million bales remained unsold, while a new second crop was expected. The reserve price was abolished in January 1959, and by August both the backlog and the new crop had been sold, although at lower rates than had previously been obtained. At the same time foreign currency reserves were guarded by a rigorous system of import licences. In June 1959 the civilian minister of Finance was able to estimate a surplus of revenue, although admittedly of the low order of £S105,000. Meanwhile the Sudan's sterling reserves rose from £S4.8 millions at the end of 1958 to £S30 millions in August 1959.

The second major achievement of the regime is the successful conclusion of a new Nile Waters Agreement with the United Arab Republic. The attempts of the parliamentary government to secure an agreement finally broke down in January 1958. Negotiations were resumed in October 1959, when the internal faction struggles in the Supreme Council had come to an end. The new agreement was officially concluded a bare month later, on 8 November. The Sudan was to receive £E15 millions in compensation for the land in the vicinity of Wadi Halfa which would be flooded on the completion of the High Dam. After its building, the allocation of water would be 18,500,000,000 cubic metres for the Sudan, as against 55,500,000,000 cubic metres for Egypt, with a margin of 10,000,000,000 cubic metres for evaporation losses. In addition the Sudan would make Egypt an annual 'loan' of 1,500,000,000 cubic metres until 1977, since this quantity is not at present required for irrigation in the Sudan. The Nile Waters Agreement was accompanied by a trading agreement between the two states.

The conclusion of the Nile Waters Agreement should mark the beginning of a new period in Sudanese-Egyptian relations. The independence of the Sudan is an accomplished fact, while the principal material cause of tension between the two countries has now been allayed. Other Sudanese problems remain. In particular, although the south is quiescent the military regime has undertaken no fresh approach to the problem of its relations with the north. Military control on the border of Kenya and Uganda has been stepped up, the integration of the southern and northern educational systems has been continued, some new ventures in economic development have been started. The federal scheme was rejected as decisively by the army officers as by the parliamentary politicians. But no regime can hope to produce a neat programme for dealing with the problem of the south; its solution will be the gradual work of economics and education and, above all, time and patience.

CONCLUSION

G*

CHAPTER XIV

CULTURE AND EDUCATION
IN THE SUDAN

THE ARABIC-SPEAKING, Muslim tribes of the northern
Sudan whom Muhammad 'Ali Pasha brought under his rule
were by no means primitive savages. True, with the decline of
Funj power, the tribe or the clan was the largest effective
political unit: true also that the towns were little more than
agglomerations of villages on sites favourable to the exchange
of merchandise: nevertheless these tribal communities of cultivators and herdsmen possessed a vigorous if rudimentary
culture, and produced a small literate *élite* who were in touch
with the civilization of the great Islamic world. The characteristic figures of traditional Sudanese culture were the poets
and the *fakis*. The poets were the commentators on the vicissitudes of tribal and individual life. Their utterances, generally
brief and intensely allusive, were given in dialect. They spoke
from the heart, and their sayings were passed by word of
mouth, and transmitted to later generations. In our own days
some have been reduced to writing, to puzzle the scholars of
classical Arabic, who cannot hear the staccato deliverance of
the Sudanese speaker behind the uncouth forms.

The *fakis* were the successors of the missionaries and
teachers of the early Funj period, and were a class as varied in
character and attainments as the clerks of medieval Europe. At
the bottom of the scale were social parasites, battening on the
credulity of the ignorant villagers through the superstition
which was common to them. More honest, if little more erudite,
were those who taught the Koran by rote to the children. But
above these were men of wider repute as teachers, who would
read religious and legal texts with serious students from all parts
of the Muslim Sudan. These *faki*-schools, of whatever degree,

were known as *khalwas*.[1] The *fakis'* authority was strengthened by their standing as Sufi adepts, for it is impossible to disentangle the Sufi from the orthodox elements in the traditional Islam of the Sudan. The most notable centre of religious teaching was the town of El Damer, where the Majadhib family had, during the eighteenth century, established what might almost be called an Islamic university, the students of which were in contact with the greater and more famous schools of Cairo and the Hijaz. Students from the Funj dominions were sufficiently numerous to have their own hostel at al-Azhar: learned visitors to Sennar from other Muslim lands were rare but not unknown.

The Turco-Egyptian conquest produced a sharp impact between the traditional Muslim culture of the northern Sudan, and the more legalistic and orthodox Islam of the Ottoman state and hierarchy. The establishment of a judicial hierarchy of *qadis* and *muftis* was, as has been stated earlier, an innovation in the Sudan: the old *faki* class found itself confronted with a new religious *élite*, the official *'ulama'*. Nevertheless the schism was not absolute. If the government paid its religious officials, it also subsidized the more distinguished members of the *faki* class. Men who had studied under Sudanese teachers continued, as in the past, to go on to al-Azhar. Sudanese entered the official religious hierarchy. Thus the old and the new religious *élites* continued to exist side by side: the older one changing little with the passage of years, the newer becoming increasingly accepted as a part of Sudanese society. Even the Mahdia, which may be partially explained as a revolt of the *fakis* against the official *'ulama'*, did not destroy the concept of a religious hierarchy dependent on the ruler. The Mahdi appointed a judge of the former regime as his *qadi al-Islam*, and under the Khalifa an elaborate system of courts and judicial officers developed.

In the same way poetry, the touchstone of Sudanese culture, shows first the impact, then the assimilation, of new influences after the Turco-Egyptian conquest. The traditional dialect poetry still survived, as it does to this day: there is indeed a body of such utterances evoked by the events of the Mahdia. But there also arose in the Sudan poets of a more formal literary type, men of some Arabic scholarship who produced odes composed according to classical canons of grammar, style and metre. This literary poetry was also transmitted orally, but was much more susceptible than the dialect verse of being reduced to writing. It was very closely associated, in the nineteenth century, with the new '*ulama*' class. Of thirteen literary poets listed by a Sudanese writer, nine held judgeships or other posts in the official hierarchy under the Turco-Egyptian regime, the Mahdia or the Condominium; one, whose panegyric on the 'Urabi revolt brought him into disfavour with the British, became an inspector of Arabic in the Ottoman Ministry of Education; and one, who had studied in Cairo, Paris and Turkey, held a series of governorships in the Egyptian Sudan. Six of them studied at al-Azhar.

Throughout this period, there was no comparable efflorescence of prose-writing. The Sudan, in contrast to most other Islamic countries, has produced only a very meagre crop of historical works, although some may have been lost in the vicissitudes of the nineteenth century, and no comprehensive, systematic search for manuscripts has yet been made. There has, however, been published a biographical dictionary of local holy men, written before the Turco-Egyptian conquest, which throws much light on the traditional Islam of the Sudan and on the history of the Funj period. A chronicle of rulers, originally composed early in the Turco-Egyptian period but continued in later recensions down to the reign of Khedive Isma'il, is particularly valuable for the period of Funj decline and the opening phases of the new regime. The characteristic form of traditional Sudanese historical writing is, however, neither the biographical dictionary nor the chronicle, but the genealogy. In this field also there is much room for a systematic search for material, as well as for the formulation of rigorous standards of criticism.

The chief remains of early Sudanese prose that are now available are the official documents of the Funj rulers and the sultans of Darfur. In the absence of field-work, any discussion of these must be on the basis of the very few specimens that have been published. The elaborate titularies and precise phrasing of Funj land-charters of the eighteenth century, clearly indicate the existence of trained clerks working according to well-established precedents. The formal chancery Arabic of both these groups of documents shows that the sophisticated archives of the Mahdist period reflect a tradition older than that of the Turco-Egyptian bureaucracy.

From the time of Muhammad 'Ali Pasha onwards, Egypt was receptive to the culture of Western Europe. The principal instrument of this reception was the educational system devised by the viceroy in connection with his remodelling of the Egyptian army and administration. Thus there developed in Egypt a system of state schools, providing the personnel for the new state, side by side with the older Islamic institutions, which were training-grounds for the '*ulama*'. This development was but feebly reflected in the Egyptian Sudan. No schools were established there while Muhammad 'Ali lived. 'Abbas I, otherwise unsympathetic to the westernizing projects of his predecessor, ordered a school to be set up in Khartoum, but his motive seems to have been to provide an excuse for banishing a distinguished Egyptian scholar, Rifa'a Bey Rafi ' al-Tahtawi, who had been the head of Muhammad 'Ali's department of translation. Rifa'a was to be headmaster of the school in Khartoum, but the project was not supported by the governor-general, while it was disliked by the Sudanese, who feared it might lead to the conscription of their sons. When 'Abbas died, and Muhammad Sa'id recalled Rifa'a, the school seems to have faded out. In education, as in other aspects of development, Khedive Isma'il endeavoured to continue the work of Muhammad 'Ali. He encouraged the entry of Sudanese students into al-Azhar, and, in 1867 and 1868, set up primary schools in Khartoum, Berber and Dongola. The pupils went into government service as telegraph and dockyard apprentices. The further history of these schools, and of one or two others which were started, is obscure.

The impact of Western ideas and Western education upon the Sudanese did not come until the establishment of the Condominium. The establishment and history of the Gordon Memorial College and other educational institutions have already been mentioned in connection with the political history of the Sudan: here it is proposed to consider in more general terms the effect of a British-inspired educational system on the Sudanese community.

Sir James Currie, who laid the foundations of the system, lacked neither ideals nor insight, as his comments on the developments of the twenties show. He was, however, working with meagre funds within limits dictated by administrative convenience. The Gordon College and other schools established in his time had a very small intake, and their curricula were consciously planned, not to give a liberal education, but to provide adequately trained government employees. The danger of creating a large educated class, in excess of what could be absorbed by the administration, was thus avoided, but by the later thirties the demand for education could no longer be contained. The government schools were supplemented by schools founded by public subscription, which did not always find it easy to maintain educational standards. At the end of the Second World War, a considerable expansion of the government educational system began. A new secondary school near Omdurman succeeded to the functions, but not to the name, of the old Gordon Memorial College. Another was opened in 1946, a third in 1949. These were the precursors of a great increase of schools at all levels, secondary, intermediate and elementary, which has continued until the present day. Yet in spite of these developments, and of assistance received from outside agencies, such as UNESCO, universal compulsory education is not yet feasible. Apart from the financial and material problems of providing and staffing schools, the Sudan has the particular difficulties of a vast but sparsely populated country, with a considerable nomadic element in its peoples.

As the Sudan climbed out of the depression of the early thirties, more money became available, and a more liberal attitude began to show itself on the part of the Sudan Government. A rethinking of the aims and methods of education was urgently necessary. The progress of educational thought in Britain was not reflected in the Sudanese schools, which were still tied to the narrow and utilitarian objectives of Currie's day. Education had long suffered from its dependence on the administration: too few British officials in the Department combined authority and professional knowledge. How much of the spirit of modern education was absent from the Sudan of those days can be seen from the reactions of a young Lebanese, an Oxford graduate, who came to teach in the Gordon College in 1926:

'. . . I disliked the Gordon College the moment I walked into it. It was a military, not a human institution. It was a Government School in a country where the Government was an alien colonial government. The [British] Tutors were members of the Political Service. They were there in the dual capacity of masters and rulers, and the second capacity over-shadowed the first. The pupils were expected to show them not the ordinary respect owed by pupils to their teachers, but the submissiveness demanded of a subject. . . . Even if the master was individually kind and human, there stood behind him, in the eyes of his pupils, the Director of Education, the Civil Secretary, the Governor-General, the Union Jack, and the power of the British Government. Behind him there also stood the District Commissioner who ruled their village homes. The master himself, indeed, would one day be a District Commissioner and rule over them and their fathers.'[2]

During the thirties, a new spirit developed in the Gordon College, and this was inherited by the secondary schools which succeeded it at the end of the Second World War. The quasi-military system of discipline was humanized. The College was no longer a barracks with some of the outward trappings of an English public school. At the same time, the British masters ceased to be political officers in embryo, and were recruited (in spite of wartime difficulties after 1939) from professional gradu-ate teachers. The gulf which had existed between the British and non-British staff was bridged, while teachers and pupils entered on a more normal and rational academic relationship. Experiment in syllabuses and teaching-methods was encouraged.

These developments were hastened by G. C. Scott, warden of the College from 1937 to 1943. Formerly a member of the Political Service, he found his vocation and life's work in teaching. His enthusiasm and liberal outlook inspired the new generation of Sudanese and British teachers. The College, which had shed its intermediate classes in 1924, and its technical workshops in 1932, acquired during Scott's wardenship the full status of an academic secondary school. In 1938 some selected senior pupils were entered for the Cambridge School Certificate, which in the course of a few years became the final examination for all secondary classes. Secondary education has, however, remained a four-year course, with nothing comparable to the work of English sixth forms. An attempt to lengthen the secondary phase, by selection of pupils at an earlier age from the intermediate schools, was defeated by the force of public opinion in the last decade of the Condominium.

The Gordon College was, however, no longer the limit of the educational system in the Sudan. Apart from the Kitchener School of Medicine, from which sixty doctors had graduated between 1928 and 1939, there was established after 1936 a group of 'Higher Schools' giving post-secondary education with the object of training Sudanese officials for the more responsible posts in government service. These Schools of Agriculture, Arts, Engineering, Law, Science and Veterinary Science were, in 1945, fused into a single institution, to which the name of the Gordon Memorial College was transferred. A number of its students took external degrees of London University. In 1951 the new Gordon College was combined with the Kitchener School of Medicine to form the University College of Khartoum. The special relationship with London continued until shortly after the Sudan became independent. The *Khartoum University Act* of June 1956 transformed the college into a degree-giving university, maintained financially by the government but enjoying administrative autonomy. The teaching staff, at first largely British, has been increasingly sudanized as qualified men have become available, but still includes many expatriates from nearly every country in Europe, and a great many in Asia. The first Sudanese vice-chancellor took office in 1958.

Before the establishment of the Higher Schools, small groups of Sudanese students had been sent by the government to foreign universities. In the inter-war years such student missions had gone chiefly to the American University of Beirut, and were composed of the most promising recruits to the Education Department. Just before the outbreak of the Second World War, the first Sudanese students came to Britain, where they were trained at the University College of the South-West (now the University of Exeter). The expansion and rising standards of post-secondary education in the Sudan during and after the following decade was reflected in an increasing flow of students to British universities and centres for specialist training, and this has in no way slackened or diminished with the coming of independence. The development of this educated *élite* has facilitated the sudanization of posts in the University of Khartoum and the schools, as well as in the various technical government services. In addition, many Sudanese students have made their way to Egyptian schools and universities, where they were particularly welcomed from the mid-thirties onwards, as tension grew between the two co-domini.

Elementary education had long been the Cinderella of the government system. The teachers were inadequately trained, and had too limited a background of general education to breathe life into the subjects they taught. Literate only in Arabic, and for the most part village-dwellers, they lacked the status of the new English-educated, urban intelligentsia, while their functions were alien to the traditional communities in which they worked. They were given guidance from the Education Department in the form of teaching-notes, and periodically their schools were visited by British inspectors, but the sparse material available was instilled by the traditional method of rote-learning, and inspections amounted to no more than a display of memorized information. A watchful eye over the schools was kept by the district commissioners, many of whom had some mistrust of education, and discouraged any developments which might threaten the traditional structure of life and authority.

The opportunity for reforms in the elementary schools was an indirect result of the Gordon College strike of 1931.[3] A committee of inquiry was set up, which was persuaded to extend its terms of reference to the lower stages of education. One of the committee's recommendations was the transfer of the Training College for elementary teachers from Khartoum into rural surroundings. The principalship of the new institution was given to V. L. Griffiths, who had been appointed as an inspector of education in 1931, after teaching experience in India. Griffiths's early tours of inspection had shown him the weaknesses and faults of the elementary school. He hoped that by giving teacher-training a fresh start, in surroundings similar to those in which the schoolmasters would have to work, the next generation of teachers would develop initiative and a sense of profession which at that time they lacked. The site he selected for his college was in open country near Dueim, which had lost its importance as the White Nile port since the construction of the railway, but was still a provincial town of some importance. The choice was unpopular with most Sudanese (as later with some British) staff. In Sudanese opinion, towns are the true centres of civilization: there is no sentimental affection for the countryside, which is synonymous with austere living, poverty and backwardness. Furthermore, Bakht er Ruda, as the site is called, is malarial, and, especially in the rainy season of late summer and autumn, far more isolated than its relative proximity to Khartoum would suggest.

Nevertheless the scheme had the backing of the government, which was still at this time strong enough to override public opinion, and the college, later known as the Institute of Education, was carried through its initial difficulties and hardships. Its original purpose was simply the training of elementary teachers, but Griffiths soon realized that they and their pupils could not be expected to adopt more enlightened methods of study without a far wider range of Arabic books than was available. So within the course of a few years, book-production became a principal activity of the staff. These were carefully tested in draft and revised, so that by 1950, when Griffiths left the Sudan, over 120 publications for the elementary schools had appeared. At the same time, and in spite of the staffing and other problems of the war-years, the objectives of elementary education had been redefined, and new teaching-methods devised which diluted, even if they could not completely eliminate, the old mechanical ways of learning. The training given in full and refresher courses was followed up by tours of inspection by Bakht er Ruda staff. From the first, there was close co-operation between the British and the Sudanese members of staff, and a vital part in the development of the Institute was played by the vice-principal, 'Abd al-Rahman 'Ali Taha, who left in 1948, after twelve years' service, to be the first Sudanese minister of Education.

While reforms were thus proceeding in the curricula and methods at the elementary and secondary levels, the intermediate schools remained almost static. Although the language of instruction in these schools was Arabic, a considerable proportion of the teaching-time was given to English. The intermediate teachers formed an important part of the Western-educated class, and transfers of staff from intermediate to secondary level were frequent. There was therefore a natural link between these two phases of the educational system, and British teachers of English in the old Gordon College (and the secondary schools which succeeded it) played an important part in training and inspecting intermediate teachers of English.

A general reform of intermediate education could, however, only be undertaken by an institution with the resources and accumulated experience of Bakht er Ruda. This new problem was first tackled in 1939, but the programme of reform met with many difficulties and setbacks. Its initiation was during the war-years, when British staff were scarce and hard to obtain. The trainees were more westernized and sophisticated than the potential elementary teachers. Coming to the Institute of Education after four years of secondary education, followed by a period of more advanced work in the Higher Schools, they did not take kindly to the austerities and isolation of Bakht er Ruda. Many of them had no real heart for intermediate teaching: they saw wider opportunities of entering secondary education or other branches of government service opening before them, as a consequence of the great expansion, and the movement towards sudanization that began during the war. As the intermediate schools continued to expand, their staffs had to be eked out with recruits from other government departments, who were given short training-courses at Bakht er Ruda. Furthermore, the intermediate schools themselves provided the bulk of the recruits for the lower grades of public service, while providing an avenue for a minority of pupils to secondary and higher education. Hence public opinion was opposed to change in the long-established pattern of studies and organization, since these might interfere with prospects of employment, or otherwise adversely affect the future of the pupils. This attitude forced the abandonment of the Brown Plan, which would have creamed off the pupils suitable for academic secondary education at the end of the second year in the intermediate schools.

Nevertheless, before the end of the Condominium, intermediate reform had overcome its first setbacks. Syllabuses were being reorganized, and text books written, on the same lines as for the elementary schools. After a period of experiment, courses had been designed to prepare the various kinds of recruits for teaching in intermediate schools. Meanwhile the expansion of education at all levels led to the foundation of branches of the Institute of Education at Dilling (in the Nuba Mountains) in 1948, and later at Shendi.

One of the special educational problems of the Sudan is that of protecting the ex-elementary schoolboy from relapsing into illiteracy, for lack of adequate and available reading-matter. Newspapers have small circulations, and reach the outlying villages but slowly, if at all. Books are expensive and hard to obtain, outside two or three of the chief towns. The style and language of literary works present difficulties to the young or unsophisticated reader. To meet the need for cheap and readable matter a Publications Bureau was opened at Bakht er Ruda in 1946, and transferred in the following year to Khartoum. In 1948 another was opened in Juba for the southern provinces. The output of these Bureaus has been very considerable, and has done much to supplement the formal education of the Sudanese. The most successful production of the original Publications Bureau has been a fortnightly youth magazine, sold through schools and local merchants. Its sales far exceed those of even the most popular newspapers. Another attempt to maintain literacy is a series of very simple illustrated storybooks, intended for those who have not even had a full elementary education.

Apart from the Publications Bureaus, there is an independent press, which has had a longer history. The rise of Sudanese nationalism in the thirties, and its intensification in the post-war period, was reflected in an increasing output of news-papers, which have been conceived primarily as vehicles of political ideas. The oldest of the daily papers still existing was founded in 1935. Before the army *coup d'état*, thirty-five daily and weekly papers were listed in the *Directory of the Republic of the Sudan*. Of these, five were founded between 1935 and 1945, twenty between 1946 and 1955, and ten since the coming of independence. Recent years have also seen the publication of literary and historical works and memoirs. A number of Sudanese scholars, graduates of British universities, have pub-lished works in English on topics relating to the Sudan.

Girls' education, in the Sudan as in England, got off to a much slower start. The comparative lack of educational oppor-tunity for women in Islamic countries has been the subject of frequent criticism by Western Christian observers. Much of this criticism has been emotional and superficial; the ascription of female inferiority to Islam as a religion is in particular a crude over-simplification of a complex sociological phenomenon. It should also be remembered that in the Sudan, as elsewhere, lack of formal education has not prevented women from acquiring a dominating position and profound influence in domestic and social life.

At the outset the Sudan Government, conscious of the dangers arising from interference with established social usages, made no provision for girls' education. The pioneer work was done by individuals outside the official system. Shaykh Babikr Badri, after fighting in the Mahdist wars, had settled down as a merchant at Rufa'a on the Blue Nile. Here the provincial authorities helped him to set up an elementary school for boys, to which he unofficially added a girls' department, at first for his own daughters. In 1910 his girls' school received official recognition, and was in due course followed by others, directly under government auspices. The demand for girls' education at a higher level was slow to develop: the first intermediate school was opened in 1938, and the first secondary school in 1949. There are now twenty-three and two intermediate and secondary schools respectively. Some Sudanese parents had for years been sending their daughters to the privately established Christian schools. Best known of these was the Unity High

School, which had grown out of a school for Coptic (Christian) girls founded in 1902 by the Rev. Llewellyn H. Gwynne, later the Anglican Bishop in Egypt and the Sudan. At first this gave primary education, but in 1928 it was reorganized as a secondary school. The entry of women into the university came with surprising speed. The first was admitted in 1945: by 1957 there were twenty-five, the majority of whom lived in a newly-built hostel.

In spite of the great increase in educational opportunity in the last two decades, the Sudanese who have received a formal education in the Western sense remain a minority. The traditional *khalwas* still exist, and for many have been the first rung in the educational ladder. Some of the better ones are subsidized by the provincial authorities (a practice for which there were precedents in the Turco-Egyptian period) and are known as sub-grade schools. Their teachers are now instructed in the use of the handbooks provided by Bakht er Ruda for elementary schools. More recently, a determined attack has been made on the problem of illiteracy. In 1948 the Publications Bureau launched the first mass literacy campaign among adults. There now exists a full-scale department for adult education in the Ministry of Education, responsible for the organization of literacy campaigns, the supervision of boys' clubs, welfare work amongst women, and experimental schemes of village improvement.

The preceding review of education during and after the Condominium period may give the impression that the Sudanese tradition has become dominated by the British cultural legacy. This is by no means true. In the first place, acquaintance with the Western, and more specifically the British, cultural achievement, as distinct from mere literacy in English, is possessed only by the *élite* who have had a secondary or higher education. Secondly, even to the great majority of this *élite*, the Western tradition and outlook remain essentially alien: there is a dislocation between their Muslim, Arab tradition, nurtured from their earliest years by their environment, and appealing to their deepest emotions, and the academic and technical skills, laboriously acquired through the medium of a foreign language.

This has produced certain tensions, both in individuals and in Sudanese society as a whole. Generally speaking, the Western-educated student has tended to solve the internal conflict by putting the two traditions into separate compartments of his being, applying the Western attitudes and response to the demands of his public and official life, and relaxing at other times into more congenial ways of thought and behaviour. Within Sudanese society, the tension takes the form of lack of understanding between the generations, a loss of authority by the older peoples, a tendency for the more immature members of the educated *élite* to acquire habits of intellectual arrogance. These are, of course, not problems peculiar to the Sudan. The difficulty of reconciling two widely divergent attitudes is paralleled by the conflict between science and religion, which has long beset the West. Misunderstanding between the generations is an ancient social theme. The Sudanese are exceptional only in the rapidity with which these conflicts have come upon them: virtually within the space of two generations, and, to an acute degree, even within the last quarter of a century.

The Muslim, Arab tradition within the Sudan is, moreover, not an inert residual deposit from the past. It is an active and developing factor, constantly stimulated by the cultural renaissance of the Middle East, which has now been in progress for about a century. As we have seen above, new elements were added to this aspect of Sudanese culture during the Turco-Egyptian period, and fresh influences began to pour into the Sudan from the time of the Reconquest. A clear distinction must always be drawn between the significance of Egypt to the Sudan as a political power on the one hand, and as the mediator of Arab and Muslim culture on the other. The political record of Egypt in the Sudan is chequered, and it seems unlikely that the Sudanese will ever again willingly accept Egyptian political control. The cultural influence of Egypt has, by contrast, been almost wholly beneficent, and the Muslim Sudanese have indeed been fortunate that, while lying on the periphery of the Islamic world, they have had as their neighbour one of the greatest centres of the Faith and, in more recent times, the principal focus of the Arabic renaissance. Culturally, the position of Egypt *vis-à-vis* the Sudan is not unlike that of France and the German states in the eighteenth century. The mediation of Egyptian Arab and Muslim culture to the Sudan goes back to the work of the missionary teachers of the Funj period. It entered a second phase with the Egyptian and Egyptian-trained *'ulama'* of the Turco-Egyptian regime. In its most recent and most successful phase, its most effective agents have been not so much persons, schools or colleges, as the abundant products of the Egyptian printing presses, Egyptian films, and the broadcasts of the Egyptian radio.

The independent Sudan is faced with a political, a social and a cultural situation each of great complexity. The integration of the north and the south, the harmonious combination of the educated *élite* and the unsophisticated tribesmen, the reconciliation of the Arab and Western cultural traditions—these are the basic problems which underlie the external phenomena of political history. As in so many other situations in the modern world, time and patience are essential to their solution. Although the political leaders occupy the centre of the stage, the work of nation-building depends less upon them than upon more obscure figures, the successors of the past saints and teachers, who since the times of Ghulamallah al-Rikabi and Dushayn have laboured to kindle the fire of learning, and bring justice to a vast and remote land.

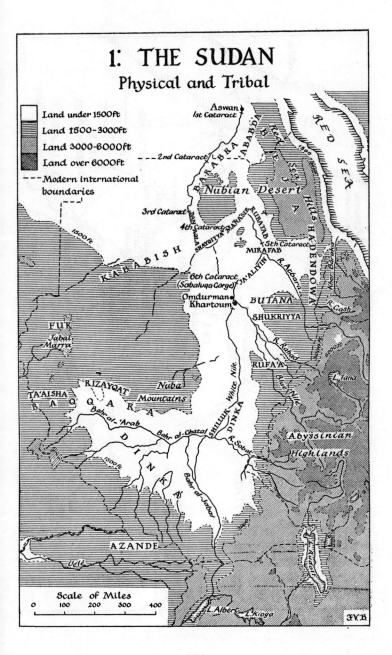

1: THE SUDAN
Physical and Tribal

Land under 1500ft
Land 1500-3000ft
Land 3000-6000ft
Land over 6000ft
Modern international boundaries

Aswan
1st Cataract

2nd Cataract

BARABRA

ABABDA

RED SEA

Nubian Desert

RED SEA HILLS

3rd Cataract

4th Cataract

SHAYQIYYA MANASIR

RUBATAB

5th Cataract

MIRAFAB

HADENDOWA

R. Atbara

1500ft

KABABISH

6th Cataract
(Sabaluqa Gorge)

JA'ALIYIN

R. Gash

Omdurman
Khartoum

BUTANA

SHUKRIYYA

R. Rahad

FUR

Jabal
Marra

RIZAYQAT

Nuba
Mountains

White Nile

RUFA'A

L. Tana

Blue Nile

TA'AISHA

BAQQARA

Bahr al-'Arab

Bahr al-Ghazal

SHILLUK

DINKA

Abyssinian
Highlands

DINKA

R. Sobat

Bahr al-Jabal

AZANDE

Uele

R. Kafu

Scale of Miles
0   100   200   300   400

L. Albert   L. Kioga

J.V.B.

207

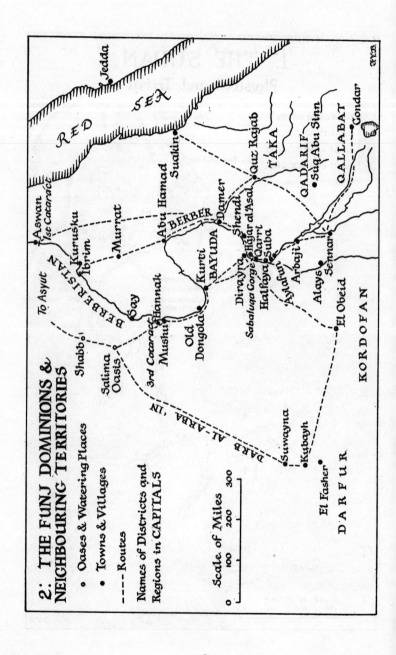

2: THE FUNJ DOMINIONS & NEIGHBOURING TERRITORIES

○ Oases & Watering Places
● Towns & Villages
---- Routes

Names of Districts and
Regions in CAPITALS

Scale of Miles
0 100 200 300

RED SEA

Jedda

Aswan
1st Cataract
Kurusku
Korim
Murrat

BERBERISTAN

To Asyut

Shabb
Satima
Oasis

3rd Cataract
Mushut
Hannak
Say

Old Dongola
Kurti
BAYUDA

Abu Hamad
BERBER
Damer
Shendi
Dirayra
Sabaluga Gorge
Halfaya
Hajar al'Asal
Qarri
Suba
'Aylafun
Arbaji
Alays
Sennar

Suakin

Guz Rajab
TAKA

QADARIF
Suq Abu Sinn
QALLABAT

Condar

El Obeid

KORDOFAN

DARB AL-ARBA'IN

Suwayna
Kybayh

El Fasher

DARFUR

208

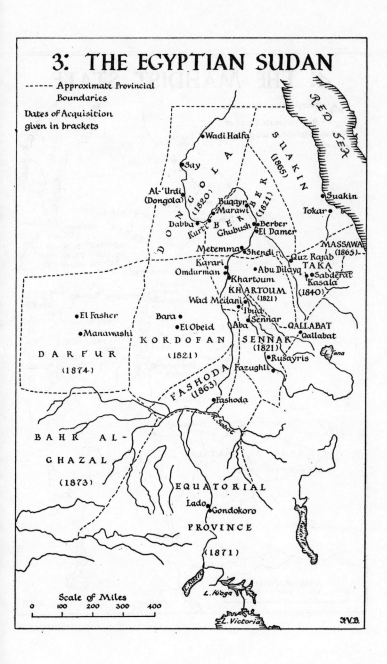

3: THE EGYPTIAN SUDAN

----- Approximate Provincial
       Boundaries

Dates of Acquisition
given in brackets

RED SEA

•Wadi Halfa

•Say

SUAKIN
(1865)

Al-'Urdi
(Dongola)

DONGOLA
(1820)

Buqayr
Marawi

BERBER
(1821)

•Suakin

Dabba
Kurti
Ghubush

Berber
El Damer

Tokar

MASSAWA
(1865)

Metemma
•Shendi

Kurari
Omdurman

•Quz Rajab

TAKA

Abu Dilayq

•Sabderat
Kasala
(1840)

Khartoum
KHARTOUM
(1821)

Wad Medani

•El Fasher

Bara•

•Ibud
Sennar

QALLABAT

•Qallabat

Aba

•Manawashi

•El Obeid

KORDOFAN
(1821)

SENNAR
(1821)

•Rusayris

L. Tana

DARFUR
(1874)

FASHODA
(1863)

Fazughli

•Fashoda

BAHR AL-

R. Sobat

GHAZAL
(1873)

EQUATORIAL

Lado•
•Gondokoro

PROVINCE
(1871)

Scale of Miles

0   100   200   300   400

R. Nile

L. Kioga

L. Victoria

H.V.B.

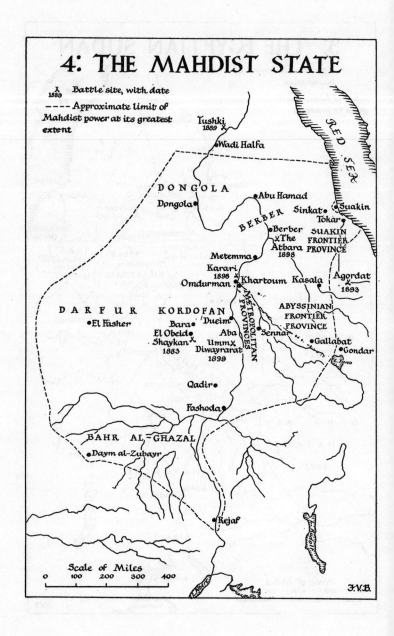

4: THE MAHDIST STATE

X 1889   Battle site, with date

--- Approximate limit of Mahdist power at its greatest extent

RED SEA

Tushki
1889 X

Wadi Halfa

DONGOLA

Dongola •

• Abu Hamad

BERBER   Sinkat •   • Suakin
Tokar •

• Berber   SUAKIN
X The   FRONTIER
Atbara   PROVINCE
1898

Metemma •

Karari
1898 X
Omdurman •   • Khartoum   Kasala •   • Agordat
1893

METROPOLITAN PROVINCES

DARFUR   KORDOFAN   ABYSSINIAN
FRONTIER
• El Fasher   Bara •   Dueim •   PROVINCE

El Obeid •   Aba
Shaykan X   Umm X   Sennar •   • Gallabat
1883   Diwayrarat   • Gondar
1899   El Fona

Qadir •

Fashoda •

BAHR AL-GHAZAL

• Daym al-Zubayr

Rejaf •

Scale of Miles
0   100   200   300   400

J.V.B.

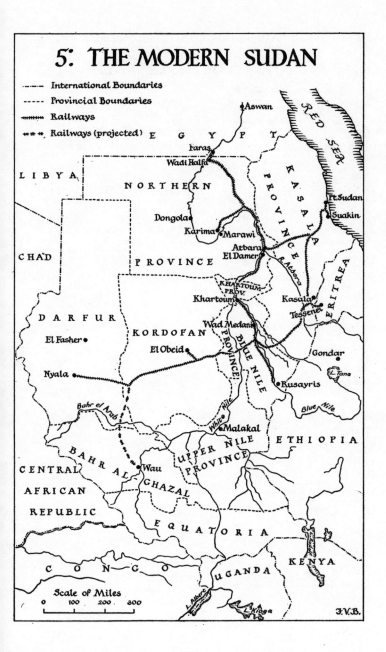

5: THE MODERN SUDAN

- --‒-- International Boundaries
- ‒‒‒‒ Provincial Boundaries
- ᴗᴗᴗᴗ Railways
- ⧓⧓⧓ Railways (projected)

LIBYA

EGYPT

•Aswan

•Faras

Wadi Halfa•

NORTHERN

RED SEA

KASALA

PROVINCE

•Pt.Sudan

•Suakin

Dongola•

Karima• •Marawi

Atbara•

El Damer•

CHAD

PROVINCE

R. Atbara

KHARTOUM
PROV.

Khartoum•

ERITREA

Kasala•

Tessenei•

DARFUR

KORDOFAN

Wad Medani•

El Fasher •

El Obeid•

BLUE NILE

•Gondar

Nyala •

PROVINCE

L. Tana

•Rusayris

Bahr el Arab

White Nile

Blue Nile

•Malakal

ETHIOPIA

BAHR AL

UPPER NILE

PROVINCE

CENTRAL

•Wau

GHAZAL

AFRICAN

REPUBLIC

EQUATORIA

CONGO

KENYA

UGANDA

Scale of Miles

0 100 200 300

L. Albert

L. Kioga

J.V.B.

NOTES

CHAPTER I: THE LAND AND THE PEOPLE

1. In 1823, the *defterdar* Muhammad Bey Khusraw was entitled 'commander-in-chief of the Sudan and of Kordofan'. Ten years later, 'Ali Khurshid Pasha was given the title of 'governor of the provinces of the Sudan', perhaps the first official usage of the term in something like its modern sense. The Ottoman sultan's *ferman* to Muhammad 'Ali Pasha in 1841 did not mention the Sudan as such, but recognized him as vassal ruler of Nubia, Darfur (which had not then been conquered), Kordofan and Sennar 'with all their dependencies'.
2. Barabra, the plural of *Barbari* (in English, Berberine) is the name given to the Nubians of this region. See further, Ch. II, note 3.
3. Habesh, from the Arabic *Bilad al-Habash*, 'the Land of the Abyssinians', was the name of the Ottoman province on the Red Sea corresponding to parts of the modern Sudanese and Eritrean littoral. The Abyssinian hinterland was never conquered by the Ottomans. See p. 25.
4. Arbaji was an important town from the sixteenth to the eighteenth century. It was visited by Bruce, the Scottish traveller, in 1772, and was devastated by its own ruler in 1783–84.
5. *Makk* was a title given to the vassal-kings under the suzerainty of the Funj sultan.
6. John Lewis Burckhardt, a Swiss by birth, visited Shendi in 1814.

CHAPTER II: BEFORE THE TURCO-EGYPTIAN CONQUEST

1. The treaty was known as the *baqt*, from the Latin *pactum*. It is of importance in Muslim law because it fell outside the usual category of treaties whereby non-Muslims capitulated to Muslims. Here, on the contrary, the terms of the treaty showed that the Nubians negotiated on equal terms with the Muslims.
2. Banu Kanz, i.e. 'the children of Kanz', because the tribal chiefs bore the honorific of *Kanz al-Dawla*, 'The Treasure of the State'. Their modern representatives are the Kunuz in Egyptian Nubia.
3. The root *barbar* has the sense of making an incomprehensible noise, and its derivatives were applied by the Arabs in Africa to non-Arabic speakers, e.g. the Berbers in North Africa, and the Berberines (*Barabra*) of Lower Nubia.
4. See above, p. 9. The accepted version describes an alliance of 'Abdallah Jamma' and the Funj under 'Amara Dunqas (see p. 19), and places the capture of Suba in 1504–5. This, however, cannot be traced beyond a nineteenth-century chronicle. Other evidence (see p. 29) would suggest that 'Abdallah Jamma' flourished in the second half of the fifteenth century, and that the taking of Suba was a purely Arab achievement, anterior to the coming of the Funj.

5. *Wad* is a colloquialism for *walad*, meaning 'son of'. It is the equivalent in Sudanese usage of the more dignified classical *ibn*.

6. The coexistence of the ancient free aristocracy and the more recent servile aristocracy was noted by Bruce:

   'At the establishment of this monarchy, the king, and the whole nation of Shillook were Pagans. They . . . took the name of Funge, which they interpret sometimes lords, or conquerors, and, at other times, free citizens. All that can be said with certainty of this term . . . is, that it is applicable to those only that have been born east of the Bahar el Abiad. It does not seem to me that they should pride themselves in being free citizens, because the first title of nobility in this country is that of slave; indeed there is no other. . . . All titles and dignities are undervalued, and pre-carious, unless they are in the hands of one who is a slave. Slavery in Sennaar is the only true nobility.' (*Travels*, Vol. vi, pp. 371–2.)

   The 'Bahar el Abiad' (*al-Bahr al-Abyad*) is the White Nile.

7. Of the Hamaj in the kingdom of Sennar, the Funj Chronicle (Arabic text, ed. M. Shibeika, *Ta'rikh muluk al-Sudan*, Khartoum 1947), makes the inter-esting statement that 'they are a group of the offspring of the Arabs who are the progeny of the Nubians, and alternatively it is said that they are a branch of the 'Awadiyya Ja'aliyin'. The former statement suggests that the Hamaj were arabized autochthons; the latter does not really contradict this, since (as has been suggested above, p. 6) the Ja'aliyin are really arabized Nubians.

8. Bruce, *Travels*, Vol. vi, p. 345.

9. *Arbab* was a title held by some high Funj notables.

10. Slatin, *Fire and sword in the Sudan*, p. 42.

11. Browne, *Travels*, p. 212.

12. *Defterdar* was the title of the chief financial official in Ottoman Egypt.

13. *Maqdum* was the title held by a personal representative of the sultan of Darfur who acted as a provincial governor.

14. *Dar al-harb* and *dar al-Islam* ('the land of Islam') are Muslim legal terms. The former is used of territory belonging to non-Muslims who have not been subdued by Islam; the latter, of territory in which Islamic law is in full force.

15. The Sufis are Muslims who follow systems of mystical devotion. They are grouped in a large number of religious orders, distinguished by varieties of devotional practice. Members of these orders are generally referred to in English works as 'dervishes', a term derived from the Turkish form of a Persian word meaning mendicant. The followers of the Sudanese Mahdi were popularly referred to as dervishes, but he rejected the term.

16. There are four recognized schools or systems (sometimes misleadingly called 'rites') of Muslim law, which are followed by the Sunni majority of Muslims. The three which will appear in this book are known, after their medieval founders, as the Maliki, Shafi'i and Hanafi schools. Their legal doctrines differ mainly on minor points. The Maliki school is generally followed in North and West Africa and Upper Egypt, whence it seems to have come to the Sudan. The Shafi'i school is strong in Lower Egypt. The Hanafi school was that officially followed by the jurists of the Ottoman Empire; hence its doctrines were applied by the courts in Egypt after the Ottoman conquest in 1517. After the Turco-Egyptian conquests in the Sudan, the Hanafi school similarly became official there. It was abrogated during the Mahdia, but restored with the establishment of the Condominium. So today the Muslim

judiciary in the Sudan officially follows the Hanafi school, although the individual adherence of most Sudanese Muslims is to the Maliki system.

17. *Qadi al-'adala* is usually translated as 'the just judge'; but *'adala* is a technical term in Islamic law, and implies good moral and legal standing. Hence Dushayn may have been remembered as the jurist who familiarized the subjects of the Funj with the concept of *'adala*.

18. Funj Chronicle, tr. MacMichael, *History of the Arabs*, Vol. ii, p. 244.

CHAPTER III: THE INAUGURATION OF THE TURCO-EGYPTIAN REGIME: 1820–25

1. English, *Narrative*, 21.
2. Waddington and Hanbury, *Journal*, 98.
3. The name of Berber was at this time applied only to the district inhabited by the Mirafab. The complex of villages on the right bank, the predecessors of the modern town of Berber, had no common name. At the time of the conquest the village of Nasr al-Din was the effective capital of the district. Fifty years earlier, at the time of Bruce's visit, the capital had been Gooz (*al-Quz*), another village in the complex.
4. English, *Narrative*, 140.
5. This was the two-horned cap (*taqiyya umm qarnayn*) which was the particular symbol of authority in the Funj state. See above, p. 31.
6. English, *Narrative*, 159–60.
7. The date (17 Rajab 1136) is given by Jabarti (*'Aja'ib al-athar*, iv, 318) who also makes it clear that the objective of the expedition was Darfur, not merely Kordofan.
8. Stories of the capricious cruelty of the *defterdar* were told to the British traveller, John Petherick, who visited Kordofan in 1847.
9. El Fasher (*al-Fashir*) means literally the courtyard before the royal palace, and was used for the successive residences of the sultans of Darfur. With the final settlement of the royal residence in the late eighteenth century, the name came to be applied to the town which grew up around the palace.
10. *Mu'allim* (Arabic; 'teacher') was the regular title of Christians and Jews under Ottoman rule.
11. Hill gives the sterling equivalent of the taxes as £2 5s., £1 10s., and 15s., respectively. He states that the current price at Sennar of a male slave was £3, while that of a milch cow was £14s. *Egypt in the Sudan*, 14–15.
12. MacMichael, *History of the Arabs*, ii, 420.
13. MacMichael, *History of the Arabs*, ii, 422, places Umm 'Uruq 'on the west bank of the White Nile close to the site of the present Commandania of Omdurmán'. Shibeika, *Ta'rikh*, Notes, p. 21, thinks that it may have been a village on the Nile between Khartoum and Shendi. The Funj Chronicle distinguishes between Umm 'Uruq and Omdurman (*Umm Durman*).
14. The name of Khartoum (*al-Khartum*) means 'the elephant's trunk'.

CHAPTER IV: SETTLEMENT AND STAGNATION: 1825–62

1. Translated from Shibeika's edition of the Funj Chronicle. The passage is omitted in MacMichael's translation.

2. Kanfu was the paternal uncle of the future King Theodore, who made himself ruler of Abyssinia in 1855 and committed suicide at the time of Sir Robert Napier's expedition to Magdala in 1868.

3. Ahmad Abu Widan was probably of Circassian Mamluk origin. He served in Muhammad 'Ali Pasha's forces in Arabia, Greece, Syria and the Sudan. Recalled from the Sudan after a difference of opinion with Khurshid, he was for a time minister of War in Egypt.

4. *Hükümdar* had long been used in Turkish in the sense of sovereign or ruler. It had not hitherto possessed any precise administrative significance, and, in the sense of governor-general, was a neologism. Muhammad 'Ali also, in 1832, conferred this title on his governor-general in Syria (information supplied by Dr M. Abu Hakima of the University of Khartoum).

5. Khurshid was appointed governor of Adana, a province at this time controlled by Muhammad 'Ali Pasha, in consequence of his successful war against the Ottoman Sultan Mahmud II. He died in 1845, in the post of governor of the Egyptian province of the Sharqiyya.

6. During the winter of 1838–39, Muhammad 'Ali Pasha paid a visit to the Sudan. His principal object was to inspect the gold-producing region of Fazughli. Disappointed with what he saw, he returned to Egypt. His visit is devoid of significance for Sudanese history.

7. Kanbal was the son of *Makk* Jawish, who had resisted the advance of Isma'il Pasha (see above, p. 38). After his death, Kanbal became a legendary figure: 'he is described, on account of his cruelty and savage deeds, constantly wandering round, without grave, rest, or peace, as the punishment of his crimes.' (F. Werne, *African wanderings*, London 1852; 177–8.) His son, Bashir, served both the Turco-Egyptian and Condominium regimes, and died in 1919.

8. Muhammad wad Dafa'allah's wife, Nasra bint 'Adlan, was a person of even greater consequence than he himself. She was the daughter of the Regent 'Adlan by a Funj princess. She held her court at Surayba, near Wad Medani, where she was visited by the German archaeologist Lepsius in 1844, and by the American Bayard Taylor in 1852.

9. These instructions should undoubtedly be linked with decrees of the Ottoman Sultan 'Abd al-Majid, who in October 1854 prohibited trade in white slaves, and in February 1857 trade in negro slaves.

CHAPTER V: THE ERA OF KHEDIVE ISMA'IL: 1862–81

1. Usually called Arabi Pasha by English writers.
2. See above, p. 58.
3. See above, p. 59.

CHAPTER VI: THE MAHDIST REVOLUTION: 1881–85

1. A supporter of 'Urabi named Ahmad al-'Awwam was banished to Khartoum after the suppression of the Egyptian revolution. He then wrote an account of recent events in Egypt, which he communicated to the Mahdi's followers. For this he was tried and put to death. His work was later lithographed in Omdurman by the Mahdist authorities. 'Awwam's book was, however, only

composed at a time when the Mahdist movement was on the verge of its final successes.

2. The original Ansar were the 'Helpers' of the Prophet Muhammad in Medina. In this, as in other instances, the Mahdi patterned his movement on early Islamic history. See above, pp. 86–88.

3. The name is usually given in English works as Osman Digna. His Beja followers were the 'Fuzzy-Wuzzies' of Kipling's poem.

4. See above, p. 31.

5. Later the first Earl of Cromer.

6. *Al-Siddiq, al-Faruq* and *al-Karrar* are names traditionally given to Abu Bakr, 'Umar and 'Ali respectively.

CHAPTER VII: THE REIGN OF THE KHALIFA 'ABDALLAHI: 1885–98

1. The name has gone down in British military history as Toski.

2. Ahmad 'Ali's successor as *qadi al-Islam*, al-Husayn Ibrahim wad al-Zahra, who also perished in disgrace, had studied at al-Azhar in the Turco-Egyptian period, and was a literary poet of repute.

3. For information on the diplomatic background of the Dongola Campaign, I am indebted to Dr G. N. Sanderson of the University of Khartoum, who has made a detailed study, as yet unpublished, entitled *Anglo-French competition for the control of the upper basin of the Nile, 1890–99, and its resolution in the Fashoda crisis* (Ph.D. thesis, London 1959), and has also kindly communicated with me on this topic.

4. Later Earl Kitchener of Khartoum.

5. The name is often distorted to Surgham.

CHAPTER VIII: THE ERA OF KITCHENER AND WINGATE: 1899–1918

1. The Capitulations were originally treaties by which the Ottoman sultans had conceded virtually autonomous status and trading rights to European mercantile communities within the Empire. With the decline of Ottoman power they had become in effect charters of extraterritoriality for any persons who could claim the citizenship or protection of European states or of the USA.

2. The Mixed Tribunals had been set up in the reign of Khedive Isma'il to try civil suits in which Europeans were concerned. They were independent of the Egyptian government.

3. The first Convention concluded on 19 January 1899, is the substantive instrument. The second Convention, dated 10 July 1899, merely extended the provisions of the first to Suakin. The texts of both documents, together with Cromer's highly important memorandum of 10 November 1898, which was their genesis, may be read in J. C. Hurewitz, *Diplomacy in the Near and Middle East; a documentary record* (Princeton, N.J. 1956), Vol. I, pp. 210–18.

4. The frontier was modified in practice by three deviations. On the Nile, the Sudan Government controlled a few miles of territory north of lat. 22° which gave the Sudan a low-water station for steamers at Faras. In the eastern desert, to permit better control of nomadic tribes, Egypt controlled some territory south of the line, and the Sudan Government a larger area

north of the line and towards the Red Sea coast. These modifications of the juridical frontier provided the Egyptian government with its pretext for action against the Republic of the Sudan in March 1958: see pp. 176–77.

5. Of other Mahdist notables mentioned earlier, Muhammad Khalid Zuqal was released from his imprisonment in exile at Rejaf by the Belgians in 1897. He went back to Darfur, where he was killed in 1903 by order of the new Sultan 'Ali Dinar. His former gaoler, 'Arabi Dafa'allah, after being driven out of Rejaf by the Belgians, also made his way to Darfur with the remnant of his Mahdist forces. He was regarded with suspicion by 'Ali Dinar, and died, or was killed, in 1915 or 1916. The last survivor of the Khalifa's military governors was Yunus al-Dikaym, who died in great old age at Omdurman in 1935.

6. See above, Ch. II, note 16.

7. See further the Conclusion, pp. 196–97.

8. £E=Egyptian pound, the equivalent of £1 0s. 6d. sterling.

9. 'Abbas II was the last khedive. His successor under the protectorate took the title of sultan, which was superseded in 1922 by that of king.

10. I am obliged for this information to Mr A. B. Theobald, formerly Reader in History in the University of Khartoum, who is working on a detailed study of the reign of 'Ali Dinar, and has very kindly allowed me here to anticipate the publication of some of his findings.

CHAPTER IX: REVOLT AND REACTION: 1919–33

1. Toynbee, *Survey of international affairs*, 1925, I, 245. The passage quoted is based on reports in *The Times*.

2. A sub-*mamur* was a (Sudanese) district official of junior status.

3. Sir James Currie, 'The educational experiment in the Anglo-Egyptian Sudan, 1900–33', II, *Journal of the African Society* (London 1935), xxxiv, p. 49.

4. The Sudanese *feddan*=1·038 acres.

5. Currie, as above, p. 53.

6. Currie, as above, pp. 54–55.

CHAPTER X: THE RISE OF SUDANESE NATIONALISM: 1934–52

1. See Conclusion, pp. 196 ff.

2. For the text of the Treaty, see Hurewitz, *Diplomacy in the Near and Middle East*, II, pp. 203–211.

3. Subsequently minister of Finance in the government of 'Abdallah Khalil.

4. Viz., the Northern Province, Kasala, Khartoum, the Blue Nile, Kordofan and Darfur.

5. The southern Sudan comprises the three provinces of the Upper Nile, Bahr al-Ghazal and Equatoria.

6. Subsequently the last British governor-general of Nigeria.

CHAPTER XI: SELF-GOVERNMENT AND SELF-DETERMINATION: 1953–55

1. See p. 173.

CHAPTER XII: THE PARLIAMENTARY REGIME: 1956–58

1. £S = Sudanese pound, valued like the Egyptian pound at £1 0s. 6d. sterling.

CHAPTER XIII: THE ARMY *COUP* AND
MILITARY GOVERNMENT:

1. The above account of events is based on private information and on the account given by Mr Peter Kilner, who was editor of an English-language newspaper in Khartoum at the time of the *coup*. See his article, 'A year of army rule in the Sudan', *The World Today*, R.I.I.A., London 1959; 15, pp. 430–41.
2. The Muslim Brotherhood is an extremist organization, founded in Egypt in 1928, which gained considerable influence during the last years of the Egyptian monarchy. It was suppressed in Egypt after the revolution, but has continued to attract many adherents in the Sudan. Its strongly Islamic ideology resembles in some respects the outlook of the Sudanese Mahdi.
3. An informant who was in close touch with the student body emphasizes that the name of Communist was a fashionable and daring label assumed by many young left-wing radicals, and that the genuine Communists were probably no more than a small handful. This is no doubt true: on the other hand, it has been said of the appeal of Communism to the Middle Eastern intelligentsia that 'it is not the Marxist ideology, but the Soviet program, which attracts'. (John A. Armstrong, reviewing Walter Z. Laqueur, *The Soviet Union and the Middle East*, in *Middle Eastern Affairs*, New York; xi5, 1959, p. 164.
4. See p. 157.

CHAPTER XIV: CULTURE AND EDUCATION IN THE SUDAN:

1. *Khalwa* (literally, 'a place of seclusion') means primarily a retreat for Sufi initiates. The Sudanese usage, to signify a place for religious instruction (and nowadays essentially the teaching of the Koran) is a surviving trace of the Sufi character of the islamization of the Sudan.
2. Atiyah, *An Arab tells his story*, p. 138.
3. See p. 137.

A SELECT BIBLIOGRAPHY OF WORKS IN ENGLISH

Introduction

R. L. Hill, *A bibliography of the Anglo-Egyptian Sudan from the earliest times to 1937* (London 1939), is comprehensive within its chronological limits. There is unfortunately no bibliography for the later years, in which there has been a good deal of writing on the Sudan. The gap is partly filled by the annual book-lists which have appeared in the periodical publication, *Sudan Notes and Records* (Khartoum) from 1948 onwards. This periodical, which first appeared in 1918, and now usually publishes two issues yearly, is a mine of information on all aspects of Sudanese studies, but its articles are of very varied quality.

No advanced specialized geography of the Sudan has yet appeared. For an introduction, Robin A. Hodgkin, *Sudan geography* (London 1951), originally written as a textbook for Sudanese schools, is useful.

There is no general history of the Sudan available in English, although short surveys are frequently inserted in more specialized works. One of these forms part of J. Spencer Trimingham, *Islam in the Sudan* (London 1949). The account given of Sudanese Islam, which forms the main portion of the book, is extremely valuable. The author was for many years an Anglican missionary in Omdurman. Richard Hill, *A biographical dictionary of the Anglo-Egyptian Sudan* (Oxford 1951), is an indispensable work of reference. A. J. Arkell, *A history of the Sudan to 1821* (London 1955), written by an archaeologist with long experience of the Sudan as an administrator, is mainly concerned with the millennia before the coming of the Arabs.

H. A. MacMichael, *A history of the Arabs in the Sudan* (Cambridge 1922), is a collection of material from classical, Arabic and Sudanese sources, rather than a systematic history. It incorporates much genealogical and tribal traditions which should be submitted to rigorous criticism. Of more limited scope is the same writer's *The tribes of central and northern Kordofan* (Cambridge 1912). MacMichael, whose other works are noticed below, (see *Part III: Condominium*), was a distinguished member of the Sudan Political Service. Another tribal history, A. Paul, *A history of the Beja tribes of the Sudan* (Cambridge 1954), was also written by a former member of the same service. O. G. S. Crawford, *The Fung kingdom of Sennar* (Gloucester 1951), is the product of wide reading (but not in Arabic) and archaeological experience. It is a valuable work of reference, but its conclusions, like most writing on the Funj, should be treated with caution.

There were few European travellers in the Sudan before the Egyptian Conquest. The journey of Charles Jacques Poncet, who visited Sennar at the end of the seventeenth century, has been reprinted by Sir William Foster (ed.), *The Red Sea and adjacent countries at the close of the seventeenth century* (Hakluyt Society, Second series, No. C, London 1949). Much material from the early travellers has been incorporated in Crawford's book, mentioned above. The classical description of the Funj sultanate in its decline was given by James Bruce, *Travels to discover the source of the Nile* (vol. vi, second edition, Edinburgh 1805). Bruce travelled from Sennar to Aswan in 1773. The earliest English account of Darfur appears in W. G. Browne, *Travels in Africa, Egypt, and Syria, from the year 1792 to 1798* (London 1799). Conditions on the main Nile on the eve of the Egyptian Conquest are described in John Lewis Burckhardt, *Travels in Nubia* (London 1819).

Part I: The Turco-Egyptian Period

The only general account in English is Richard Hill, *Egypt in the Sudan, 1820–1881* (London 1959), largely based on unpublished material, including the Egyptian archives. It contains an important bibliography.

Accounts by travellers become increasingly numerous in this period. *A narrative of the expedition to Dongola and Sennaar* (London 1822), by 'an American in the service of the viceroy', was written by G. B. English, an officer in the Egyptian artillery at the time of the Conquest. John Petherick, *Egypt, the Sudan and Central Africa* (Edinburgh 1861), describes early travels in the Bahr al-Ghazal. The writer, a Welsh mining-engineer, traded in the Sudan. Sir Samuel W. Baker, *The Nile tributaries of Abyssinia* (London 1874), and *The Albert N'yanza* (London 1877), are records of exploratory journeys, which throw some light on conditions in the Sudan. Baker's *Ismailia* (London 1874), is his account of his mission to the southern Sudan on behalf of Khedive Isma'il. T. Douglas Murray and A. Silva White, *Sir Samuel Baker, a memoir* (London 1895), contains some interesting material. A modern biography has been written by Dorothy Middleton, *Baker of the Nile* (London 1949).

The immense literature about Gordon in the Sudan began in this period. It is surveyed in Richard Hill, 'The Gordon literature', *Durham University Journal*, New series, xvi/3 (1955), pp. 97–103. The essential study of Gordon's work in the Sudan is Bernard M. Allen, *Gordon and the Sudan* (London 1931). Material on Gordon's activities before the Mahdia may be found in G. Birkbeck Hill (ed.), *Colonel Gordon in Central Africa, 1874–1879* (London 1881). The career of Romolo Gessi, Gordon's lieutenant in the Bahr al-Ghazal, is described in Romolo Gessi (ed. Felix Gessi), *Seven years in the Sudan* (London 1892). Another Italian servant of the khedive described his adventures in Gaetano Casati, *Ten years in Equatoria* (London 1891). For the biography of the last khedivial governor of Equatoria, the German-born Emin Pasha (Edward Schnitzer), see Georg Schweitzer, *Emin Pasha, his life and work* (London 1898).

Part II: The Mahdist State

A general history, based mainly on the Mahdist archives and other unpublished sources, and on the Arabic history of Na'um Shuqayr, is P. M. Holt, *The Mahdist state in the Sudan, 1881–1898* (Oxford 1958). This contains a bibliography. A. B. Theobald, *The Mahdiya* (London 1951), draws its material chiefly from English published sources, and devotes most space to the military conflicts between Mahdist and British or Egyptian forces. Mekki Shibeika, *British policy in the Sudan, 1882–1902* (London 1952), deals most fully with the events and diplomatic background of the Mahdia to 1885. The writer is a Sudanese historian.

Among contemporary works in English, three form a group on their own, F. R. Wingate, *Mahdiism and the Egyptian Sudan* (London 1891); *Ten years' captivity in the Mahdi's camp, 1882–1892, from the original manuscripts of Father Joseph Ohrwalder* (London 1892); and Rudolf C. Slatin, *Fire and sword in the Sudan* (London 1896). For a critique of these, stressing their significance as war-propaganda, see P. M. Holt, 'The source-materials of the Sudanese Mahdia,' *St. Antony's papers, Number 4; Middle Eastern Affairs, Number One* (London 1958), pp. 107–118. An independent record of a European prisoner of the Mahdia is Charles Neufeld, *A prisoner of the Khaleefa* (London 1899). For events in the south, in addition to the books by Casati and Schweitzer, mentioned in the previous section, see A. J. Mounteney-Jephson, *Emin Pasha and the rebellion at the Equator* (London 1890). A. Egmont Hake (ed.) *The journals of . . . Gordon . . . at Kartoum*, covers only a part of the siege of Khartoum, and is a pathetic revelation of Gordon's state of mind, rather than a source of major importance. The Reconquest produced an immense amount of journalistic narrative, of which G. W. Steevens, *With Kitchener to Khartoum* (Edinburgh 1898), is a fair specimen. Sir Winston Churchill, *The river war* (London 1899; many later eds.), is a literary masterpiece.

Biographies of persons important in this and the following period include H. C. Jackson, *Osman Digna* (London 1926). The author at the time of writing the book was a member of the Sudan Political Service. The laudatory account of Kitchener in Sir George Arthur, *Life of Lord Kitchener* (London 1920), may be compared with the treatment in Sir Philip Magnus, *Kitchener, the portrait of an imperialist* (London 1959). Wingate's career has been described by his son, Sir Ronald Wingate, *Wingate of the Sudan* (London 1955). Cromer's attitude to the Sudan is revealed in his *Modern Egypt* (London 1908).

Part III: The Anglo-Egyptian Condominium

Accounts of the Condominium period have chiefly been written by former members of the Sudan political service and tend to lack detachment. The most informative are Sir Harold

MacMichael, *The Anglo-Egyptian Sudan* (London 1934); and *The Sudan* (London 1954); J. S. R. Duncan, *The Sudan, a record of achievement* (Edinburgh 1952); and *The Sudan's path to independence* (Edinburgh 1957). The accounts of the Sudan in successive editions of *The Middle East: a political and economic survey* (Royal Institute of International Affairs, London 1950, 1954, 1958), may also be compared. A scholarly study by a Sudanese is Mekki Abbas, *The Sudan question* (London 1952).

Factual surveys of events at two critical periods in the history of the Condominium are given in Arnold J. Toynbee, *Survey of international affairs*, 1925, i (London 1927), pp. 232–69; and George Kirk, *The Middle East, 1945–1950* (London 1954), pp. 116–43. Both are publications of the Royal Institute of International Affairs.

Much valuable material is contained in a biography of the civil secretary, Sir Douglas Newbold, by K. D. D. Henderson, *The making of the modern Sudan* (London 1953).

Materials for the study of the social and economic development of the Sudan under the Condominium may be found in articles in *Sudan Notes and Records*, but much still lies buried in departmental archives. Four books deal with special aspects of the subject. J. D. Tothill (ed.), *Agriculture in the Sudan* (London 1948), is a collection of monographs by experts, edited by a former director of Agriculture. A detailed study of the Gezira Scheme, written by the first chairman and director of the Gezira Board, is provided by Arthur Gaitskell, *Gezira, a story of development in the Sudan* (London 1959). The scope of Saad ed Din Fawzi, *The labour movement in the Sudan, 1946–1955* (London 1957), is defined by its title: the author was a distinguished Sudanese economist. An account of the public health service, by a former medical officer in the Sudan, is given in H. C. Squires, *The Sudan Medical Service, an experiment in social medicine* (London 1958). For developments in Muslim law, see J. N. D. Anderson, *Islamic law in Africa* (London 1954), pp. 301–21.

Part IV: The Republic of the Sudan

No study of the Sudan since independence has yet appeared in English. Chronologies of current events and occasional articles may be found in the periodicals *The Middle East Journal* (Washington) and *Middle Eastern Affairs* (New York). These are also useful for the preceding period.

Official literature in English is also produced by the Sudanese Government, and is obtainable from the Sudanese Embassy in London. *Sudan* is a monthly magazine, while the current issue of the *Sudan Almanac* is a useful handbook. The unofficial *Directory of the Republic of the Sudan* contains, among other information, short biographies of notabilities.

The earlier history of Communism in the Sudan (down to 1954) is given in Walter Z. Laqueur, *Communism and nationalism in the Middle East* (London 1956), pp. 63–69. For its influence on the Labour Movement, see Fawzi, *The Labour Movement in the Sudan*, pp. 118–21.

Culture and Education

J. Spencer Trimingham, *Islam in the Sudan* (see above, p. 221), gives an account of the traditional Islamic culture of the Sudan, and of the influences which have impinged on it in modern times. Specimens of dialect poetry, proverbs and excerpts from the biographical dictionary of holy men, mentioned in the text, may be found with translations in S. Hillelson, *Sudan Arabic texts* (Cambridge 1935). MacMichael, *A history of the Arabs in the Sudan* (see above, p. 221), incorporates other material from this dictionary, and an abridged translation of the chronicle mentioned in the text, as well as genealogical documents. The cultural history of the Sudan in the Turco-Egyptian period is virtually unknown to Western writers.

Some insight into the educational system in the early years of the Condominium is given by Humphrey Bowman, *Middle East window* (London 1942). The author served under Sir James Currie from 1911 to 1913. A hostile view of the Gordon College in the late twenties is given in Edward Atiyah, *An Arab tells his story* (London 1946). Atiyah's novel, *Black vanguard* (London 1952), is a fictionalized social study of the Sudan in the later years of the Condominium, and is very relevant to the subject of this chapter. Atiyah, of Christian Lebanese descent, was a teacher in the Gordon College and later an intelligence officer of the Sudan Government. Information on the rôle of the Anglican Church in the Condominium period is given by H. C. Jackson, *Pastor on the Nile* (London 1960).

The new spirit which entered Sudanese education in the thirties and forties is reflected in some of the comments of the civil secretary, Douglas Newbold, as given in K. D. D. Henderson, *The making of the modern Sudan* (see above, p. 225). Newbold's liberal and enlightened attitude towards education greatly encouraged the new developments. The aims and history of Bakht er Ruda, the most characteristic educational foundation of this period, have been described by its originator and first principal, V. L. Griffiths, *An experiment in education*, London, 1953.

INDEX